FIRST
PERSON
MORTAL

FIRST PERSON MORTAL

Personal Narratives
of Dying, Death, and Grief

LUCY BREGMAN
and SARA THIERMANN

PARAGON HOUSE

First Edition, 1995

Published in the United States by

Paragon House
370 Lexington Avenue
New York, NY 10017

Library of Congress Cataloging-in-Publication Data

Bregman, Lucy.
    First person mortal : autobiographical narratives of dying, death,
  and grief / Lucy Bregman, Sara Thiermann.—1st ed.
      p.   cm.
  Includes bibliographical references and index.
  ISBN 1-55778-714-X—ISBN 1-55778-715-8
    1. Death—Psychological aspects. 2. Terminally ill—
Psychology. 3. Grief. I. Thiermann, Sara. II. Title.
  BF789.D4B72 1995
   155.9'37—dc20
                                                 94-24383
                                                   CIP

Manufactured in the United States

CONTENTS

PREFACE

ON THE WALLS OF THE HOUSE WHERE I GREW UP were a number of photographs of a beautiful four–year–old boy, my older brother Bruce, who died a little over a year before my twin brother and I were born. He had been my parents' only child and was said to have been so precious to my father that he could not see the need for more children. Beyond that, and the fact that Bruce had died of an illness that was soon after treatable with the new "wonder drugs," I knew very little. Even after I had children of my own, when my mother and I had more in common, I never heard her speak about his illness and how his short life ebbed away, about what it was like to lose a child, or about how it had broken her heart and changed her life. There had always been a deep sadness in her eyes, but I don't think I clearly saw it until a few years ago, when I went in search of my mother's story— more than twenty years after she died. I had heard a colleague, the bereavement coördinator for Childrens' Hospital here in Philadelphia, tell about the death of her own young son from leukemia. As I listened to May, for the first time I heard my own mother speaking about her grief. I looked through the stacks of photographs that my father, an amateur photographer, had taken of all of us as we grew up and found more fragments of her story. But there were still many pieces of the story missing.

Reading John Gunther's *Death Be Not Proud* when I was sixteen years old marked the beginning of my conscious interest in first person accounts of death and dying, and although years went by before this interest was actively rekindled, images from that narrative stayed sharply etched in my memory. Gunther tells the story of his son Johnny's brave struggle with a brain tumor. Many of the girls at my boarding school read Gunther's book that year because Johnny had been a student at Deerfield Academy, one of several nearby boys' schools that shared social events with our school—and because most of us found something romantic in the notion that, had we been born some years earlier, we might even have known Johnny.

Soon after I was married, my maternal grandmother, Clara, died. She had played a pivotal role in my life. For me, she was one of those people whom *Readers' Digest* refers to as "The Most Influential Person in My Life." My mother was her only child, and they appeared to have had an extremely close relationship. They used to call each other long distance on Sundays to do the *Times* crossword puzzle together over the telephone. During Clara's final illness, my mother frequently traveled to New England to be with her and to manage her affairs. Even though the silence following her death left me feeling empty, at that time I remained unaware of my own hunger for stories.

Over the years, autobiography continued to hold a special fascination for me, but it wasn't until I was given the opportunity to teach an interdisciplinary course in death and dying for upper–level undergraduates at Temple University that I rediscovered this particular genre of personal narrative. It was a "coming together" time for me. I had long been fascinated by twentieth century European philosophers like Martin Heidegger, Jean Paul Sartre, and Gabriel Marcel, in part because of their forthright acknowledgement of our finitude. I thought seriously about pursuing a degree in philosophy. At the same time, I had found an "everyday" kind of groundedness in Buddhist thought, particularly in the matter-of-fact way one's dying is integrated into that worldview. Teaching the death and dying course allowed me to pull together resources from these varied disciplines, and I delighted in the quest for new and exciting materials each semester. Not so gradually, it dawned on me that this was where my real passion lived (although it was to be a while before I became fully aware of how and why I found myself there), and I went on to complete an advanced degree and post–doctoral work. I finally set upon a career path that led me to work with persons who are dying and bereaved.

Lucy Bregman directed the death and dying courses—thus began our long friendship and eventual collaboration. Along the way, her zeal for our shared areas of interest was profoundly rewarding. We began by exchanging new ideas, articles, and books for the death and dying courses. Then, Lucy taught a fascinating graduate course on spiritual autobiography that added fuel to the fire. She agreed to be my advisor for my doctoral dissertation, and although narrative analysis was only peripheral to my doctoral research, we were, by then, completely immersed in stories of illness, grief, and dying. Lucy included commentary on these narratives as a literary genre in her book, *Death in the Midst of Life.* At that time, Lucy thought perhaps we had enough material for a journal article. But the prospect seemed ominous to me, since both of us were insatiable and more books kept finding us. Summers proved to be an especially productive time for finding, reading, and sharing books. We met weekly to exchange our latest finds and to log our written comments and impressions.

The narrative thread seems to connect certain moments in my life: my youthful interest in autobiography, my use of first person accounts in the death and dying course, and the enthusiasm Lucy and I shared through our digging into stories of illness, dying, and grief. What I began to notice was the way I sometimes tore into the books, which I would then have to go back and reread more objectively. It was as if I thought I might find some hidden information that would light darkened windows and open locked doors. I now know I sought in others' words the stories I had not heard when I needed them— such was my hunger for narrative.

It is interesting how one's projects and one's life become indistinguishable. From my doctoral work on non–traditional spiritual approaches to working with the dying, through hospice and hospital experience with patients and families, narratives are at the heart of my work. Case conferences depend on narrative. On hospital ethics committees, dilemmas are told and resolved through narrative. Whether working with individuals, families, or health care professionals on issues of loss and bereavement, the importance of narrative is undeniable. Grief can and must be shared through its telling.

These authors and their stories have become more than just interesting to contemplate—more than mere acquaintances. Many have become teachers, whose most potent lesson is that the very stories I grasped so tightly because I thought they spoke to me alone, are in fact the ones that point to the universality of the human experience of death and loss. Of course, Lucy and I both have our particular favorites—wonderful men and women we wish we had met before they died and authors with whom we have had daydream conversations. The best part is knowing we haven't read the last one yet.

Sara Thiermann
Radnor, Pennsylvania
Autumn, 1994

Chapter One

THE INDIVIDUAL DIES

THIS IS A STUDY OF FIRST-PERSON NARRATIVES OF ILLNESS, dying, and grief. Accounts of "How I endured a life-threatening illness," "How I cared for my dying loved one," and "How I mourned the death of a loved one" are proliferating in America today. Many are intended to be inspirational. Others protest the American medical establishment and voice "the patient's perspective," medicine from the bottom up. Some inform, providing readable advice about what to expect if you've had a stroke, or some other medical condition that requires special care. Yet many do not claim any special wisdom, or directions for successfully navigating the turmoil and suffering. Perhaps, as one author put it, "we all hope for . . . a recipe, we all believe, however much we know we shouldn't, that maybe somebody's got that recipe and can show us how not to be sick, suffer and die" (Shin 1980, 6). A few reject all goals of inspiration and hope: even when help was given, even when help was there, "Hospice helped us graciously. Hospice was a godsend. And *still* we were in hell" (Rubin 1982, 197). Yet telling the story, sharing with others—anonymous others at that—the day-by-day chronicling of this hell, is considered worthwhile and even a moral obligation.

Our interest in these narratives initially developed out of the spirit of sharing works we came across as death educators, and it steadfastly grew into this collaborative effort. Lucy Bregman is a professor of religion and psychology at Temple University. Both Lucy Bregman and Sara Thiermann have taught death and dying at the university level for a number of years. Sara Thiermann has extensive experience in hospice programs, as a bereavement counselor in the hospital and in private practice, and, as a member of a hospital ethics committee, her work focuses on decisions near the end of life. We have collectively, as might be expected, lived through the final illnesses and loss of parents, other family members, and dear friends. In addition, both of us have life experience with mild chronic illness. As might be surmised from the above, growing out of our experiences in death education, a multidisciplinary perspective informs our work.

We believe that these many accounts form a genre, a special subdivision of the voluminous "death and dying" literature. They are also, with few exceptions, a relatively recent phenomenon. What is their importance for understanding how Americans are reenvisioning death? How does the appearance of this genre express our new awareness of death and dying? What are the links between death and spirit, death and the quest for ultimate meanings, that appear within this genre? How can a closer look at this type of writing illuminate the experience of life-threatening illness for Americans today? These are some of the questions we will address here.

As we realized that our work together was leading us into a book-length project, we asked ourselves: Who should read this work? Why and how should it be used? Hospice team members, particularly those interested in the interface between illness and spirituality, will find that these narratives offer a perspective different from the usual formulaic versions of "life's end stages" offered in most theoretical and descriptive hospice literature. Death and dying counselors, pastoral care personnel, and oncology social workers are some who will find these works a valuable resource (not just as a list of "good" and "bad" books) and, in some, a useful model for the utilization of the power of story (both in the hearing and in the telling) to aid in healing and personal growth, not to overlook the importance of the life-review process for end-of-life meaning-making. Academics teaching multidisciplinary death and dying courses (at the university level, in medical humanities, in the didactic clinical pastoral education settings) will find these books important: for their depiction of the humanistic elements of life-threatening illness and the patient's experience of medicine's response to it; because many generalizations about American society's views of death and religion are too simplistic; and because this literature reveals (at a "softer," nonstatistical level) emergent attitudes toward death and transitions in assumptions about health and faith as they intermesh with medicine—seen *not* from medicine's privileged frame for illness and death. For all who are ill or whose family member or loved one's illness and dramatically declining health has ever been a primary life event, these books may serve as a map, support, companion, witness or even vindication. For all who turn to them, they underscore the importance of the voice of the first person singular.

A paradox of the discussion in America today of death and dying is the coexistence of two seemingly contradictory themes. The first theme is familiar: "Americans deny death," a dictum that even today is repeated by almost every popular writer and many scholarly ones. Terms such as *repression* and *taboo* also appear again and again to characterize our culture's attitudes toward death, usually contrasted with the more "accepting" and "natural" views of the past. Take, for example, Elisabeth Kübler-Ross's nostalgic opening scenes of the dying Swiss farmer of her childhood, in the early pages of her classic *On Death and Dying* (5–6). The man died at home, surrounded by family and neighbors, at peace. "Why do I describe such 'old-fashioned' customs?" she asks rhetorically. Because this scene sets the stage for her depiction of the terrible struggle endured by her dying, hospitalized patients in the late 1960s to remain human beings amid an atmosphere of bureaucracy and denial. Accusations of denial persist today, even in an environment where some specific practices have changed, and where the movement of "death awareness" has flourished for several decades.

The second theme is that of talkativeness about death. During the past generation, an immense amount of literature, media focus, and public education has drawn our attention to issues of dying, grief, illness, and death. The flood of this material, beginning with the publication of Kübler-Ross's *On Death and Dying* in the late 1960s, has yet to subside. Samuel Southard, in a recent survey, attributes its rise to the "post-Vietnam ethos" (Southard 1991, p. xxx) which included a distrust of the technical expertise and an interest in patients' rights.

Associating the beginnings of this trend with a certain political climate may make sense, yet interest in thanatology, and the popularity of first-person narratives of death and illness, continued unabated when the conservative 1980s replaced the more liberal decades of the 1960s and 1970s. There is no sign that interest in such personal histories has slackened in the 1990s.

Early in the current era of public awareness of death, a leading researcher noted this paradox of denial and talkativeness, and wondered:

> Perhaps it is an error to read in this new awareness a major transformation of the zeitgeist. And yet this willingness, this eagerness, to discuss death openly has gone far beyond the ranks to those touched in any immediate way by the specific problems of medical technology. (Steinfels 1975, 2)

Does eagerness to discuss and read about death signal a "major transformation of the zeitgeist"? Are the days of denial and repression truly over?

Our study starts from the premise that a mere "yes" or "no" answer to these questions is impossible to give. We must go beneath the level of rhetoric that terms such as *denial* or *acceptance* take for granted. Personal narratives, first-person accounts of "How I endured a life-threatening illness," and "How I mourned the death of a loved one," may be among the most powerful evidence for the shift Steinfels was already able to see. Whereas works by professional thanatologists may reach only a professional audience, first-person narratives such as Jill Ireland's *Life Wish* and Gilda Radner's *It's Always Something* were best-sellers, indeed reaching far beyond the ranks of those touched in an immediate way by medical technology (although, writing before the "patient's perspective" view of medicine had become common, Steinfels was probably thinking of medical professionals when he wrote the above lines). Authors of new narratives read the older ones, too, and sometimes consciously craft their stories to fill the gaps left by the existing literature:

> Sick people need a literature of their own. Misery loves company—if it's good company. And surprisingly enough, there isn't much good company in this rapidly proliferating field. (Broyard 1992, 12–13)

But if the popularity of this genre signals a new era of acceptance and the end of denial, why then do so many authors' struggles to retell their experiences witness to the continuing repression and denial of death, its banishment from our society's vision of what human life is about? Why are so many revealing personal narratives *necessary* if a new zeitgeist is truly here?

A second question relates to the possibility of a new zeitgeist in regard to death. In Western culture, death has, for thousands of years, been viewed in religious terms, and funerals, burials and mourning practices occurred under religious auspices. By the mid-twentieth century, that was no longer consistently the case. The detachment of death from religion is a reality taken for granted, from which current thanatology literature begins. The "secularization" of death means that Kübler-Ross and all her less-well-known colleagues could approach the topic as a psychological, interpersonal, or socio-logical reality, without directly addressing its spiritual meanings. Yet, just as claims about society's overall secularization have been vigor-ously disputed (Hammond), so too is an easy assessment of religion's role in the process of dying, or in the encounter with death, chal-lengeable. How do the first-person narratives shed light on the spiri-tual dimension of the struggle against suffering, illness, and death? We will show that a new understanding of religion or spirituality must be gained before a full answer to this question is possible. Perhaps the autobiographical genre itself can be seen as a vehicle for particular forms of emerging personal religiousness.

Our starting point is that, works of first-person writing about ill-ness, dying, and grief can be seen as attempts of contemporary persons to wrest human meaning from marginal situations, situations about which our society has much to say medically but little to offer otherwise. Because there is now greater awareness on the part of medical sociologists of how necessary the patient's perspective is for the practice of medicine, a space has been cleared to interpret these works as "illness narratives" and "narrative bioethics" (Kleinman, Frank, Brody). However, we find this alone does not go far enough to interpret their function and appeal. We examine them not specifi-cally in the context of medicine, but in a more generalized frame-work of the study of contemporary, emergent forms of spirituality and meaning-making. However, this perspective is also a bias, as we will find, for the message many authors wish to convey is that their experiences are too painful to be encompassed by any coherent, consoling meaning at all.

Death and the American Worldview

To set the stage for our investigation, we must begin at a slightly different starting point from the psychological death and dying literature which Bonnie Miller-McLemore refers to as the "Kübler-Ross Discussion" and is the starting point from which most popular authors begin. Psychological language (such as "denial") lays the problem at the door of the individual, or treats society as if it were a giant individual with drives and desires and defense mechanisms parallel to those a therapist postulates as being at work in clients. Although some or all individuals may, at times, indeed rely on denial as a defense, this would not be an obstacle, were it not for attitudes, beliefs, and images shared by all, for which terms such as *zeitgeist, worldview,* and *sacred cosmos* seem more appropriate. These point to what all members of a society share, or, at the very least, to the dominant group's vision of reality and human expectations. Each member of that society will then have to do the best he or she can to interiorize the available worldview, and struggle with the discrepancies within it and reality.

Perhaps the following quote, from Thomas Luckmann's *The Invisible Religion,* published in 1967, is still true:

> Death does not appear even as a subordinate topic in the sacred cosmos of a modern industrial society . . . The 'autonomous' individual is young and he never dies. (114)

Luckmann, writing before the current flood of popular literature on death and dying, was chiefly concerned with the structure of modern industrial societies and the way religion functions within them. Such societies are divided into public and private spheres. The public sphere is the realm of work, economy, and large-scale institutions, the realm of Max Weber's "bureaucratic rationality." The private sphere is what is left over, and exists in the interstices of the public. It is here, in the haven of what remains, that the individual is left to construct his/her personal identity, and ultimate meanings. This

process, which Luckmann likens to "shopping" for identity fragments, appears to give each individual a huge range of choices, and,
so, a sense of autonomy.

> To an immeasurably higher degree than in a traditional social order,
> the individual is left to his own devices in choosing goods and services,
> friends, marriage partners . . . even "ultimate" meanings in a relatively
> autonomous fashion. In a manner of speaking, he is free to construct
> his own personal identity. (98)

Hence, religion in modern society is no longer a matter of large
institutions and traditional meanings, but an invisible and radically
deinstitutionalized process of meaning-making that operates within
the private sphere.

There are three major discrepancies for us to notice. One is between the real power and reach of the public sphere, and the sense of
autonomy that the private sphere permits and encourages. This is
what Luckmann the sociologist finds so disturbing. The sacrosanct
quality of autonomy as a value hides the very restricted range of the
private sphere within which autonomy is exercised. The next discrepancy is that of an absolute separation between public and private
spheres. It is unlikely that an important human event in one sphere
will not impact the other. We will meet both these disjunctions when
the protagonists of our narratives leave home and enter hospitals,
which menace both the individual's belief in his/her autonomy, and
also the neat separation of public from private. As many authors
discover, getting sick is not just a private matter; public policies about
health care, insurance, allocation of resources, and funds for research are as intrinsic to the experience of illness and dying as are
one's own innermost beliefs. A small portion of the works we will look
at make it their primary concern to address these questions, but even
some of the least political authors become aware of them.

But there is, of course, a more basic and obvious discrepancy lying
at the heart of Luckmann's sarcastic description of the young and
"autonomous" individual who "never dies." Where does that leave
the real human being who *does* die? How could any belief so directly
at odds with the reality of the life cycle flourish? If contemporary
society's vision of the person is still as Luckmann described it back in
1967, then no wonder all of us find ourselves helpless and confused

when we are forced to encounter death and, indeed, any experiences that remind us of the body's frailty and inevitable destiny. If we all share a worldview in which this deathless, ever-young person is a central fixture, then death, illness, and injury come as disruptions, as chaotic events that damage us not just physically but at the level of our "ultimate meanings." Intimations of mortality, to use the title of one first-person narrative, subvert the reality of the autonomous individual who is young and never dies, and so the entire sacred cosmos is put in jeopardy. That no such deathless individual ever existed or could exist is a major lesson that the authors of all our narratives had to learn. They learn it only by knowing that they themselves, or those they love, are not such imaginary, fantastical, deathless persons.

First-Person Narratives

This account opens the way for us to understand why personal narratives flourish as responses to this problem. If personal meaning is a private-sphere matter, a process of "identity construction," then the fascination with autobiographical narratives may lie in their revelations of others' attempts to construct and reconstruct identities in the light of threatening new realities. What many authors of these stories of suffering, illness, and dying manage to do, is continue the same process of personal meaning-making that all of us, according to Luckmann, are inevitably forced into by the peculiar structure of modern industrial society and its bifurcated worldview.

Because of the "do-it-yourself" quality of private sphere identity formation, we do not need a pattern or formula that can be imposed on each and every one of us. That was how traditional social orders managed the problem of identity. One appropriated a universally shared ideal of what a "good dying" was, and tried one's best to live up to it. Historical researchers, such as Philippe Aries in *The Hour of Our Death,* document how such ideals satisfied the needs of persons in the past. Although a certain degree of this hope for a universal model remains, as the book jackets assure us that the narrative in question will provide "inspiration" and "help for others who share the same burden," what the reader actually encounters is something very different. We do not, in an autobiography, encounter a universal ideal. Instead, we meet real, individual selves, particularly families with unrepeatable histories and memories. From them we learn how others manage; we want a recipe for a process, not a finished product. Hence, our fascination with first-person accounts, with the struggles of others as individuals, reinforces our belief that everyone is unique, that each of us is different enough from all others so that no common formula is possible. Yet all protagonists struggle against problems that—whatever the specifics—have in common the disruption of the sacred cosmos, the dominant worldview, and its concomitant vision of the deathless, autonomous individual.

This fascination with the person, the individual, the uniquely "mine," is by now widely taken for granted in today's America. In chapter 3, "Why Write a Personal Narrative," we will explore the nature of autobiographical writing, and what such accounts may or may not accomplish. Why, for instance, should we even be interested in hearing the details of Violet Weingarten's, Nan Shin's, and Jill Ireland's chemotherapy treatments, or learning of the fluctuations of Stewart Alsop's platelet count? As readers, we are prepared and willing to learn more about these peoples' bodies than we know about our own (how many of us know our platelet count or even our own blood type?) let alone more about their families and inner histories than we are likely to know about most of our best friends. We plunge as readers into often very intimate details of families and individuals in crises, in pain, coping desperately and/or courageously with major illness and death. Some of these people are celebrities prior to their illness, but stories by persons who are unfamous follow the same pattern. What do we hope to learn from this immersion? Perhaps because we know, all along, that there is no such thing as a deathless, ever-young person, we need to find out how to confront and reconcile ourselves to this knowledge. How can we ourselves do what these authors accomplish? Not to become them, but to remain truly ourselves even when our "sacred cosmos" and identity are under attack, as attacked they surely will be, sooner or later, since their tenets conflict directly with the real trajectory of human life.

First-person narratives are an arena of struggle, then—the efforts of those caught immediately in the failure of a worldview to recreate themselves and a meaningful cosmos. Ironically, the authors are, for the most part, still entangled in the fabric of the same failed world-view and must rely upon its central motifs in their efforts at reconstruction. Far from truly escaping from the limits of society's invisible religion, they often continue to embrace it. Although many raise questions about the meaning and extent of autonomy, there remains a pervasive trust that staying in control is the key to meeting life's problems. For example, all protest America's denial of death, and the portrait of the deathless, ever-youthful person that goes with this. Hence, the way that death is acknowledged is by speaking of it as a last occasion for the exercise of autonomy. Book titles such as *Last Wish* and *A Death of One's Own* exemplify this. We will discuss the issue of autonomy, correlate of which may be isolation, in chapter 5.

Attentive readers may have noticed a fourth discrepancy in the key passage of Luckmann. Is the "his" in the description of the autonomous individual simply an insensitive use of "generic male language," or is there a gender bias built into our picture of the person that overlooks the very different experiences of women? Perhaps women are more used to limits on their autonomy, or less likely to worship autonomy in the first place? Not only many illnesses, but caretaking for the sick is a gendered experience in American society. If there is a normal expectation implied in regard to death at all, it is that men die first, and women take care of the sick and dying. But how gendered is dying? Are the accounts written by women significantly different from those written by men? In chapter 6 we will look more critically at gender and identity and try to explode some of the more facile stereotypes about male and female spheres, aptitudes, and psyches.

What all dying protagonists face is the gradual destruction of their lives and their bodies, and the overwhelming interest of the death and dying literature is in dying, not in death per se. Kübler-Ross, once again the pioneer in making this topic accessible and acceptable, notes that there is almost nothing about death in her book, and states "We have learned that for the patient death itself is not the problem, but dying is feared" (1969, 268). Is this because dying can be "managed," worked through, while death is, and remains, a black hole into which all meanings vanish? Certainly the secular quality of the death awareness movement and of most of the autobiographies emphasizes this bias toward what can be coped with, and what lies firmly within the realm of this reality. Moreover, the narrator or protagonist often insists, rightly, that so long as he/she is alive, that is what is happening. "This is a book about life, not death," some of the book jackets claim (although this can be a reassurance to potential buyers that the book will not be too depressing!). Even life on the brink of death still qualifies. Nevertheless, something must be said about death, and in these accounts its negation appears in two forms: as destruction, and as loss. The destructive features are mutilations (loss of a breast) or disfigurements (loss of hair through chemotherapy), but these symbolize, unavoidably, the totality of bodily destruction that lies ahead. Loss is a far more dominant way to encounter death; indeed, some theories of the sick role and of dying make loss the only motif. We will look closely at just what is lost and how in chapter 7. That so many of these works are written to record the last months of a beloved person's being, and memorialize him/her through the text, is one reason why loss becomes the most powerful and overarching motif for encountering death.

We have mentioned the roles and definition of religion as a focus for our study. Luckmann's work, *The Invisible Religion,* was a sample of a sociologist's quest to move beyond conventional definitions of religion as tied to specific content (belief in God) or institutions (churches). Although his attempt may not be successful, many others have tried to express an emergent, personal, not-always-contained-by institutions sense of the sacred, the transcendent, and the ultimate. Today, this is most often captured by the term *spirituality,* while *religion* refers to the public, communal, historical force. But even with this shift in vocabulary, the central issue remains: because only a few of the authors of autobiographies report that they attend church or synagogue, and a large proportion make no explicit references to God or any other higher power, can we then simply label these accounts secular or irreligious? While the majority of authors sense that in their encounter with the border of human life, they have met a mystery, a more ultimate and real reality that dwarfs the world as they had previously known it. But it would be a mistake to claim that this insight alone leaves them more spiritual. Often, the reality they meet is a nightmare, and the struggle with it is a daily agonizing battle that yields no fruit beyond itself. In chapter 8 we will carefully consider the questions these possibilities raise for the nature of contemporary religion.

Limits of the Study

A word should be said about what autobiographies cannot tell us, and what we the authors disclaim trying to demonstrate. These auto-biographical narratives are special kinds of documents. Like diaries and journals, they are written texts; those who cannot write, or to whom writing is an entirely painful task, will not produce them. Those who belong to an oral subculture may sing, tell stories, and even today make videos—but they will not *write* their tales. Thus, any study that confines itself to published, book-length first-person narra-tives, misses out on the fullness and totality of American ethnic diversity.

But we, in our search through the sources, also began to wonder: where are the accounts from middle-class African-Americans? From the suburban grown children of South Philadelphia Italians? Why has no Amy Tan appeared to write the nonfictional story of her Chinese-born father's struggle with cancer? The absence of these— and it is a very glaring absence—suggests that the experiences cap-tured in a death and dying autobiography must be particular and individual, but also considered by publishers as sufficiently middle-American so that readers will not absolutely refuse to link their own experiences with those of the protagonists. Curiously, the journal of a Swiss law professor dying of cancer (Noll, *In the Face of Death*) meets this criterion, as do many accounts of Jewish families. The sole ac-count in this genre written by an African-American woman, Audre Lorde's *The Cancer Journals*, might seem to challenge this generaliza-tion; Lorde is a black lesbian feminist poet whose story of her breast cancer surgery follows many of the conventions of the genre while remaining a thrice-marginalized person as she asks, "How many black lesbian feminists do they have in Reach for Recovery?" (37).

What this tells us is that these narratives are not good sociological data about "how we die in America today." But neither are they merely "what publishers believe the literate book-buying public wants to read about how we die in America today." There is a wide range of lifestyles, locales, and values represented in these works. True, New York and the West Coast are overrepresented, but there is a big difference between the social environment of Paul Monette's *Borrowed Time: An AIDS Memoir* with its angry, saddened portrait of affluent gay life in Los Angeles, and that of Seattle native Patti Trull in *On with My Life*, about her adolescent bout with mutilating bone cancer, which conveys an exuberant, clean-cut outdoorsy normality. Moreover, the heavy overrepresentation of professional writers and journalists among the authors makes one even more suspicious of trying to rely on these texts as if they were sociological data.

What of the readers of these narratives? Here, too, we must take a very cautious stand. Who reads these books, and who do their writers expect to read them? This is a question that, within the methodology of this study, is difficult to answer directly. Some authors are widely known—Norman Cousins' *Anatomy of an Illness*, for example—while others, although they are gems, are relatively obscure. Within the texts themselves, we find references again and again to Cousins; his book is mentioned by Joseph Heller as one of the two books he had with him in the hospital (the other was Jane Austen's *Emma*). From internal evidence, we can say with confidence that many authors expect that their work will be read by: other sick persons, "This tale will not tell anyone how to cope but it does bear witness to what goes into coping. That witness, I believe, is enough" (Frank 1992, 5); or those caring for the sick, "Care itself is inseparable from understanding. It must be symmetrical . . . Listening to another, we hear ourselves" (49); by medical professionals (they hope) who need to learn how medicine looks from the patient's point of view; by the literate middle-aged who may be in good health now themselves, but who are beginning to recognize that the deathless ever-young image they hold of themselves is an illusion. People want to tell about their extraordinary experiences, although perhaps not all of us regard our own experiences with life-threatening illness as extraordinary. Anatole Broyard does, "For a seriously ill person, opening your consciousness to others is like the bleeding doctors used to recommend to relieve the pressure" (Broyard 1992, 22). Throughout his book, *Intoxicated by My Illness*, he seems to be saying that being heard and understood in the midst of illness is one of a patient's primary needs. There appears to be little appeal to the younger adult reader; nor, we suspect, to the elderly, for whom the disruptive aspect of death is no longer an acute issue.

The ideal reader, however, remains a generic figure. Male authors occasionally remark upon how their illnesses changed their views of women, as if suddenly reminded that women readers outnumber men. But then, women authors, as well, sometimes self-consciously, mention how easily women can talk with each other, as if to explain to puzzled male readers what otherwise might seem surprising. Jewish authors will briefly explain any religious practices, although so few of these are mentioned (in spite of the high percentage of Jewish authors) that no one could gain from this genre even a glimpse of traditional Judaism's rich ceremonial life. There is less need for explanation by authors writing as Christians, whether because Christian practices are simply more familiar, or because those that appear in the texts—taking communion, prayer with and for the sick—are themselves generic.

Although there are some genuine exceptions to this characterization of the ideal reader (no one uninterested or uniformed about transpersonal psychology would be able to make great headway through Ken Wilber's passages in *Grace and Grit*, his book about his wife's ordeal with breast cancer) his/her generic, educated, and white middle-class status is balanced by an assumed ignorance and fear of disease. In the case of cancer, it is taken for granted that the readers are ill-informed, carrying nightmarish pictures in their heads not only of the disease but of the treatments for it (some of these pictures, alas, are true). Heart ailments do not receive quite this attention, as the popular view is that these are somehow "better" than cancer; strokes fall somewhere in between. In the case of AIDS, an assumption of ignorance and fear of the disease is certainly more justifiable, and the accounts succeed only halfway—they help dispel ignorance, but not fear; the AIDS narratives are the most horrendous of the whole collection. When it comes to rarer conditions, such as ALS, hemophilia, lupus, and Guillain-Barre syndrome, the author-as-educator takes over. A reader presumed culturally literate may nevertheless believe that human livers come in pairs (Maier 1991, 25). But the autobiographical genre is not the best place to learn about disease itself; rather, one discovers "illness," or as Frank puts it, "the experience of living through the disease," (Frank 1992, 13) the recognition that "more is happening to you than you discuss with most physicians in most medical settings," (Frank 1992, 15) and of nearness to death.

There is, of course, a final and absolute limit for us as the investigators into these narratives of illness and death. It has been our fantasy, from time to time, to imagine the deceased narrators and protagonists all together at some kind of social function or support group for the recently dead, located in an afterlife realm where the residents are still interested in themselves and their families. How would all these dead husbands, parents, lovers get along? What would they have to say to each other—and to us? What might they now know that they did not know at the time they wrote or were written about? Would Simone deBeauvoir's "maman" have anything in common with the mothers of Betty Rollin, LeAnne Schreiber, and Joan Gould? What about C.S. Lewis's and Ken Wilber's young wives? Would the remarkable husbands of Lois Snow, Gerda Lerner, and Lael Wertenbaker find similar experiences to share, beyond the fact of being dead? What messages, if any, would they have for us today? This fantasy, kept separate from our serious beliefs about life beyond this life, sustains us in awareness that being "near death" is nevertheless *still living*, and that all tales of the dying are still told by those yet alive. In our fantasy, even the least introspective, self-aware, deceased protagonist now knows more than the wisest living authors. Or perhaps not "more," but he or she knows differently, knows in a manner or from a place that is not available to us. We, the living readers, remain rooted here, in the midst of life, but through our reading, learn from others as they approach its edge, its ending.

Chapter Two

"HOW I ENDURED
AND LEARNED
FROM . . ."

IN THIS CHAPTER, WE WILL SURVEY and summarize the range of first-person narratives we have discovered in which illness, dying, and grief make up the chief subject matter. Here, we will provide an overview of the "data" for the rest of this study. Because a tremendous amount has been written about autobiography as a genre in the last twenty-five years, we will take up the question "Why write an autobiography?" in the next chapter.

Both the Library of Congress classification and the Dewey Decimal classification catalogue books that explicitly focus on illness according to disease. All the works by and about cancer sufferers are in one section, those on AIDS are in another. Because many of the first-person narratives do not carry "cancer" or any other disease label in their title, they may be catalogued by libraries under "diaries and journals," or "memoirs," or even "theologies of suffering." Both catalogue systems mix books about cancer for the public with books by cancer sufferers, so that the disease dimension is further emphasized simply by what one finds nearby on the shelf. In contrast, bookstores may or may not have a "health" section that is willing to include such obviously downbeat items as narratives of illness and death. On the other hand, these may wind up under "biography and autobiography," and this is especially so, of course, if the author is a celebrity.

We have found that neither the library nor the bookstore approach is particularly helpful in grasping the range and types of these narratives. Why not? First, because it seems that the disease classification overemphasizes the medical dimension of narratives that may, in fact, contain a bare minimum of medical information. Even those that provide much factual information do so in furtherance of a narrative that is not a medical text. To read a first-person narrative such as Stewart Alsop's *Stay of Execution* is, to put it bluntly, a clumsy way to learn about rare blood cancers. It is true that all the narratives of AIDS share certain features that reflect the realities of the disease, and also, to some extent, the realities of its epidemiology. But even here, a focus on the disease dimension may overlook other, more profound similarities between Paul Monette's *Borrowed Time: An AIDS Memoir* and Elizabeth Cox's *Thanksgiving: An AIDS Journal.* Such a classification also minimizes the fundamental differences between examples such as these, differences of quality, truthfulness, coherence.

As for "biography and autobiography," our sources lie closer to this rubric, except that they differ from conventional examples of these genres in one major point. Biography and autobiography are normally conceived of as covering a life. Our narratives cover not a whole life, but a life towards its death, or a life recovering from the death of another. Like Mark's Gospel, eight of whose chapters deal with the last week of its protagonist's career, these somehow violate the ordinary allocation of attention we usually expect of biography. They condense the pre-illness existence of the protagonist and/or narrator into a chapter or two, so as to provide sufficient background for the main drama of dying. There are some exceptions to this, but the allotment of space means that even major cultural accomplishments are sometimes telescoped into a few preliminary pages.

In order to provide ourselves with a better starting point for analysis of this literature, we began to think in terms of *stories*, for that—and not medical texts or case histories—is what these works are.

From this insight, we looked at who was telling the story, and from what time-perspective. There are some stories that can only be told by the dying protagonist; in others, the narrator is the one who watches his/her beloved die, and writes (or edits) sufficiently long after the death so that the fact of the death is known right from the start of the tale. Then, there are those where the death is also known from the beginning, but where the principle interest lies in the survivor's recovery. From the perspective of these works as literary documents, this kind of distinction makes more sense than those of libraries or bookstores.

But the "who" of storytelling is never so straightforward as the "what" of a disease. Each work has an author, a narrator, protagonists, an ideal reader, and a writer. Although those who deal exclusively with literary autobiography have generated refinements among these categories, for our purposes we limit ourselves to the above five. Who are they? The *author*, as we will use this term, is the agency in control of the final written text, ordering and editing it. The author has *authority* of his/her text. In cases where there are two authors listed on the book jacket, there may indeed be only one author in this literary sense. The other is a conarrator who contributes chapters to the finished project. The *narrator*, however, is the voice that functions as storyteller, a voice directly heard within the text. Moreover, as we increasingly realized, the narrator's perspective is the *only* one to which we have direct access. Even if the narrator claims that he or she is writing a "biography" of a now-dead beloved, that lost person is seen by readers only through the eyes of the narrator. The narrator is not (literarily) the same as the protagonist, even if they share the same name. The narrator may know how it all turns out (although not always); the protagonist rarely, if ever, does. The protagonist acts in ways that you, the reader, find perfectly understandable for an individual under stress; the narrator comments icily on "his own" responsibility, immaturity, denial. Or, in other cases, the narrator insists how wonderful, courageous, and admirable the beloved was; while you the reader, on the other hand, discover only a shadow figure dominated by a narrator who crowds his/her beloved out of the story.

There is also, in these narratives, the *reader*; not you, the flesh and blood person who bought this book at the local shopping mall, but the reader for whom the author is writing. This is tricky; for whom are these people writing? How does what is purported to be a private journal of a very private experience get to include a reader? Did the reader get added only as the journal was edited for publication? Having already introduced the generic reader in chapter 1, we will return to this topic again in chapter 3. For now, the reader as understood here is a figure indirectly within the text, and in the case of many journal-style works, the first and foremost ideal reader may share the same name as the protagonist, narrator, and author.

Finally, there is the *writer*, who is a flesh and blood human being, outside the text. We assume that the writer is there—or if the writer is dead, that an editor will tell us how soon after the manuscript was completed the writer died. The writer has a postpublication career, which can lead to poignant or ironic complications (Monette survived the death of his beloved to write several other books and reveal other close relationships; Tsongas survived not only cancer but his own retirement, and briefly reentered politics).

Because these narratives of illness, death, and grief are true, we tend to lump together protagonist, narrator, author and writer. It is an important fact of the genre that one, and only one, human being is, so to speak, really there. No one suggests otherwise (we found no account which raises the question of ghostwriting in a serious way). But for the purposes of our classification, it helps to have these distinctions in mind. Remember, we are dealing directly with texts here, and only indirectly with persons.

Type I: "How I Came Close to Death and Recovered"

The most ancient and best-known Western autobiography is probably Augustine's *Confessions*. Here, the successful churchman, soon-to-be bishop of Hippo, recounts to God the tale of his earlier wanderings, restlessness, sins. Having fled far from God, he sought happiness in all the wrong places. But God—Augustine then realized—was always seeking him. When, after many years of misery, Augustine finally turns and repents of his distorted desires, he finds and is found by the one true love, the one goal, the one reality he had missed before. Writing the tale of his sudden, dramatic conversion fifteen years after the event took place, he looks back on an episode whose meaning has had time to jell. He is also able to sum up and evaluate his current situation, free from almost all of the pains of his tumultuous earlier years. This plot provides the model for almost all Christian conversion narratives and a wide range of secular auto-biographies as well. Although critical interpreters have tried to un-dermine Augustine's own brilliant reconstruction of life's meaning (for example, by showing how perhaps he had not changed as much as he thought he had), the paradigm of a conversion from a death-like existence to a new and miraculously better life retains its power.

It is an interesting question how this paradigm of death and re-birth is indebted directly to the central Christian passion narrative of Jesus' death and resurrection. Augustine himself does not really rely on this, but uses imagery closer to birth and childhood. The figure he sees at the time of his conversion is Lady Continence, "a fruitful mother"! (Augustine 1993, bk8, 11) Once created and set as a literary genre, one does not need to be Christian to write this kind of autobiography. Having said that, however, there is always the hint that Christian language of death and rebirth will dominate an ac-count of miraculous recovery, unless the author has some specific alternative perspective on which to draw.

The most fortunate narrators, past and present, are those who can use this time-tested model and fit their stories into its framework convincingly (see Hawkins 1990). Not only does that mean that in their own eyes the outcome is unequivocally good, but they do not need to create a new literary genre in order to tell their story. They can become new Augustines by retelling their own life trajectory in terms of downward or wayward slide, followed by dramatic turn-around toward the good. They go down toward death—physical and often spiritual—but emerge reborn, given new life. Oliver Sacks's *A Leg to Stand On* is a brilliant example of this type, and Norman Cousins's *Anatomy of an Illness* is the best known of all illness narra-tives. What really counts is the sense of miraculous turnaround, brought about by will, but even more by dependence upon some mysterious, non-ego force that works for healing. And the protago-nist's survival to the point where he/she can begin work as author, and—like Augustine—look back from a point of relative safety to become the narrator of the perilous journey.

Thus, what marks narratives such as Agnes DeMille's *Reprieve*, Mar-vin Barrett's *Spare Days*, and William Stringfellow's *Second Birthday* is more than just survival: it is a sense of profound joy and gratitude at the conversion from death to life. Barrett's closing episode serves to epitomize this. After having been treated for cancer, he suffers a heart attack and apparently a clinical death; he is revived in the hospital. A few days later, his astonished doctor stands by his bed, and stares at his now conscious and alert patient. The young doctor shakes his head and exclaims both to Barrett and a troop of medical students: "Dead. Dead." There had been no vital signs. But Barrett knows that what was really meant was: "Alive. Alive!" (Barrett 1988, 198) And the book has got to end right here, for after this ultimate turnaround, everything else would have been anticlimactic.

But is full medical recovery in any way the criterion for fitting one's story to this plot line? NO! What counts as new birth or conversion may be very far from what any doctor might consider full recovery. And most of these narrators know this. Titles such as *Reprieve* and *Sweet Reprieve* tell this side of the story. Agnes DeMille never recovered her old life after a massive cerebral hemorrhage; her return took a long time and was filled with losses, diminishments, and insults, including a coronary attack well into her recovery process. Yet she is able to say of herself, "although I looked like an old woman and could barely walk and needed help for every physical thing I did, I yet felt like a little child, young and fresh and full of vigor" (DeMille 1981, 205–206). Her book ends with her triumphant return to the concert stage under new terms, all hers. And Frank Maier tells us what his doctors told him: "Transplant recipients are never cured, they just trade a terminal disease for a lifetime of medical management" (Maier 1991, 255). But in that condition he finds a sense of purpose as a transplant publicist and in work with organ donor families. As for finding ultimate meaning in his new life, the former *Newsweek* bureau chief crows, "I can honestly say that I am more suited for being a grandpa than anything else I have done in life." But because diseases like cancer recur, even an author who closes his/her book on a disease-free note is never sure that its sequel will be called something like *On With My Life* (Patti Trull). At this point in time, the narrator tells us, "I am over the worst; I am *Recalled by Life* [Sattilaro's title]. I am reborn." Life never promises more than a life-time guarantee on anyone.

What features of this type of narrative are most characteristic and noteworthy? First, it is biased toward survival, and only survivors write them. As those who have researched the literature on the Holocaust have learned (see Young 1988), narratives by survivors are not the same as those written during the time of Nazi rule. Survivors are not a cross-section of the total population affected. They start the story at a point in time, and select incidents to include which may not have seemed especially significant when they first occurred, but which later (and from the post-Holocaust time of writing) appear ominous. "Had I but known . . ." the narrator tells his/her readers, "I would have done what I could to escape." Survivors also have been given time to separate out appearance from what seems certain to have been underlying historical reality. They are passionately concerned to contribute to the total record of an historical reality. That they did not experience this without blinders at the time is part of their tale.

Without comparing the magnitude of sufferings or in any way suggesting a broad-based analogy between having a terminal illness in America and being a Holocaust victim, this same lesson of how to read survivors' narratives can be applied to our sample. First, there are no AIDS survivors; cancer, stroke, heart disease, liver failure— yes. There are no AIDS survivors, however, because long-term, no one has survived AIDS. Someone can be HIV-positive for a long time, as Elizabeth Glaser and Paul Monette prove, but they are not AIDS survivors in the same way that Barrett is a heart attack survivor, or even in the sense that DeMille survived a stroke.

The survivors are also entitled to present themselves as not only feisty but successful. What they did as protagonists *worked*, or they wouldn't be writing as narrators. Max Lerner presents himself, in his dual role as protagonist and narrator, as the kind of person who could stand up to two cancers and a heart attack—and win. In his *Wrestling with the Angel,* there is no doubt who is going to come off best: "I may stumble into darkness suddenly. But death will catch me in motion . . . still invested with the *mysterium tremendum* of life, death, and love, of God and the cosmos—which at this point is the only way I know of transcending death" (Lerner 1990, 144). Agnes DeMille did not accomplish what she did in the world of dance without the character of a charming rhinoceros. Moreover, as a dancer, she tells us, she had a life-long habit of disciplining her body, so that physical rehabilitation after her stroke was, in her own eyes, *easier* for her than it would have been for a normal, phlegmatic, flabby person. Patti Trull, the youngest of our authors, tells how she survived adolescent cancer and leg amputation, but also how she went on to ride a bicycle and ski regularly, not to mention start a career as a therapist in the very hospital where she had been a patient.

Feisty is our word; angry, determined, powerful are the words that come to the minds of the narrators. Audre Lorde was diagnosed with breast cancer in her late seventies and survived for fourteen years. She was angry at racist, patriarchal, homophobic America before the cancer diagnosis, and she becomes angrier still as she recovers. After sensing disapproval in her doctor's office for her refusal to wear a breast prosthesis, she rants against society's images of women as decorative sex objects:

> When Moishe Dayan . . . stands up in front of parliament or on TV with an eye patch . . . nobody tells him to get a glass eye . . . The world sees him as a warrior with an honorable wound. . . . Well, women with breast cancer are warriors also. I have been to war and still am. . . . I refuse to be reduced in my own eyes or in the eyes of others from warrior to mere victim, simply because it might render me a fraction more acceptable or less dangerous to the still complacent who believe if you cover up a problem it ceases to exist. (1980, 59–60)

Whether or not we agree with her stance, we as readers feel Lorde is entitled to make it, and entitled to her anger. She's gone through hell, and survived. We grant to those who have gone through certain outrageous sufferings the right to present themselves this way.

Does feistiness as a character trait add to one's chances of survival? While this literature could not possibly give us an accurate scientific answer to such a question, it is worth raising precisely because Cousins, followed by several others nearly as influential, believes that feistiness does help. The passive patient is the one most likely to give in to death, while the one who remains feisty will make it, and get better. Or so goes the contemporary myth, most frequently associated with Carl Simonton and Bernie Siegel, whose writings on overcoming cancer are familiar to many, many of our authors (and probably to their readers, as well). Unlike Augustine, Cousins *does* take credit for his conversion from death to life, and recommends an attitude of taking responsibility for one's own as a substantial element in that same recovery. None of the survivors would categorically deny this, yet many of them are reluctant to endorse it. Stroke recovery may involve will and attitude—in fact, it almost certainly does. But the severity of the stroke limits what is possible. May Sarton's stroke was much milder than DeMille's (she mentions no lasting physical disability), which, in turn, may have been less severe than that of Eric Hodgins (see below). An even more somber consideration is that all the narrators speak of fellow sufferers who did *not* survive, and who struggled just as hard as those who did. We will return to a discussion of the influence of Cousins, Simonton, and Seigel in a later chapter.

There are only a few cases in which survival, understood existentially rather than medically, is in question. One of the oldest accounts, written in 1964, is Eric Hodgins' *Episode: Report on an Accident Inside My Skull.* This is a document of a pre-CAT-scan stroke, but also of suicidal depression, hospitalization, and finally, and very tentatively, of new life. The author is at pains to tell us, in an appendix ("Why Eric Can't Spell"), that he is still unable to write normal English, and the entire manuscript had to laboriously be corrected before publication. In short, his identity as a professional writer has been drastically and permanently damaged. In what sense, then, can we speak of Hodgins as a survivor? Because as a narrator, he can, like Augustine, look back and see that he was once lost, close to death—and now is back, headed in the right direction. There is the possibly of another stroke, but he is no longer considering suicide. And this is enough to qualify.

Survivors are free to look back and see warning signs they missed at the time. This, in fact, is how a number of the stories begin, with seemingly innocent physical sensations that only later were understood as warning signs or symptoms of a major disease. Because early detection remains the single best way to survive cancer (short of never having the disease at all), these play a critical role in the plot when cancer is the illness. "Had I but known what some odd symptom really meant, I would have rushed to the doctor, insisted on multiple tests, etc." The narrator is safe now, and free to comment on how very foolish he-as-protagonist was at the time.

But not every odd bodily feeling is an early warning sign of anything, and our authors know this. The narrator must admit that guilt overshadows his or her memories. "If only I had noticed x, I would have gone for treatment sooner," easily becomes a broken record. "Had I but known" is really not a very productive line of thought, nor does it correspond to the feisty and hopeful character narrators give to protagonists. It should be mentioned that a few of these ignored-at-the-time symptoms are so truly alarming that the narrator's as well as the protagonist's judgment is questioned. What kind of person could laugh off a loss of consciousness and coordination while driving on a Chicago expressway (Maier)? The answer will be "Only an idiot like myself," but the mud sticks to both the narrator and the protagonist. For many narrators, this additional explanation is needed: a whole generation of American men (and some women) were raised on the belief that the only manly way to handle bodily ailments was to ignore them.

The plot that holds Type I narratives together requires a buildup of suffering, and a large amount of suspense as to *how* the protagonist will survive. Perhaps to offset the foregone conclusion of recovery, reprieve, or new life, many of these accounts take the form of journals. A journal or diary offers just that day-to-day sense of immediacy, of being in the midst of struggle rather than past it, which authors of all four types of narrative prefer. So there is no necessary relationship between the outcome and the choice between a continuous narrative and a journal format. Some authors combine the two. The journal, described by one theorist of autobiography as the "precipitate" of each days events (Weintraub 1975, 827) is ideal for documenting the up-and-down jagged trajectory of illness and its treatment. A good day is followed by a bad one: physically, emotionally, psychosocially. Small events that were once too insignificant for recording (such as a walk around the block) now loom very large, and a journal that is filled with such gives the reader and the narrator a vivid picture of the shrunken world of the protagonist. Or, perhaps the proper way to describe this phenomenon is that as the world of the sick shrinks in scope, it expands in distinctness. A short walk, a visit, a "good day" now really count, as they never did before. A day-by-day journal may capture these while omitting descriptions of the more gradual, but relentless, failing of the body.

In the pattern described above, cancer sets the plot for gradual deterioration and insidious onset. Those narratives that deal with sudden onset disorders—stroke, heart attack, Guillain-Barré Syndrome—adapt the plot so that the physical assault, trauma, insult, or episode is the start of the protagonist's misery. His/her real trauma comes as the extent of the damage becomes known, or its duration is recognized. Strokes come on fast, but the psychological adaptation to them is what the narrators really chart. In all cases, there is a gradual sense that one's body, and with it, one's self, is permanently damaged, changed for the worse. As we all see, it is this drama of the traumatized, disrupted, wounded self that lies at the core of all forms of illness, dying, and grief narratives.

How does the turnaround come? Is it, as in the Augustine conversion paradigm, a *sudden* shift? The Barrett example certainly suggests that it can be, humanly if not medically. But it is misleading to see this as a necessary ingredient in narratives that follow this paradigm (Christian evangelists in the past wasted a lot of time arguing over whether or not conversions had to be sudden; there is no point at all in settling the question by defining a true conversion as a sudden event). "Getting better" is more descriptive of the normal course of events narrated. At some point, the protagonist suddenly realizes he/she has made it, at least for now.

At this point, the protagonist has emerged as a new person. This is the other dimension of the paradigm, obscured, in part, by the contemporary emphasis on feistiness as a long-term character trait. The new person may have experienced a dramatic paradigm shift: the world lived in now, what counts now, what is seen now, is very different than in the "before." Agnes DeMille reevaluates her career, her contribution to dance, and discovers a wisdom that comes with letting go of her long-term ambitions: "And I suddenly was aware that I was happy, happy in a way that I had not been before. Happy in the moment, contented, trusting. It was enough somehow" (DeMille 1981, 201–202). Other ambitious protagonists face the ending of their careers, so that writers (Hodgins), politicians (Tsongas), and newsmen (Maier) emerge disencumbered, whether through choice or the exigencies of illness. Even if the term "new person" is too strong to capture the real flavor of the change from pre- to post-illness self, almost all of the authors attest that there has been some change.

A few protagonists end their adventures by embarking on what amount to new careers, devoted in some way to helping others similarly afflicted. Patti Trull becomes an occupational therapist for children with cancer; Frank Maier speaks on behalf of transplant recipients and organ donor families. Once again, Norman Cousins is the outstanding example of this, since after *Anatomy of an Illness* he is best known for his advocacy of patient-oriented therapies. Yes, he did do others things before, such as edit *The Saturday Review,* but that is no longer how he will be remembered by the majority of Americans.

To test the theme of new life, and how much we the real readers and even the ideal reader within the text expects that theme to be present, we cite one example of a narrative where the protagonist's close encounter with death failed to have any such effect. *A Coronary Event* is coauthored by the sufferer of a heart attack (Lesher) and his doctor (Halbersham). Lesher, although at one point a very sick man, recovers physically through exercise, willpower and, (perhaps) medical technology. Readers—including the ideal reader within the text—expect him to be changed by this experience, to have dropped some of the competitive and compulsive Type A personally traits that he and others accept as having led to his heart crisis. But not only has he remained the same *qua* protagonist as he was before, but as narrator he defends himself against the reader's hopes for him. He convincingly tells us that he likes himself just the way he is and always was, that he admires his own personal style too much to abandon or alter it, and that if we expected anything else, we can just forget it. He *knows* the reader's expectations, as well as the medical prognosis. He bucks the paradigm. And his readers are—legitimately, we believe—disappointed. Surely to have come so close to death, and to have emerged as a survivor, ought to have carried with it some wisdom, insight, or sense of new values—something to justify the writing of the tale.

Yet to be a survivor is an accomplishment. These persons have earned the right to tell their stories in a certain way. We admire them, perhaps exaggerating their special qualities and strengths or overlooking the downside of feistiness. But as in the case of Holocaust narratives, when the total picture is dominated by survivors' accounts, it becomes skewed. Moreover, the real tragedy of the nonsurvivors is compounded. Not only have they lost their lives, their experiences are lost from historical memory as well. They are doubly obliterated. This is true as well of illness narratives; those who did not make it outnumber those who did. Because they are nonsurvivors, does that mean that their stories should be eclipsed and held in lower esteem than those we have discussed? Sadly, writers such as Cousins, Simonton, and Seigel might be used to legitimate such a stance. But to do so distorts the deeper wisdom of illness and dying. However, the telling of these stories—of those who struggled and hoped, but who died anyway—is more difficult. The classic Augustinian framework does not fit.

Type II: "How I Grew Closer to Death"

A stay of execution is not a reprieve. It is a postponement, not a reversal. The narratives in this category document a downward slide that may be slowed, but is never truly reversed. The narrator travels inexorably toward death, and by the time the story closes, the protagonist, as well, realizes that this is the only possible outcome. Or is it the reader—the real reader and also the ideal reader built into the text—who knows for sure that the protagonist will die? In works that follow this pattern, the final pages may be in the form of an epilogue, added by a relative or even the publisher. "Mr. X died on Month/Day/Year, in such-and-such hospital. After his death, the journal you have just read was found and edited by his wife for publication." The plot is not one of recovery but of discovery, of the unfolding of the inevitable ending to the protagonist and readers alike. This is not as clear-cut a plot line as in Type I, but it offers a potential—if fragile—structure or framework for the narrative nevertheless. And although one would expect that accounts in this category would provide unprecedented insight into death as an inescapable fact of the human condition, this is not the case. The problem of how to wrest a coherent and meaningful narrative out of one's slow drift toward death is formidable.

The very best of these works show awareness of just this challenge, and deal self-consciously with the problem of structure. Stewart Alsop's book, *Stay of Execution*, for example, begins with an explanation of the issue of author and narrator:

> Part of it was written by a me lying in bed at NIH . . . Part of it was written by a me released from NIH . . . feeling pretty rotten . . . Part of it was written by a me sick to death . . . Part of it was written a few weeks later by a euphoric me suddenly feeling better . . . And part of it was written by a me—the me now writing—faced with a recrudescence of the mysterious disease and again in fear of an unwilling expedition to that undiscovered country from whose bourne no traveler returns.
> (1973, 10–11)

Each "me" referred to represents a "stage" in the progression to-ward death: the first still in denial, the second depressed, the final "me" stoic and courageous. By offering the reader this explanation, Alsop, the author, gains control over the product in a way parallel to that in which Alsop, the narrator, gains a measure of control over the dying process. But Alsop was given time and strength to become his own "author"; others were not.

A second solution to the problem of structuring the narrative is that of Violet Weingarten. *Intimations of Mortality* is the journal of her chemotherapy, not her illness and dying, she tells us. It becomes both, but the chemotherapy has a beginning and a prescheduled ending, and this frames her story. Still another structuring device is to focus the plot on acceptance of death; the story can end when the protagonist is willing to renounce all hope for cure or physical heal-ing and trust God completely, as does David Watson in his *Fear No Evil*: "I still don't know why God allowed it, nor does it bother me. But I am beginning to hear what God is saying" (1984, 130). This is, in its own fashion, as Augustinian as a conversion narrative, for the narrator can report something—his protagonist self—transformed by grace, and ready to finish the story.

As emphasized in our discussion of Type I, the criteria used for traditional autobiography favor narratives with clear plot lines, with something accomplished, with survival as the outcome. A tale where no one survives and where no clear spiritual rebirth occurs will be—by this standard—flawed. Add to this the bias toward survival fueled by the universal human fear of death and failure, and even more specifically by contemporary alternative medicine (cancer therapies that stress *The Power Within* the patient to overcome the disease); those who do not survive are double failures. They not only succumb to the disease, but they can hardly achieve the clear narratives of those who recover. They lose twice over, when judged by conven-tional standards. These standards may tyrannize, further marginaliz-ing the already-suffering. But a protest against them is not always fruitful. Our biases run deep. The above three authors—Alsop, Weingarten, Watson—do challenge these, at least up to a point. Others do not. It is worth repeating that "Success is none of the names of God"—and nowhere should this be more true than in each individual's encounter with death.

Let us look more closely at the twin challenges faced by authors whose illness is terminal, and whose narratives must encompass and include their own impending deaths. They must undergo the same cancer treatments as those who will recover, and medically it is hard to say that they suffer more. The medical model of aggressive treatment gives the patient something to hope for, and the narrator something specific to write about ("this is the journal of my chemotherapy"). Therefore, in some ways, the saddest and most threatening narratives are those where the illness involved includes virtually no treatment; medically such sufferers are considered to be beyond hope. Murphy's creeping and completely unstoppable paralysis, in *The Body Silent*, is the clearest example of this. Yet with or without crisis-oriented medicine, the protagonist must gradually recognize that a fighting spirit does not always bring results. This includes even what one may label a religious version of feistiness, the contemporary belief—held by Watson initially and associated with the charismatic movement—that God *always* will heal, if one's faith is sufficiently strong (Murphy 1987, 25). At the level of the illness, feistiness must give way to a stoic heroism, or to despair. Fully aware that medically nothing can stop the progression of the disease, the partly paralyzed Murphy awaits the complete shutdown of his major bodily functions without anger, fear, or self-pity. He had earlier in his life triumphed over alcoholism entirely on his own, but this final condition is unfightable. "I did (and still so) know what could happen to me, but I also knew that there wasn't a damn thing I could do about it" (25). Alsop, too, remembers a near-miraculous escape from death during World War II; he knows by the time he as narrator retells it that one such adventure is all he will have. The failure of miracles and feistiness is itself worth charting; but this cannot by itself bear the full weight of the narrative. Something more has to happen, within the person and within the narrator's story.

We have deliberately used the word "stoicism" because this so well characterizes the ideal of Alsop, the best-known author of this category. It is a cultural ideal, exemplifying dignity in the face of unavoidable suffering. A stoic recognizes and renounces self-pity, self-preoccupation, and anger at fate or the failure of medicine. Significantly, a stoic outlook appears gender-biased toward males, unless one specifies what a woman's version of stoicism would look like. Violet Weingarten provides this; she knows she will die, but her version of stoicism is to focus lovingly and exquisitely on the minute, day-to-day adventures of her life as an author and a grandmother, and to keep her *Intimations of Mortality* strictly private. Her family (according to the afterword) was astonished at her awareness of her impending death and pained that they had not been able to share some of it with her. She never discussed it with any of them, and denied herself exorbitant preoccupation with the medical details of her illness. She had a good relationship with her family and with her very empathic doctor, Mark, yet to judgmental outsiders it may seem that she was in denial, merely trying to be a good patient, and not be a burden to her loved ones. Together, she and Alsop represent both literary success as narrators, and the ideal of a stoic encounter with death.

However, a stoic and heroic person is not necessarily a lovable one. Admirable, yes, but not necessarily as filled with the vitality and interest in others that Alsop and Weingarten display. In the extreme cases, someone who transcends human weakness through self-control may fully succeed in encountering death, but loses the reader somewhere along the way. Not his own ideal reader, who remains impressed by the protagonist's achievement, but the real reader, the reader who stopped reading long enough to ponder, "Would I like to know this person? To put up with him even when he's not sick?" Alas, uncharitable as it may be to admit this—after all, these people were *dying*!—Type II yields a disproportionate number of dislikable protagonists and narrators. We cannot warm up to Peter Noll, the heroic Swiss law professor and philosopher who refuses cancer treatments and lives out the remainder of his life *In the Face of Death*. In this case, the reason for our negative impression lies in the nature of his reasoning. His decision is based on an ethic of absolute control; *any* dependence on doctors or other experts threatens his freedom. In contrast, most authors feel that one may fight the domination of the medical establishment, but still admit that absolute control is a chimera. Besides, Noll seems to reserve the right to impose on others (friends, daughters) for necessary care, and his stoicism blends with a heavy stream of anger at colleagues, society, family. His categorical refusal of cancer treatment that may have saved his life is less puzzling when it is viewed as an act of hostility, not solely as an heroic stance of independence and autonomy.

To return to the double burden of the terminally ill narrator, we must ask, Is the difficulty one of how to suffer fatal illness, or how to organize the narrative of one's experience? Is the problem with Noll, at the level of his personality as a controller, or is it a function, in part at least, of the dilemma he faces as narrator? What can be the plot of a tale which ends posthumously, with the narrators death "off stage" postbook? Alsop, Weingarten, and Watson handle this deliberately, and intentionally craft stories that work as narratives. They are, we believe, the three most likable narrator/protagonists of this category, the ones whose own versions of stoicism convince the reader. What prevents the narrators of others in this category from succeeding at this level? (And note how "success" reemerges as a criterion, in spite of our critique!)

The fragmentary nature of a few of the narratives is one element in the answer. Put simply, jottings scribbled by a sick person at 2 A.M. do not make a compelling work of literature; if there is no insight, no sense of progression toward stoicism, the readers interest will wane. Alas, being on the path to death is not a sufficient guarantee of an author's ability to hold our attention. The very unedited quality that is intended to convey authenticity can undermine itself. (We will discuss this more fully in a later chapter, dealing with the nature of autobiography.)

Another way to say this is to find stoicism revealed at the level of literary activity. The author's dispassionate pruning involves careful cutting away of all that clutters his/her central meanings. By contrast, self-pity is filled with clutter; at 2 A.M., when you are feeling sick, even long-ago hurts and insults loom large. Note that an author who has recovered can see and say this via the narrator, while one in the process of dying glimpses it only sporadically.

But no, this is insufficient as an answer to the question of narrators' success. Violet Weingarten and Stewart Alsop are just as clearly dying as are Noll and Murphy and others; yet they remain self-critical writers all the way through. Perhaps another part of the answer is that, while self-conscious as authors, they are not self-consciously trying to become role models for the dying; the heroism is not on display. They write about themselves, but show such vitality and involvement in recording the doings of others, the feel of places they have lived, that they defeat the central autobiographer's demon: the threat of narcissistic self-preoccupation. The narratives that fail as narratives may do so, in part, because they succumb to this.

In chapter 3 we will examine more closely this dilemma of auto-biographers. Meanwhile, without a tale of recovery to relate, which might directly inform and inspire other sufferers, the narrators of Type II stories face the issue of narcissism less sure of their purposes. The professional writer may reply: I've written about everything under the sun, why not write about my own dying? The anthropologist, Murphy, gives his own variant of this reply: "Anthropology had made me into a voyeur of all things human" (Murphy 1987, 67). It is an anthropologist's vocation to study through participation-observation all possibilities of the human condition. Comedienne Gilda Radner offers her reply: She wants to turn a cancer diagnosis into comedy; "If I'm going to have it, I've gotta find out what could be funny about it" (Radner 1989, 168). Only a few can say clearly that they wish to report what life *In the Face of Death* feels like, and of these, fewer still have managed to do so.

Type III: "How I Tended and Cared for My Dying Loved One"

Statistically, the enormous majority of death and dying narratives fall into this group. No matter how sad the ending, it is easier to tell the story of another's dying than to chart one's own. The caretaker, after all, survives the terminal illness, and so lives on to write the ending as the authors of Type II narratives did not. Besides, he or she can avoid the dilemma of narcissistic self-preoccupation by claiming that the real story is that of the protagonist, to whom the finished book is often a memorial. The survivor appears in the story as caretaker, someone who (with few exceptions) shelves his or her own needs during the period of the beloved's dying. The result is a double self-effacement, which marks off this category from the other three main types we discuss in this study.

The story of the dying beloved does not have so clear a religious prototype as does the narrative of illness and recovery. Plato's dying Socrates, memorialized in *Crito* and *Phaedo*, is the earliest historical model for how an individual's dying becomes an occasion to convey the truth of his or her unique life. Or perhaps early Christian tales of martyrs, ordinary men and women whose bravery and defiance of death transformed them into spectacular exemplars of faith, become remote ancestors of today's Type III narratives. Not to mention those many nineteenth-century deathbed scenes so beloved of popular writers and so sentimental and unreal by twentieth-century standards. All of these may play their part in shaping the stories we will discuss here.

But it is equally true to say that the part played by these models from the past is negative. Modern dying is *not* like those death scenes from Dickens or *Uncle Tom's Cabin*, nor is dying of cancer in a hospital today anything like dying by public execution for one's beliefs in the ancient world. Contemporary authors know these models, and find them useless and even revolting. Those authors who portray voluntary deaths by active euthanasia do so to show how humiliating and violating modern death-through-disease can be (Rollin's *Last Wish*), not to glorify death itself. Those authors who portray long, drawn-out death by disease in such a way as to make the beloved appear no less saintly than Little Eva or St. Stephen must also explicitly reject the romanticized disembodied purity of such models.

In fact, there runs through much of this literature two telling motifs that reveal the disjunction between present and past. The first is aesthetic: the grittier, the less prettied-up, the more relentlessly depressing are the situations portrayed, the more authentically will the final story become a tribute to the truth of dying, and to the now-dead beloved as well. This ideology can work to convey the experience of caretaking, especially at home, just as much as it conveys the experience of terminal illness. The risk is that the resulting book will swamp the reader to the point that he or she puts it down in revulsion and despair. A second, and deeper motif is that *no* models, in principle, could fit the uniqueness of an individual person's death. It is not just a case of outdated or inappropriate models, but of the whole belief that models can substitute for the reality of the concrete, unique person's experience.

This motif of personal uniqueness fits one of the fundamental goals of Type III narratives. The memorializing of the dead beloved figures prominently in all of them. By this we mean that the narrator seeks to overcome, through the act of storytelling, the loss of the dead person, and to defeat time through vivid remembering and recording. *The Absence of the Dead Is Their Way of Appearing* (a phrase taken from Simone Weil) is the title of one such memorial (Trautmann 1984); but through the process of writing, the dead are made present again, in some new space, within a text, if no longer within ordinary life. Yet they are present as dead, lost forever. To tell the story honors them, in the manner of a Victorian monument. It cannot be confused with returning them to life.

In order to erect this monument, the narrator must convince his/ her ideal reader that the dead beloved was indeed unique, marvelous, and unreplaceable as a person. Not perfect, but utterly precious. This person stands alone; there will never be, nor could there be, an exact duplicate, or a replacement for him or her. The narrator closes the book with the promise that never, never will the dead beloved be forgotten. He or she assures the reader that the life and death of this man, woman, or child has significance worth remembering. How could any model based on someone else's dying really fit?

In spite of this strenuous assertion, there are obvious similarities among the Type III autobiographies of the beloved's dying. The story can open with the death itself, or with the narrator now bereaved; it then moves back into the history of the relationship between dying protagonist and caretaker(s). We know right from the start what the ending will be, at the level of the plot. Another device is to begin the story with the last healthy moments, before the symptoms of the terminal illness appeared. In the cases of husbands and wives (see below), this is frequently an account of the couple's last healthy vacation, as if to underscore the carefree quality of the pre-illness existence they unthinkingly enjoyed. As the illness progresses—and the majority of these accounts deal, as before, with cancer and other long-term painful terminal conditions (AIDS, Alzheimer's, and ALS are some of these)—life becomes more restricted. The caretaker and the sufferer both move into another reality, severed from that of ordinary healthy life. Being on the moon is one author's reference to this space: lifeless, cold, alien, and in exile (Monette 1988, 2).

Yet the existence of the "moon" of terminal illness is only one side of the story. For the narrator, writing retrospectively, it is astonishing how life elsewhere seems to go on. Other family problems, career commitments, and even national events that once would have loomed large are now reduced in subjective size, but must be handled somehow. More significantly, the image of the moon does not fully capture the sense of life, of vitality and enjoyment that occasionally wells up even in the midst of sickness. Suddenly, in spite of cancer or AIDS, everyone is laughing. Or friends plan a picnic, and although it physically stretches the resources of the dying person, it is a memorable event, a temporary return to earth's surface from the moonscape.

As the illness closes in on everyone, tension builds within the narrative. Often this tension takes one form: Which will happen first—the death of the sick person, or the emotional collapse of the caretaker? To the protagonists within the story, this may have been a real question at the time. Even though it is unlikely that a caretaker who did suffer emotional collapse would write such a narrative (although there are a few) the suspense generated is believable. Especially when what is stressed is the harrowing day-to-day routine of caretaking.

Finally, the sick person is ready to die, and does so, most often without special fanfare, insight, or enlightenment. But also, without special agony—or rather, without agony above and beyond what he or she had already endured. There are a few, but only a few, beatified death scenes in these works, scenes that blend Little Eva with New Age spirituality in a romanticized vision of dying as spiritual fulfillment. Given the prevalence and popularity of out-of-body, near death accounts in American popular culture, it is their absence from the deathbed scenes of Type III narratives that ought to be emphasized. To the survivors, the deaths are expected but not joyful. For the caretakers who had anticipated relief and release (and who had frequently prayed for the death of the beloved), the actual death brings only numbness and loss. The narrative ends here, or with a memorial service soon after the death. The best endings, storywise, do not prolong the tale past the immediate aftermath of death.

Within this plot line, the real content of Type III narratives is played out. They are intended to tell the story of someone else's dying, yet the narrator inevitably sees the whole thing through his or her own eyes. The only story we know is that told by the survivor, whose agony as a survivor is different from that of the dying. Wise narrators recognize this, right from the start, and move the center of gravity from the dying person alone, to the relationships among the protagonists. What dying can reveal is the nature of these relationships, their real worth and meanings, their hidden nuances. Thus the history of the relationships, told from the perspective of their final stages, is the true focus of many of the best Type III narratives. Stories of illness in itself are not worth telling—in contrast to the library classification schemes!—but marriages and ties between generations most definitely are.

The most common relationships covered are those of dying husband, cared for and survived by his wife, and dying mother, cared for by her daughter. This probably reflects demographics, in a society where men die first, and women are the anticipated caretakers in all family deaths. We have found a number of male caretaker narratives, some very good, but in each of these the situation is acknowledged as unexpected, unusual. In Type III, then, the majority of authors are women. The story of the dying husband is also the story of the whole marriage, told from the wife's point of view. The story of the dying mother is simultaneously the daughter's tracing of her identity through time, her trajectory as a daughter of this particular woman, and as a woman who is herself a mother.

The variations of this pattern include husbands caring for dying wives (Meryman, Wilber); men caring for aging parents (Rosenfeld, Roth, Malcolm); and gay men caring for lovers (Monette). There is also a whole subcategory of narrative, parents writing the story of their child's death. Here again, it is mostly mothers who write (Lund, Levit), although the most famous example of this is John Gunther's *Death Be Not Proud.* This is also one of the earliest modern examples; were Johnny Gunther alive today, he would be sixty-three years old!

In the case of spouses and parents, memorializing, as we define it, is not hard to achieve. It becomes much harder in the case of a teenager, and almost impossible in the case of a child. When someone's biggest step into the shared world of adult life was to complete second grade before disease took over her body, the protagonist's uniqueness is hard to portray convincingly. It is easier to turn her into an implausible, preternaturally angelic being such as Little Eva:

> Sometimes I think Alex cared so much for everything around her because she sensed it was all she would have—that her elementary school would be junior high and high school and college, as well as her job, her husband, and her family—everything outside of the home she lived in for all of her life. (Deford 1986, 108)

Stories of teenagers who died struggling to graduate from high school (Gunther 1947) or experience one first and final romance

(Lund 1974) are more tellable, but the narrator must again and again insist to his or her ideal reader that the dead person was truly unusual.

In the tales of adults, what is really being memorialized is the relationship itself: the marriage, the family life, as lived over a period of time. The dying of one partner forces a review of the whole relationship, at least in the mind of the survivor/narrator. As the title of one of Madeleine L'Engle's works suggests, a marriage is a two-part invention (L'Engle 1988); it is continuously being reinvented up to the death of one partner. And beyond, as in the case of L'Engle and her husband Hugh; theirs was a relationship that would not be ended by death, but will resonate down through the years in their children, in their community. For a middle-aged woman, her mother—now dying—remains in one sense an element in her self, and a fusion between self and mother emerges in this group of narratives (Schreiber 1990, Gould 1988). Even Simone deBeauvoir, whose relation to her "Maman" was anything but companionable, shares a partial submersion in her mother's identity and is surprised by it. Gould reflects on this fusion between parent and child:

> A child needs parents to give him life and to nurture him—but a father or mother has an equally urgent need for a child to complete the parent's life and give him a proper death, through the consummate act of seeing him whole. When I was able to see my mother whole, I was able to finish this book. (Gould 1988, 5)

There is, however, a class of narratives in which the focus is less on relationships and more on the day-to-day tribulations of caretaking. To let the other know what it is like to care for someone with AIDS or for a dying elderly parent, is, or can be, as "worthy" a goal as to record the specific relationship. Here, it is no longer the uniqueness of the deceased which counts, but the anticipated typicality of the situations. "Worthy" is placed in quotes here to signify our awareness of the problem besetting these narratives. Self-sacrificing women caregivers who write to memorialize their husbands and marriages are on safe ground, morally, in our culture. Those who write bitter diatribes around the theme of how rotten caretaking can be, or who focus on "how bad *I* had it," risk losing our sympathy. To make this type of narrative succeed, the storyteller must anticipate this problem of self-pity, and accommodate to it. It is not enough to address her ideal reader every so often by saying, "You think this is repulsive to read about—you should try living through it!"

One way to overcome this problem is to write a "just the facts, ma'm" documentary account, renouncing both interpretation and the self-indulgence of normal emotional responses. When we examine the nature of autobiographies and why people write them in chapter 3, we will have more to say about this strategy. Of all Type III narratives, Barbara Peabody's *The Screaming Room* best exemplifies it. Her son Peter is dying of AIDS; she is his caretaker, and has promised to nurse him until death. The relationship between mother and son, however, is not the book's primary focus. Written when few medications for AIDS were available (it was published in 1986), it documents the symptoms of the disease, its ravages on the mind and body, its hopelessness and horrors. Peter suffers eleven months of convulsions, diarrhea, fevers, pneumonia, mental disorientation; he is hospitalized six times, but dies at home. Peabody's narrative takes the form of journal entries, blow-by-blow descriptions of caring for her son, never knowing which new and horrible symptom would appear next. We learn what this meant *to her* principally through the book's title: the journal on which it is based was her only source of relief from the constant ordeal of caretaking.

The risk is that accounts of the stress involved in caretaking can be glibly labeled "self-pity." "See how awful this was for me!" seems inappropriate when it is someone else, after all, who actually suffers the symptoms of illness. A skillful, self-aware narrator is able to acknowledge this, yet never take advantage of it. Gerda Lerner, for example, writes of her husband's death (*A Death of One's Own*) from what is admittedly her own perspective as one whose earlier experiences with death came in large part through the Holocaust. To take care of her husband, Carl, she must review not only their marriage, but even more privately, her own unmourned family losses.

An account of terminal illness in what is now popularly called a dysfunctional family will, alas, memorialize the anger, hurt, guilt and grief of several decades, often without the narrator being quite aware that this is what is happening. With a certain level of insight, the family's history of unhappiness is not an insurmountable obstacle for the narrator of a Type III story. Simone deBeauvoir's *A Very Easy Death* is both a tribute to her dying mother and a diatribe against Maman's clinging to a set of self-destructive hypocritical values. DeBeauvoir recognizes this, as does Joan Gould, whose conflicted relationship with her mother is not resolved, but accepted for what is was during the time of her mother's dying: "to my astonishment, a time came when I stopped agonizing about our relationship and realized that on a more significant level, it didn't matter whether my mother and I liked each other or even loved each other or not; there was a deeper bond than liking or not-liking between us" (Gould 1988, 5). In contrast, the works we find truly painful to read are those where anger over a failed relationship spills over into the narrative, covering page after page with a dark stain of resentment. "We were in hell," declares one such narrator—and sharing this hell with the reader can become itself a goal. Righteous indignation over the isolation of caretakers, at the stigma of AIDS, over the entire philosophy our society holds that keeps the terminally ill and their families on "the moon"—all of these, justifiable in themselves, can be the occasion for this other, more depressing resentment.

Although a book such as Peabody's is relentless and anything but fun to read, it is easily distinguishable from a memorial to the dead person's failures and betrayals. Nor does it dwell on the failures and selfishness of other family members who refused to help with caretaking. One author even listed the names of the family's ex-friends, those who deserted them during the illness. What message can such tales convey? What meaning do they offer readers? These are questions all autobiographies must answer, but in the case of certain dysfunctional Type III narratives, they become more urgent. The common belief is that writing itself will serve as a catharsis, as in Peabody's *The Screaming Room.* But in the works that express mostly resentment and a sense of being ill-used by fate and family, no release from crisis, no "moving beyond" it, really occurs for the author or for us. Even by the time the author, now free to edit and rewrite the manuscript, could have been able to gain insight into what he or she really felt before the death, nothing has changed. Perhaps what such accounts challenge is our deep assumption that suffering ought to be meaningful, that so much pain must be worth *something* beyond adding more pain to the world's total. Narratives that flatly defy all these expectations, whose narrators and protagonists remain deep in hell, are deeply disturbing indeed.

Yet the overwhelming majority of Type III narratives do not fail at the level of meaning and insight. They work, memorializing the dead beloved and the relationship. A strange testimony to how well these work is that it is possible to imagine the dead protagonists now joined together (our "support group for the newly dead") and sharing their own experiences and memories. The husbands, the mothers of middle-aged daughters, the dead teenagers—memorial-building creates this picture. However precarious as eschatology, it can be sustained, because each narrator did convince us that the dead beloved was and remains unique, a person forever unlike any other person. If the absence of the dead is their way of appearing, then the act of storytelling, of memorializing, keeps the dead from utter invisibility and extinction.

Type IV: "How I Mourned (and Learned to Live Again)"

Type III narratives, the most frequently written category, end with or immediately after the death of the beloved. The family comes home from the hospital. Or they sit exhausted, as the men from the funeral home remove the body. Perhaps there is a final scene of a memorial service. Is this the end? No, everyone in and out of the story is aware that a long period of grief will follow. Indeed, nothing will ever be normal again. No matter how anticipated the loss, no matter how grateful everyone is that the sick person has finally died, mourning follows death. In the words of C. S. Lewis,

> Bereavement is a universal and integral part of our experience of love. It follows marriage as normally as marriage follows courtship or as autumn follows summer. It is not a truncation of the process but one of its phases, (1963, 59)

It would be perfectly possible, in the light of this, to see the Type III narratives as themselves part of the work of mourning, just as erecting a gravestone is an acknowledgment that the death is final, has really occurred.

However, this is not our view of relationships, as Lewis himself admits. The usual view omits the final stages, and sees mourning as loss and violation rather than integral to the experience of love. Type IV narratives tell of the process of mourning and must struggle to explore this paradox. These stories have an altogether different plot structure than any but the tales of Type I. As we will see, death as loss is almost the only way death makes sense to Americans. Hence, narratives of bereavement, of gradual coping with and acceptance of loss, fit into this motif, and so into our study. They share with other death-and-recovery tales (Type I) a clear plot structure, and with Type III the project of memorializing the dead beloved. But there are not very many of them: mourning is less glamorous and dramatic than dying. And those that do exist fail proportionately more often than do narratives of Type I and Type III.

The mourner has been touched by death, very deeply touched—but knows that he or she is still alive, and is obligated both to mourn, and to return to life. The story of mourning is one of immersion in death, and a gradual reconciliation to the loss, along with movement into a new stage of his or her existence without the lost beloved. This is a sufficiently distinctive structure so that few narrators of Type III tales attempt to combine them with Type IV (Meryman in *Hope,* Albertson in *Endings and Beginnings* try this, with unclear results). Readers, real and ideal, want the closure of the Type III ending before beginning the further sufferings Type IV promises. Yet it is clear that narratives of mourning belong in our general category of "first person mortal" stories of death and dying.

Additionally, a distinct, inevitable element in mourning is intensive, obsessive replaying of the death of the beloved. The survivor-protagonist torments him or herself by trying to answer the following questions: How well did our relationship stand up under the final illness? How did we cope with the failure of medicine? What were his or her last conscious words, last gestures? Where were our friends and family during this time?

While the survivor focuses profoundly on these concerns, she or he is faced with new, current problems: loneliness, moving, financial readjustment, and so on. It should be stated quite clearly that Type IV narratives are primarily tales of widows and widowers, the death of a spouse being the situation that poses the most drastic changes in one's physical circumstances as well as one's emotional world for an adult. Because of this, a tale of mourning must move back and forth between the past, which is fixed and gone, and the present, which is chaotic, empty, and frightening. One hopes that at the close of the narrative, the present—and a dimly seen future—emerge as real and meaningful in their own right. Yet the self does not throw off the past, nor break loose from it. It becomes a permanent part of the self, but no longer the total self.

Mourning is a transitional state, in our society at least. We do not expect widows to entomb themselves along with their dead husbands. Nevertheless, the lack of social space to mourn, or generally recognized guidelines for how mourning should proceed and when it should end, lies behind each one of the Type IV narratives. In opposition to the viewpoint voiced by Lewis, our culture views bereavement as unnatural—the truncation of a relationship. The expectation is that the mourner will "get through it" as quickly as possible, will get on with her life, or prepare just as quickly and quietly for her own death. This, combined with the self-isolation basic to the mourning process, burdens all the protagonists unbearably. Lewis's suggestion of a "leper colony" for mourners (1963, 11) is the exact equivalent of "the moon" of terminal illness.

How do the protagonists endure existence in such a spiritual leper colony? As narrators, they may still be in the midst of occupying it, as was Lewis when he wrote *A Grief Observed*. This work, by the way, was not published under his own name during his lifetime, a poignant testimony to the shame he and other mourners fall prey to. In contrast, Laurie Graham's *Rebuilding the House* is a more typical Type IV narrative. Unlike Lewis, who died himself within two years of his wife, Graham is able to write knowing that she has a future of new relationships on this earth. Hence the emphasis on "rebuilding," on hopeful activity—even though the central theme is clearly that of mourning.

The basic allegory in which a house or home represents the self is established immediately and maintained throughout. As the young widow of a much older man, she moves into a dilapidated house they had jointly owned but never lived in. Her task of rebuilding her life and identity is expressed via her plans for new drainpipes, clearing the gardens, rebuilding the porch, and so on. Like the house, George, her husband, was old and far from perfect, but she loves them both. Graham as protagonist shares her fears that the house will suddenly collapse, burying her inside its ruins. As narrator, she knows these fears are groundless architecturally, but massively real existentially. As the remodeling comes to a close, we learn that she and George had already bought an apartment for her in Paris, where she will indeed take up her life post-mourning. Yet the rebuilt old house is indeed an achievement: "I realize now that my fears about the house grew out of my feeling that I had lost control of my destiny. That if your husband can die, anything can happen to you" (Graham 1990, 142). It was necessary for her to live there, at least for a while.

Graham's story may work so well because the central allegory directs attention simultaneously to two levels, and balances memories of George with scenes of broken drainpipes. Without this sense of a rooting in physical reality, the autobiographer's nemesis of self-pity looms particularly grievously through any extended depiction of mourning. Yet self-pity is an authentic part of mourning, and any account that glossed over it would be psychologically unreal. Disgust over his own self-pity troubles Lewis; it is this which may have prompted him to publish the original *A Grief Observed* anonymously. The narrator must recognize—as both Lewis and Graham do—that the ideal reader for whom he or she writes is owed an apology occasionally on this account. "How dreadful anyone must think me! Here I am alive, while my beloved is dead. I am sorry for myself, when I should be sorry for him."

Other author-narrators are not similarly troubled, and like some of the caretakers of the Type III narratives, lose the reader's sympathy along the way. Mourners share a notorious inability to distinguish trivial from catastrophic situations—everything appears catastrophic. But precisely this kind of patronizing statement betrays a shallow and facile assurance that we know how objectively worthy each situation or problem must be. A skillful narrator, on the other hand, challenges this assurance. He or she convinces us that to the bereaved protagonist, each and every decision is a major one. Every choice, every movement, requires an immense amount of energy, and exhausts the protagonist for the next major task.

But narrators less skilled at storytelling, or still locked into the stance of the mourner, will not be able to convey this with the proper sense of embarrassment or apology. They won't believe that an apology might be necessary, that readers might be bored to hear how agonizing a decision it was to buy new drainpipes. Thus a feature of the mourning process itself, exaggerating the significance of one's daily routine, one's minor adventures in coping, becomes a sign of that same narcissistic self-preoccupation we have noted earlier. Tedious pages can be devoted to "How I arranged the details of the funeral," "How I decided to stop wearing my wedding ring," and "How I decided to adopt a kitten," as if all of these situations were of intrinsically equal significance to the narrator and his or her ideal reader. In a few of these accounts, just as in a few of the dysfunctional Type III accounts, we learn details about the protagonists that we wish we didn't know. Surprisingly, given the intensely personal nature of these stories, we find ourselves responding this way rarely. Once again, a skilled author—one fully in control over the final narrative—can make sure his or her narrator apologizes to the ideal reader within the text, and says (sometimes in so many words) "Do you really want to know about this? Probably not. I'm sorry, but I felt I just had to put it in."

One central area which appears very difficult to write about, with or without apologies, is the formation of the new sexual relationships after the loss of a spouse. The protagonist is caught between a world that holds out the goal of forming new ties, and the risk of appearing a traitor to the dead beloved. He or she naturally worries about this. Moreover, the narrator so often expresses this thought, and defends new involvements, that this ambivalence overshadows the portraits of the new lovers who appear as protagonists in these stories. We meet "B," the new love, and are primed by the narrator to view him or her principally as "A's" replacement. "B" never jells as a character in his/her own right, and in some cases is even left nameless—a final indignity in a personal narrative.

It is far easier to direct readers' attention back into the relationship being mourned. The spouse is now dead—just as are the dying protagonists of Type III narratives. The mourner can, however, more freely and flagrantly idealize the relationship; we are not getting a clear, day-by-day account of a fatally ill person's sickbed behavior, or even anything that purports to be such. Idealizing in all types of stories creates a credibility problem for the narrator, who must repeatedly assure the ideal reader "We had a perfect marriage," or "She was a beautiful, expressive, magical woman," while telling actual incidents that inadvertently destroy this view. Once again, the insightful narrator will distrust and renounce idealization, accurately identifying it as one of the pitfalls of mourning. Both Lewis and Graham deliberately want to remember the flaws of their dead spouses, and as a narrative strategy this works to ensure that we love H. (Lewis' dead wife) and George all the more. Moreover, an over-idealizing narrator who is also self-preoccupied emerges as a dislikable, immature personality, thereby undermining the idealization. "Her husband must have been a real jerk, if he married someone like her," we think to ourselves.

Any successful Type IV narrative must conclude that mourning is a terminable, not interminable, condition. The conclusion is often marked by an act of closure on the part of the protagonist. She or he does something that brings mourning to an end, such as writing a letter to her dead husband (such as in Jill Truman's *Letter to My Husband* and Xenia Rose's *Widow's Journey*). Note that in American and British culture, this is a therapeutic device; it is not a claim about the ontological status of the dead. The narrator tells us, "This is the conclusion of my mourning and of the story I wish to tell." Even Lewis, who claimed he stopped writing as he ran out of notebooks (!), concludes with an awareness of his wife's spiritual presence; she is still a fact of his reality. A story of mourning that simply faded out, as do several Type II narratives, would be a disaster. Yet, even with a conclusion to both mourning and its narrative, Type IV autobiographies appear more difficult to bring off than do those of the other major categories.

Type V: Journalists' Accounts

We now turn to a more debatable subfield of "first person mortal" narratives. In all of the above four types, we have taken it for granted that the author/narrator has an intense, intimate relation to the protagonists in the story. These are all narratives of families, of persons bound together through ties of birth and sex as well as death.

There exists, however, another kind of personal narrative of illness and dying; that of the journalist, reporting on the sufferings of those with terminal illness. Depending on how this is done, the result can be a set of short, almost first person accounts of "what its like to have AIDS" or "my battle with cancer." While there are a large range of legitimate reasons for writing narratives of Type I through Type IV, only one can be given for a journalistic exploration of this kind. To tell the world what the reality of sickness or its overcoming are like is virtually the only justification for such an intrusion into the intimate lives if strangers. And intrusive it must be: the journalist must learn and be able to tell information that is ordinarily only shared by intimate family and friends. The journalist's assumption—and that of his or her subject and ideal reader—is that the value of such information outweighs the violation of privacy. (Privacy is of course always an issue in autobiography, but it becomes even more so here because obtaining the information in the first place is the issue, not just sharing it.) In order for this motivation to be convincing, there must be something unusual, previously unknown and important to learn. Important for society at large, or for those of us not stricken by the diseases involved. Although Americans have now become accustomed to investigative reports on just about any topic, we need to remind ourselves how justification for Type V narratives is required, and rests on a narrower base than that demanded by all of the other types.

Who is the journalist, and what gives him or her the right to "tell all," an "all" that even family members are reticent to share with one another? To be journalist is both the author's social role and the narrator's stance of relating to his or her subjects. As outsider (non-family member and non-friend) the journalist has "subjects" for his or her writing, and, in fact, initially AIDS or cancer is "an assignment" among many possible assignments. The individuals chosen for interviews are selected as typical or illustrative of a category of persons ("cancer sufferers who fought back"), never because they are unique or unrepeatable, as the ideology of Type III narrators holds. A journalist is bound to his or her subject, then, by fascination with the assigned topic, but only rarely and inadvertently by ties of personal bonding.

Yet it would be a mistake to envision the journalist in terms of some standard of scientific objectivity, detachment, or disinterestedness. No journalist writing about AIDS or cancer aspires to become that mythical fly on the wall, who hears and observes without any intention or ability to influence the flow of events. Illness journalism is advocacy journalism, a moral act of giving voice to those whose voices otherwise might not be heard. The assumption is that once we meet—via journalist's interviews—the human sufferers, we the public will no longer be so indifferent, so ignorant, so stingy with funds for research and other services. The ideal reader of all journalistic accounts is *persuadable* along these lines, even if the real readers may not be.

A journalist focuses upon categories, and selects subjects who either typify the sufferers from a particular condition, or who seem particularly likely to persuade readers of the rightness of the advocate's goals. But it is the same journalist-narrator who conducts all the interviews, and writes all the stories. This poses a dilemma. A series of such interviews will sound too similar: the journalist can dominate the words of the protagonist-subject and we will feel cheated of the experience of meeting a living, real person. Or the journalist can "let the subject talk," and the result is unfocused, rambling, and uninteresting. Professional journalists seem to err on the side of too much control; an amateur, such as Petrow (*Dancing Against the Darkness*) falls into the second trap. There is no better way to recognize the storytelling achievements of all the authors of Types I through IV narratives than reading such meanderings.

Because AIDS has appeared so recently as a "new disease," and because of its peculiar epidemiology, it is seen as horrible, mysterious, and stigmatizing, as well as terminal. AIDS is the clearest focus for journalists' narratives. George Whitmore's *Someone Was Here: Profiles in the AIDS Epidemic* can serve as our illustration. Whitmore wants to cover the "human face" of AIDS; not just the medical news, but the persons affected by the disease. And so he visits and interviews two gay men: one an AIDS patient, and the other his "buddy," who visits and tries to support and encourage him. Ironically, the follow-up to the original story shows the mysterious arbitrariness of the disease: the original patient has outlived his "buddy," who himself has died of AIDS. Whitmore also interviews imprisoned drug addicts, and the social workers (including a nun) who try to help them. Finally, there is the mother of a young Hispanic man who died homeless and addicted in San Francisco early in the epidemic. Whitmore the journalist is the voice of all these persons, their advocate in print. Only in the epilogue does he tell us directly what we, the readers, suspected all along: that he himself is HIV positive (Whitmore 1988, 205–206). His work on the stories that make up this book was a way to help himself come to terms with the disease.

Whitmore's very striking title has significance not only for his particular study, but indeed for all first-person narratives. All of them might well be titled *Someone Was Here*; the "here" of the moon of terminal illness, or the leper colony of mourning. We will examine this dimension of autobiographical narrative in the next chapter.

The special responsibility of an advocacy journalist such as Whitmore is to assume the role of voice and pen for those who will never write autobiographies of their own. He will tell the stories of persons who are too sick, too undereducated and inarticulate, or already dead. If one's task is to capture the human face of AIDS or of any disease, then these persons' stories are as much parts of that face as are the tales of those fortunate enough to survive, or to have loved ones able to memorialize them in print. This may be particularly important in the case of AIDS, because the epidemic has hit hardest in some sectors of the population with the least access to written media.

On the other hand, the above task is substantially different from that of Barbara Peabody, whose work *The Screaming Room* also documents the human face of AIDS. A journalist interviews subjects; Peabody nursed her own son. The journalist finishes one assignment and picks up another; Peabody is morally bound to stick with Peter until he dies. A journalist initially chooses from a range of potential subjects those who typify the illness that is the real focus of the story; no one could write a work such as *The Screaming Room* on this basis. The burning intensity of the mother-son bond keeps the reader going through ever-more-harrowing scenes of suffering and deterioration. Curiously and ironically, then, *The Screaming Room* is a far more powerful advocacy work on behalf of those suffering with AIDS than is Whitmore's otherwise excellent account. Whitmore assumes, as do all advocacy journalists, that his ideal readers are persuadable, that ignorance, indifference, and even bigotry will melt away in the face of his narrative. Because he wrote originally for *The New York Times*, this may have been an accurate assumption politically. But to persuade more socially conservative readers to raise their awareness of AIDS, *The Screaming Room* would be a surer bet. Its topic is unmistakably not homosexuality or drug addiction; it is the tale of a mother taking care of her dying son.

And so this overview of the "first person mortal" narratives of dying and death ends in a question about the purposes and goals of such writings. Are they all, fundamentally, advocacy journalism? Or memorializing of an individual dead beloved? What role does information about a disease, a medical entity, play in such literature? Or is a basic aim of these works something different altogether, something that Whitmore's title, *Someone Was Here*, captures as well if not better than do most of the others?

Chapter Three

WHY WRITE A
PERSONAL
NARRATIVE?

The Nature of Autobiography

In the middle of the night, the sleepless caretaker of a dying loved one picks up a pencil and pad, and begins to write out her feelings of anguish, loneliness, and fear. Or a long-established habit of journal-keeping continues, but the focus for the recently diagnosed writer now becomes "my chemotherapy" rather than "my new novel," or *Intoxicated by My Illness* rather than Anatole Broyard's usual musings on literature for *The New York Times Book Review*. From these beginnings, there is a long road to the published book-length works we reviewed in chapter 2. All of the published autobiographies, however spontaneous they may appear to the reader, have passed through *some* editorial hand. Moreover, even the journal format itself has much more structure than one might at first imagine. Most regular journal writers organize their entries by day, and each entry becomes "the completed precipitate" of the day's experiences (Weintraub

1975, 827). This becomes even more apparent when the entries are made late at night, during times of insomnia and personal isolation.

These jottings and journals are initially "the screaming room" for those who keep them. They are a place—very often the *one* place— where pain is let loose, and where the person who is otherwise expected to be stoic and in control may become immersed in feelings. The journal may be the last bastion of privacy for the sick person made suddenly dependent upon others. Sometimes memories of happier times flood the sufferer, and writing in the journal becomes a substitute or an accompaniment to sessions with the family photograph album. In other cases, what gets written out, night after night, are detailed and vivid descriptions of the minutiae of illness and caretaking, recorded while they are still fresh and before the next day's similar onslaught wipes them out with a new and possibly more painful layer.

From these beginnings, then, grow full-scale published autobiographical narratives. It is important for us to start this chapter with this observation, because some of the many current theories of autobiography examine solely the finished product, and are elaborately *uninterested* in a question such as "Why does someone write an autobiography?" Theories of literature that deny the "author's intention," or deny that "author" is a meaningful category for analysis may work well to grasp some kinds of autobiographical writing, but not, we believe, those that are the subject of this study. Far from vanishing, these authors/narrators/protagonists wish to be present to us: *Someone Was Here* will indeed be a major theme in this chapter. And although the flesh-and-blood writer's motivation for writing may remain, qua Kantian thing-in-itself, a mystery to us, the explanations offered by editors, authors, narrators, and protagonists abound, and we will take them seriously.

Autobiography as a genre, or genres, of writing has generated an enormous amount of interest in the past thirty years, and there exists a rich critical bibliography on this topic. (See Ross 1991 for a fine recent example of how this flourishes.) Some of this attention is concerned with autobiography as a literary product, other interest is in the usefulness of personal narratives for the historian, psychologist, and so forth. A focus on autobiography in the study of religion reveals how doctrine, life experience, and social environment relate to each other in unique and sometimes utterly striking ways. The autobiographies of ex-slaves, of Native Americans, and others from cultural situations that are now and forever gone add to this fascination with the genre.

Obviously not all of this literature is relevant to the category of "first person mortal" narratives we examine here. Some of the generalizations based on the autobiographies of "famous men," including those by celebrities, do not hold for our writings. However, to balance this, we find that some of the more recent generalizations about women's selves and women's autobiographies seem equally irrelevant to an appreciation of the materials reviewed in chapter 2. Adding to the confusion, very sophisticated literary analysis often claims for the autobiography genre works such as T. S. Eliot's *Four Quartets*, which would not ordinarily be considered as such (Olney 1972, 230–316). Bearing this in mind, we will try to present some of the central themes that run through most of the literature about autobiography.

One such theme is that autobiography is principally a modern, post-Enlightenment form, and is premised on the uniqueness of the individual and his or her experiences. This individual, moreover, dwells in history, feeling he or she would be a different person if born twenty years earlier or later. Whether this is "really true" or not is an unanswerable question; it is part of a set of beliefs about selfhood that make personal storytelling into modern autobiography.

> Every existence was marked by its singular locus in space and its moment in time. It had to be understood in terms of its specified setting and its unrepeateble development. . . . It had its very own story. (Weintraub 1975, 846)

A correlate of this, the other meaning of "uniqueness," is the unity of the personal, experiencing self. There must be some "I" who tells the story. Very recently, this emphasis on the self's unity has come under fire as a masculine ideal unsuitable for the selfhood of women (Henking 1991, 521–23). But persons too fragmented or multiple to fit this model will not be found among our authors, male or female.

One of the questions a naive reader invariably wants answered after reading an autobiography is, "Is it true?" Is the "very own story" we read by someone else about him/herself a true story? In what sense can autobiography be false? Here, contemporary theories of autobiography have clarified the various issues that perplex the reader of personal narratives under the heading of "truth." Roy Pascal's *Design and Truth in Autobiography* takes a good look at the "elusiveness of truth" (Pascal 1960, 61ff., 179ff.). The first issue, that of factual truth in autobiography, arises most often in cases of memoirs, where the narrative covers public historical events (Weintraub 1975, 823). The assumption is that readers read memoirs to find out "what really happened during the Watergate scandal," and not to discover Nixon's, John Dean's, or Gordon Liddy's deepest levels of personal reality. Discrepancies among accounts mean that "someone's lying"; everyone will be looking for such discrepancies, and the authors know this as they prepare the work for publication.

But when one moves from memoirs to "true autobiography," the issue of truth shifts. In our stories, for example, the issue of who was given the prognosis for the life-threatening illness is one that might be parallel on the surface to who knew about Watergate, but is really a very different kind of concern. We, the readers, are interested in "who knew" the lump was cancerous because of what this knowledge reveals about the relations among the protagonists, doctors, and family members (not one of our works was written to provide evidence for a malpractice suit; this would indeed provide a closer parallel with memoirs and would be very different from the materials we have surveyed). Discrepancies from one account to another—as in the very different opinions held by Johnny Gunther's father and his mother on whether their son knew he would die (Gunther 1947, 162, 220)—reveal lack of communication much more than they do a "cover-up" of damaging facts. After all, persons with lots to cover up ordinarily need not write autobiographies.

But truth in autobiography remains a valid concern, albeit redefined so as to focus no longer on factual accuracy. We ask that the narrative have an internal consistency, and that it not violate too many of our basic assumptions about how people behave. We ask that the protagonist and the narrator who bears his or her name be recognizable as "the same person." We ask that the narrator's direct description of another protagonist not conflict too greatly with the character of that protagonist as revealed through his or her actions. Instances of autobiographical "falseness" almost always cluster around one of these requirements. For example, the narrator appears convinced that he or she behaved reasonably and compassionately, while in the story the protagonist who bears the same name repeatedly threatens to sue doctors, quarrels with family members, and becomes intensely and passionately concerned with the loss of hair or a breast, rather than loss of life. The inconsistency jars us, although articulating this problem is a lot more difficult than identifying factual errors in memoirs. In contrast, a narrator whose stance toward him/herself as protagonist is to recognize immature and selfish behavior and apologize ("I am a notoriously flaky and hysterical person; even my friends tell me this") will be "truthful" and so gain our allegiance up to a point. Paul Monette, the narrator of *Borrowed Time*, provides an excellent example of this truthfulness, while Martha Lear of *Heartsounds* fails to recognize her own immaturity qua protagonist.

Because so many of the narrators memorialize and idealize the dead beloved, there is ample opportunity for the second kind of untruthfulness. The narrator tells us repeatedly what a wonderful person "X" was, how ideal their marriage was, and how loving a father, colleague, fellow human he was, and so on. Yet in the story, we find the same idealized man lying to friends, angry when they fail to penetrate his lies, and repeatedly engaged in obnoxious one-upsmanship in all his encounters (Roni Rabin's *Six Parts Love* is the unfortunate example here). In another case, repetitious assertions that "We had the perfect marriage" are belied again and again by the lack of communication shown by both protagonists as one dies unaware of what the other was really thinking and feeling. (Elizabeth Cox's *Thanksgiving: An AIDS Journal* sadly illustrates aspects of this situation.) We know that something is wrong when the person within the story is simply not recognizable as the person the narrator keeps telling us about. As a general rule, those who write autobiographies must be aware of such occasions for falsehood, because either one can be deadly to the credibility of the entire narrative.

Another way the naive reader frames the question of truth is to ask, "Is the person who wrote this book really like this? He sounds just wonderful; but is he really?" We have several times been assured by those who know the authors in real life rather than in print that "He's really an awful person; but then his whole family was crazy" (or similar remarks). The issue of the autobiographical self is, however, a much more complicated matter than that of matching "self-in-the-text" to some flesh and blood individual. Olney, writing a generation ago (in *Metaphors of Self*), laid the foundation for awareness that the self within autobiography was a creation, a construction, an achievement of the author-narrator. This self never truly existed before the narrative was written:

> The self expresses itself by the metaphors it creates and projects, and we know it by those metaphors; but it did not exist as it does now and as it is before creating its metaphors. (1972, 34)

The story told is basically a story of how the self came into being, a process that is completed only when the final chapter of the autobiography is done. The self, which we assumed we had as a given prior to writing, becomes a self of text, never born until he or she emerges within the storytelling process. Olney divides autobiographical writing into two categories: the kind written by authors who know, in however shadowy a fashion, that the above is the case, and those who believe that their self exists as a finished product prior to the writing. Writing then merely records the history of how this self came to be who it is, but does not constitute the self. All but a very few of the narrators of our collection are, by that definition, naive. Reflective and introspective as they may be, they are not concerned with the question Olney's theory poses.

And yet, a moderate version of Olney's perspective is enthusiastically endorsed by most of our authors: to tell one's story is vital to becoming a self. Recall the Weintraub quote: within the modern historical consciousness, every existence has "its very own story." "Finding one's own voice," a major feminist theme, appears to have pervasive impact far beyond feminist authors. It suggests how personal narrative and personal empowerment can go together. Only the self who tells a story knows that he or she has a story to tell, is someone worthy of being the protagonist in one's own narrative. Storytelling about others—one's mother, for example—is of value insofar as one is able to see oneself as separate from the other yet incorporate that person's wisdom into one's new, valid, and articulate self. Even the most degraded and damaged self, when speaking through the narrative of a personal story, will gain a victory over those who exploited, victimized, and silenced him or her. To tell one's story is to dare to challenge one's oppressors. (For a volume of women's narratives that blasts the reader with this ideology, read *The Stories We Hold Secret*, edited by Carol Bruchac, Liona Hogan, and Judith

McDaniel). Storytelling from this vantage becomes a sacred act; authority is transferred from external figures and forces, to the newly discovered authentic and interior self. Once again, although this is frequently cited as a feminist theme, it is impossible to link it to gender in our collection of narratives. Men and women, Americans and Europeans, the dying and the bereaved, all partake of this mystical belief in the power of stories.

Nowhere does this ideology about storytelling, taking off from Olney's and other's theories about autobiography, ring more loudly than when confronted with experiences that previously shamed one into silence. Rape, incest, and homosexual experiences are obvious examples; in our collection these are replaced by mistreatment at the hands of "the medical establishment." Doctors who silence or patronize their women patients; nurses who blame the hospital patient for loss of his or her own body control; chaplains who offer incredibly uncomforting and inappropriate consolation—all of these figures appear in these works. Moreover, the mutilating nature of cancer and its treatments is also shaming. The anger against both doctors and their treatments wells up in many of these narratives, as we shall see in chapter 4 ("Medicine from the Bottom Up"). Before jumping to any overgeneralized conclusion, however, let us state clearly that no matter how frequently anger and empowerment appear as twin motifs in these narratives, they are not the dominant tone of first person mortal autobiographies. And although we have labeled the above theory about storytelling and "finding one's voice" *feminist*, survivors of any serious illness, the dying and their caretakers, and the bereaved all find themselves silenced and sent to the moon. A male stroke survivor writing bitterly of his experiences in the early 1960s (Hodgins, *Episode: Report on the Accident Inside My Skull*) illustrates all of these preoccupations much more intensely than do several women authors who had strong prior feminist commitments (Gerda Lerner, Mary Kay Blakely).

Rather than speak of a feminist perspective here, then, we might say that the cluster of hopes surrounding the autobiographical project—hopes loosely based on the perspectives of Olney—hinge on the set of ideas about the autonomous and unique individual we charted in chapter 1. The autobiographer is the constructor of individuality, of an identity that was not given, but created over time. Belief in this individual's worth and uniqueness permeates the process. Each story must be told because each self is different; one breast-cancer narrative cannot stand in for all, nor is one dead teenager the same as every dead teenager. *A Death of One's Own* (Gerda Lerner's title) affirms this individual uniqueness, and the freedom of the autonomous person to tell his/her story up until the moment of death. (Somewhat ironically, the actual death covered in Lerner's book is that of her husband Carl, although she is much more aware than most narrator-caretakers that the story is always *hers*.)

For the test of this ideology of storytelling and empowerment is that it is able to encompass even the most fearful and potentially meaningless experiences, those that threaten to disintegrate the self. The storyteller's work of construction races against the destructive work of cancer or AIDS. In *In the Face of Death*, Peter Noll will not accept the loss of freedom, to him a worse disintegration than that of his body. What remains is the constructed, created self of the text; the embodied person is gone. Insofar as death is destruction as well as loss, these autobiographies triumph over it, in part if not in full.

Where this sense of finding a voice of one's own in conjunction with experiencing a death of one's own (or a death of one's beloved) differs from the model developed by Olney is in the relative naiveté of most of the authors of our works. They, like Olney's naive autobiographers, assume that the self is formed before the writing begins. They are by and large uninterested in the ongoing construction/creation of the self in the process of writing. They assume that their job is to tell the story, not to reflect intricately upon the storytelling project or the way the "who" of the telling emerges. The experiences changed them, often dramatically; the telling of these experiences gives voice and empowers, but never literally creates a self who was never there before.

One way to test this generalization, is to notice how naive most narrators are about their own stance and principles of selection for what gets told. Very few recognize explicitly and dwell on the fact that "It might have been told otherwise," or that meanings are not necessarily given by the events themselves. Admittedly, almost all of them allow for some degree of subjectivity, with remarks such as "When I showed my sister this passage, she was astonished that I could remember everything that was said that day, but she thought I had missed the point of what was not being said." Here we have a glimpse into the intermediate stage of the final narrative—and also into the narrator's character, as he or she dutifully shares the written draft with family members. But much more rarely do we find explicit concern with the author's authority to dominate the structure, to determine whether the ending will be one of triumph ("he died a death of his own") or sadness ("he died a long lingering death"). Gerda Lerner's work is one among the few that addresses this explicitly, which is interesting, given how many of our authors are writers by profession.

> The ending I have just written is not untrue, nor is it quite the truth. As everything memory serves up, it is a slice of the truth, a layer, a segment. . . . There is another ending, the nightmare version. (Lerner 1974, 267–68)

Perhaps there is so much ambivalence within the narrative that additional ambivalence included in it about the storytelling process and the self it brings forth would just be intolerable.

Reasons for Writing: Surface Reasons

These preliminary attempts to place our collection of narratives within some current understandings of autobiography do not really answer the question, Why do persons write *this kind* of autobiographical narrative? What is it about a narrative of illness, dying, and death that requires a special justification? Or should it be obvious that these central human experiences require less justification than writing, say, the history of one's real estate or stock market transactions? When we ask this question, we should look first at the specific answers given by the authors of our texts. Here we find a strange conglomeration of truthful and not-always-truthful (in the sense of truth discussed earlier) replies.

Among the frequently cited reasons for writing such intensely personal narratives as these are: to inform others about the disease process or the reality of caretaking; to encourage others who share this situation that it can be endured with hope and courage; to advocate changes in the health care system, such as endorsing hospice; to plead on behalf of sufferers for more public funding. Information and self-conscious inspiration are promised here. In discussing these reasons, we do not wish to make them sound phony or shallow. Some diseases, particularly AIDS, hemophilia, and ALS, are either new, especially frightening, or relatively unknown. Guillain-Barré Syndrome, the subject of Joseph Heller's *No Laughing Matter*, is another, as is cystic fibrosis described in Frank Deford's *Alex: The Life of a Child*. Authors are aware that medical ignorance is pandemic, and respond by educating their readers. Is the disease contagious? Curable? Hereditary? How is it transmitted? What risks are run by caretakers? Ample evidence for massive medical ignorance is presented within these texts. Frank Maier, a victim of liver failure, is consoled by a friend: "Don't worry; you can always use your second one" (Maier 1991, 25). (How many educated adults really confuse the liver with the kidneys? Probably more than we expect!)

An especially useful example of this form of medical education is the advice given to stroke victims, and their families, by those who are stroke survivors. Agnes DeMille, Eric Hodgins, and Douglas Ritchie do not have much in common as persons, but all three offer similar advice about how to move, how to speak, and how to explain one's limitations to others. Betty Ann Spohr's *To Hold a Falling Star* is filled with practical nuggets for those who care for Alzheimer's sufferers. Occasionally, this advice can be offered in what one may call the second-person-inspirational tone, as in Xenia Rose's tips for widows in *A Widow's Journey*. The "you" addressed within the text is obviously in need of advice, and the story comes to a halt as the narrator dispenses this liberally.

Medical education can take the form of warnings against the medical profession and advocacy of alternative treatments. Anthony Sattilaro wrote his *Recalled by Life* to extol a macrobiotic diet as a treatment for cancer. The Zorza parents wrote the story of their daughter's death to recommend hospice as a way to die. The most famous of all these is Norman Cousins' *Anatomy of an Illness*, the work mentioned most by our other autobiographers. Cousins was diagnosed with a very rare disease shared by none of our other narrators, but his recipe of laughter, will power, and a positive active role in his own treatment is adopted by sufferers with almost any life-threatening condition. Even those who did not recover seemed to find it useful; it appears at the bedsides of two such wildly different characters as Joseph Heller, the novelist (alongside Jane Austin's *Emma*), and David Watson, the British evangelist (alongside the Bible). Cousins' book is, however, barely autobiographical after the first section. It is read as personal narrative, but even more frequently for self-help, as are Bernie Siegel's *Love, Medicine and Miracles* and the Simonton's *Getting Well Again*. The example of Cousins suggests not only a literary tradition within the genre, but also how the function of education can actually shade off into self-help and away from personal narrative. For, by the standard of nonfiction, the information value of most of our collection is actually pretty low. True, one can learn about the more unusual diseases, but a straight text for lay persons (equivalent to *The Asthma Sufferer's Handbook*) would provide more recent and complete information. Ironically, none of the AIDS narratives are strong in providing information about the disease. Autobiography is not a particularly suitable vehicle for the kind of detailed medical information necessary to be an activist or Cousins-like participant in one's own treatment.

However, some forms of advocacy are very compatible with this genre. Elizabeth Glaser's *In the Absence of Angels* tells the story of her family's infection with the AIDS virus, including the death of her small daughter Ariel; the book's purpose is to advocate research for pediatric AIDS, and the address of the author's organization is given on the jacket so that contributions can be mailed there. Similarly, the Massie's and Deford's accounts of hemophilia and cystic fibrosis are urgent pleas for funding to fight these diseases. These hope to succeed not just by raising money, but more realistically, in creating a climate of public sympathy and awareness. Once we know what AIDS can do to a family like the Glaser's (white, affluent, and conventionally married) we will presumably be less likely to condemn other sufferers.

To our minds, a sinister variant on this goal is revealed in the small group of autobiographies that advocate active voluntary euthanasia. These intend to create the same climate of public sympathy and awareness for a practice that, when advocated more blatantly, is perceived as ethically dubious. The direct advocates of active voluntary euthanasia know they must defend their view against very serious criticisms, from ordinary persons as well as medical, ethical, and religious leaders. They must engage in argument and rebuttal, for instance, by trying to show that this practice, if legalized in the United States, would not have the consequences that followed in Nazi Germany. No such burden is placed on the autobiographer, who must only convince the reader that for this person, at this time and place, euthanasia is the only humanly possible solution. Not that this always works; Betty Rollin's *Last Wish* diffuses our sense that there is some-thing wrong with active euthanasia, but relocates it onto the charac-ters themselves; we are scarcely aware of the import of what's happening as Ida Rollin, Betty's mother, manipulates her daughter and son-in-law into helping her kill herself. Such stories, because they convince at some level other than that of argument, objection, and rebuttal, create a climate of sympathy that may pave the road for hasty or misguided policy decisions.

What makes us label all of the above reasons for writing "surface" reasons? It is not that they are unworthy, or that the authors are necessarily insincere if they offer these as their reasons for writing. Only a few authors seemed insincere at this level, making themselves vulnerable to the charge that they wrote their book to pay their hos-pital bills. Perhaps a few of these books were published for no more reason than that the authors were celebrities, but that is the pub-lisher's problem. Jill Ireland's *Life-Wish* and Gilda Radner's *It's Always Something* have earnest purposes that compete with those of the educator-inspirers.

Our reason for delving beneath the above collection of purposes is that none of them seem to warrant the use of personal narrative rather than other nonfiction genres such as self-help. When persons write autobiographies, they do something that could *not* be duplicated by any other kind of writing. Even those narratives that stress the educa-tional purpose contain so much more that they are focused on per-sons rather than diseases. It is the Massie family, and not hemophilia, that is the true subject of *Journey* (once again, in spite of the library classification). Finally, many of the very best of the genre deliberately eschew any goal of medical education or the direct, specific advocacy of any cause beyond compassion for all the protagonists of the story. When we turn to the deeper reasons for writing, we find that these are shared across the board by those who purport to offer medical educa-tion, or advocate alternatives to contemporary Western health care— and by those who neglect such goals completely.

Writing as Bearing Witness

During the genocidal rule of the Khmer Rouge in Cambodia, any-one who wore glasses would be singled out for death. Why? The assumption was that such a person would be able not only to read, but to write—and could therefore keep a record for posterity of all the horrors witnessed and endured. The twentieth century saw not only the institution of death camps, but also an unprecedented number of literate witnesses to them. Under such conditions, obtaining even the minimum physical materials for writing, such as pencil stubs, was a challenge. Diaries were smuggled out of the Warsaw Ghetto, or buried, or preserved against all odds. There was a burning drive to record the events, the conditions, the experiences; not just to let the world "out there" know the truth, or to prepare the ground for postwar legal prosecutions, but to engage in the reality of one's sufferings as more than a passive recipient. To bear witness was to retain some spark of human spiritual dignity against an environment of overwhelming horror and degradation.

The theme of bearing witness goes back to the era of the Maccabees, and the Jewish struggle against the religious persecution of Antiochus IV. To bear witness to the Lord and his Torah meant to suffer death as a martyr (the Greek word for "witness"); the main point was not death, but faithfulness to God displayed by those who refused to commit idolatry. Their loyalty and courage was "written in God's book of life," and they were the first of those promised resurrection from death in the world to come. This distinctly Jewish concept of "witness" was one of the sources for the Holocaust victims' intense concern with "witnessing," whether or not all those who died in the Holocaust should be counted as witnesses in the traditional sense of martyrs (those who die "for the sake of the Name" in Judaism). Moreover, in modern usage, those who survive are clearly as much witnesses as those who perished.

Why have we wandered into a discussion of the Holocaust, when none of the deaths recorded in our collection of narratives even begin to resemble those of Auschwitz? We are *not* going to claim that they do, or that dying in a hospital in America is, or possibly can be, as horrible as dying in a concentration camp. There is something morally repulsive about such a comparison to others' sufferings, and we refuse even to start. But it is impossible to discuss the theme of bearing witness to suffering as a reason for writing without explicitly mentioning the primary locus of this activity in our century, the Holocaust. Reasons for writing *are* parallel, even if the experiences cannot be legitimately compared.

Arthur Frank directly invokes this theme in his illness and recovery narrative: "This tale does not tell anyone how to cope but it does bear witness" (Frank 1991, 5); he returns to this theme again and again: "I want what I have written to be touched as one touches letters, folding and refolding them, responding to them" (4). In his forward to Broyard's book, *Intoxicated By My Illness*, Oliver Sacks (the author of one of our recovery narratives) comments, "First Broyard found himself making a narrative for himself. And then, almost at once, for others too" (1992, xiv). Not medical education or self-conscious inspiration for others, but the basic claim: "Someone was here. It really happened. I testify that it did." The experiences that such witnesses record are so existentially overwhelming, so foreign to their own and others' "normal" sense of what is real, there is a fear that they themselves afterward (let alone others) won't believe this really could have happened. Sufferings that threaten one's basic identity, the indifference or hostility of those who purport to help, or of society at large: there is something ineradicably wrong with letting these go unwitnessed and unrecorded. To tell the sufferer "Don't dwell on it; forget it and get on with your life" is to do double harm. To silence a witness compounds the original evil inflicted, whether that came by human hands or by disease.

The impulse to bear witness to suffering appears rooted in a tragic awareness that humans forget and repress whatever threatens a vision of a just and orderly world. A just world is one where those who win and those who lose deserve their fates, and where only the winner's memories are preserved. In a just world, disproportionate, undeserved, and terrifying suffering simply do not happen. Or, if they do, they are not really undeserved, or there is some ultimately benevolent purpose that justifies whatever they endured. To bear witness to one's sufferings can mean to take a stand against such assumptions as these, even if one does believe that some meaning can be gained from wrestling with one's experiences of suffering.

Today, those who suffer from extended terminal illness, or illness that is life-threatening and painful to treat, feel compelled to bear witness to their experiences. They are living reproaches to the "just world" view, as well as to the modern industrial worldview's vision of the autonomous individual who never dies. Their most common designation is as victims and this, paradoxically, wreaks further harm by eroding their sense of agency. To become a witness—whether one lives or dies—is to move beyond the sheer passivity of having things happen to you. It is a way to remember, and in remembering to retain humanity. Anatole Broyard captures this as he recalls the writings of British psychoanalyst D.W. Winnicott:

> D.W. Winnicott began an autobiography that he never finished. The first paragraph simply says, "I died." In the fifth paragraph he writes, "Let me see. What was happening when I died? My prayer had been answered. I was alive when I died. That was all I asked and I had got it." Though he never finished his book, he gave me the best reason for writing one, and that's why I want to write mine—to make sure I'm alive when I die. (1992, 29–30)

Terminal illness, to many of these witnesses, is a place of exile from normal life, in a culture where no one ever dies. In chapter 2 we used Paul Monette's image of "the moon," which invokes not only strangeness but lifelessness. It is a place where normal life's rules don't hold, and the sufferer must learn a whole new set, rules unknown and incomprehensible to those still healthy. The hospital environment for our authors is often a moonscape (albeit noisy and terrifying as well as alien). The high-tech diagnostic equipment, the machines of the intensive care unit, the loneliness of isolation on the bone marrow transplant unit, and the many physically distressing cancer therapies add to this picture of a place outside of earth. Even when the protagonists are deeply committed to modern medicine, and are in no doubt that the wielders of the expertise and equipment are benevolent, there is something frightening and soul-shriveling about the whole hospital situation.

Nor is the sense of being in exile ended when the sick person returns home. As we saw in chapter 2, the experience of extended caretaking is as isolating and disruptive to one's sense of normality as being sick can be. Caretakers witness from a distance those events that preoccupy others (national elections, graduations, holidays). So long as the sick person needs their help, the rest of life fades to background noise. Moreover, the lack of extended family in contemporary America (about which we will have more to say in chapter 5) very much increases the pressure on close family members to be there continuously for the sick person, and this in turn augments the sense of exile from ordinary life. As Elizabeth Cox cared for her husband, who was dying of AIDS, she observed in her journal:

> I'm feeling angry and isolated this morning. Wondering when life will be fun again. Angry that nobody has called and said all the right things to make me feel better; nobody has offered to do the things that would make me feel cared for and secure—though what those might be even I don't know. . . . Sometimes I feel that maybe I am isolating myself, because there are times when I have such feelings of anger toward healthy people. I am desperately jealous of everybody else's life. (Cox 1990, 183)

Not everyone keeps a journal during such times. But those who published journals, or books based on them, claim that writing does something more than serve as a "screaming room," although it performs a cathartic role for many. To write is to record, to remember what took place *now* while it is still fresh. To write preserves what would otherwise be lost, and this includes the knowledge of suffering that it is somehow important for the author to preserve. It is a knowledge of suffering, not of disease and its treatment, however:

> I write to the younger self I was before the illness overwhelmed me. I write to a self not so many years younger but a gulf of experience away. . . . I want to tell my self-before-illness that his fears are legitimate. (Frank 1991, 6–7)

Frank, whose book is half personal narrative and half a discussion of the role of personal narratives in medicine, presents an interesting example of this. His heart attack was an event in his life that, although medically alarming (he was in his thirties at the time) did nothing to radically change his life or his perceptions. He was a researcher on medical sociology, and he continued to be such; this alone would have not prompted him to write a personal narrative. It was his second illness, testicular cancer, that exiled him from past assurance:

> I may have bounced back from a heart attack, but with cancer I was going to have to sink all the way through and discover a life on the other side. Cancer was not going to be an incident; I would have to experience it. (28)

Cancer and its treatment are what led Frank to bear witness to the experience of being seriously ill in this society. Cancer mutilates the body, and he identifies with the marked and mutilated bodies of others who have endured the disease (the bald child who returns the stares of others with courage and honesty). Thus, it is not disease, the medical entity, but the extended experience of life-threatening illness that forces Frank the patient to become Frank the witness, the narrator of an autobiography.

The case of AIDS sufferers is an even more clear-cut example of how bearing witness to the experience of illness lies at the heart of why persons write such narratives as those we examined in chapter 2. In a sense, all of the narratives involving AIDS, and all of the journalists' accounts of the disease, might well be titled *Someone Was Here*. This, the primordial witness' cry, demands that we attend and remember, that we acknowledge to the witness, "Yes, you *did* experience this." It also questions us, the listener or reader: "And where were *you*, while I was here?"

AIDS particularly fits this pattern of bearing witness for two reasons. First, its stigma: it has entirely replaced cancer as the most feared disease, whose sufferers are most likely to be shunned and made to feel that they deserved to get sick. And, second, its epidemiology: while the majority of those with the disease belong to groups where many others have it (hence the phrase "the AIDS community") the rest of us have been, up until now, relatively removed from its devastations. (Note: although most Americans now know at least one person who has died of AIDS, those in "the AIDS community" may know literally hundreds.) Moreover, AIDS destroyed not just individuals, but their way of life, the gay subculture of the 1970s. Randy Shilts' *And the Band Played On* and Andrew Holleran's *Ground Zero* focus profoundly on this aspect of the epidemic, bearing witness to individuals and to activities and to institutions that are now dead and gone:

> The bomb seems the best metaphor. . . . "Oh," people say when they learn someone left New York in 1983, "You got out before the bomb fell," Well, not really, he wants to reply. The bomb fell several years before that. Only we didn't know it. The bomb fell without anyone's knowing the bomb had fallen, which is how it destroyed a community that now seems—looking back—as extinct as the Mayans. (Holleran 1988, 25)

Curiously, even a reader who finds these activities and institutions thoroughly repulsive may appreciate the moral impulse to bear witness to them shown by both of the above authors.

Once again, we wish to avoid drawing parallels with the Holocaust on the level of actual sufferings. But a parallel does exist at the level of reasons for writing, and with it a source of potential confusion. Holocaust journals not only tell the world "someone was here," but they were sometimes written with the hope that they could be used later as evidence in legal proceedings against Nazi war criminals. They were seen by those who kept them as direct evidence of atrocities, and the temptation has been to treat them as "just the facts," as raw historical data without cultural setting or precedent. After all, what could look more unadorned than a tattered document written with a pencil stub and kept in a coffee can by associates of the journal-keeper? It is hard to think of such written works as cultural documents requiring the same skills of interpretation and analysis as any other cultural document would. James Young, in *Writing and Rewriting the Holocaust,* explodes this ideal of raw historical data when he looks at journals and diaries from this period. Even the above-mentioned Warsaw Ghetto journal is one person's interpretation of a situation that the historian knows "better" because of more complete information available from both sides (Young 1988, 25–30). Ironically, some writers of journals were being systematically deceived by their own hopes as well as Nazi assurances of safety.

Yet the one who writes to bear witness does not want to be deceived, and often wishes to record what happened as if it were unprocessed factual reality. Not all of our authors of death and dying narratives would accept this, and almost all admit that the real story is not just what happened medically, but what happened to themselves as persons. Nevertheless, it is a function of a witness to include specific facts that make for historical veracity. This urge may account for one peculiar feature of our accounts. Although not usually medically informative, these accounts contain a plethora of medical test results. Narrators record their platelet or T-Cell counts, or the results of biopsies, as if this information mattered to the storytelling itself. As Stewart Alsop recognizes, it does not; it is boring to read about—yet he continues to report on it. Medical tests yield facts, yield undisputed evidence that the protagonist is really deathly sick. They are perceived as intrinsic to the task of bearing witness, evidence that indeed that "someone was here."

Memorializing the Dead

When someone died in traditional cultures, there was a standard, set way to mourn, known and practiced by the entire community. There may have been unmourned deaths, such as those of individuals believed to have been witches, but even in such cases, the community knew what to do. By the nineteenth century, mourning in our culture included elaborate special clothing, a lovely cemetery plot that could be visited regularly (for those who could afford it, at least), and a whole theology about the afterlife that emphasized consolation and the continuation of family life in a home-like Victorian heaven. Scarlett O'Hara may have danced while she was still in mourning— but most people didn't, and besides, she is herself the product of twentieth century popular imagination. Moreover, in small communities the dead person was usually *missed*—his or her absence was noticed by everyone, although perhaps not always truly regretted. Life went on, but the dead were not completely forgotten, not at least until all who remembered them had themselves died. (At which point some African societies believe the dead become ancestors, an impersonal group who live in an alternative time, contrasted to living, remembered time.)

None of the traditional practices of mourning, nor the assumptions about the dead and their continued presence, have survived into the world depicted in our narratives of death, dying, and bereavement. After the viewing (if there is one) and the funeral, there is literally nothing that the family and friends of the deceased *must* do, and it is quite possible to omit any ceremonies at all. Even if the person who died was in his or her time a celebrity, a long illness preceding the death lets others fill the same social niche, the same job slots, before the actual death. The dead just vanish, and the family is left to bear the loss without having socially sanctioned rituals for doing so. Although some of these generalizations may not hold true for all contemporary Americans—some African Americans may converse with their dead via dreams, and in some ethnic communities extended families still support the immediate mourners—they shape the backdrop against which the majority of Type III and IV narratives are written. In the world of the educated, upper-middle class, mourning is no longer anything but the most privatized and often shameful experience. Shameful because the mourner is in invisible exile— bewildered as to how to live in the country of the bereaved.

Memorializing the dead person, and one's relationship to him or her, thus becomes a private or, at most, a family endeavor. Not everyone does it by writing a book about the dead person's last illness, of course. There are countless other ways—including finishing projects begun but not yet completed by the dead person. Some of the Type II narratives discussed in chapter 2 qualify for this (Anatole Broyard's wife edited his writings to produce *Intoxicated by My Illness*; J.R. Money's friends found a publisher for his unedited jottings, *To All the Girls I've Loved Before*). Another related method is to literally revisit the places of the relationship, places saturated with memories for the survivor. To replay the past in this way immerses the mourner for a while, but appears to meet some compelling need for closure and resolution, to acknowledge that the bereavement is indeed, as C.S. Lewis wrote, the final stage of love and not its truncation. Family photograph albums and, today, videotapes, can substitute for travel through ordinary geographical space. And, we have already referred in passing to writing letters to one's dead spouse or child.

The curious thing about any of these activities is that they have no direct social consequences whatsoever, and people are neither obligated nor forbidden to do any of them. They exist in the private sphere of personal choice and individual or familial identity formation. To continue to communicate via letters with one's dead spouse does not conflict with one's religious beliefs, nor does it support them; such actions (when carried out as described by widows Xenia Rose and Jill Truman) are not intended to convey any belief in the afterlife existence of the dead spouse. They are not bolstered by any Western cultural tradition (as they would be in African and some East Asian contexts).

Thus, to memorialize by writing the history of the relationship, especially of the terminal illness that led to the death of the beloved, is in continuity with these otherwise entirely private practices. The difference, of course, is that to publish such a personal narrative is to go public, to reveal to the outside world matters that would ordinarily never be shared beyond the family. Of course, a fancy grave monument also memorializes the dead in a public manner. But that kind of memorializing is alien to most of the authors of autobiographies. Not only is the stone grave marker obviously not a valid substitute for the living person in their eyes, but the very qualities of public, impersonal, communal worth that such markers seem to claim for those buried beneath them are *not* those that matter most to the autobiographers.

And so we have the personal narrative that memorializes what is more private, most uniquely real, and most missed about the dead person. Not Carl Lerner the author of film scripts, but Carl Lerner Gerda's husband is the protagonist of *A Death of One's Own*. Likewise, the spouse or child of the dying protagonist, who may be a public person, such as Philip Roth the novelist, appears primarily as a relative, a family member, a private person caught up in the same dilemmas of caretaking and grief as the completely unknown families. An interesting case of this is Lois Snow's *A Death with Dignity*, which tells of the death of her husband and of the hospice-style care he received from a visiting team of Chinese health experts who flew all the way to Switzerland to assist with his illness and ended up helping him die. Edgar Snow was an expert on China, and his wife's memorializing narrative is also intended to advocate the "Chinese way of dying" she experienced. But the narrative itself does not dwell on his contribution to Western understanding of Chinese people and history; he appears primarily as dying husband, and the Chinese appear as his friends and helpers. Any political implication or motivation for their visit is simply not part of the story she tells, and would be as out of place as an extended discussion of the benefits and failures of the Chinese Cultural Revolution.

Does memorializing achieve its goal? Its goal is not to bring the dead person back to life, but to remember him or her, and share this memory with others. The message of the memorialist is not the "someone was here" of the witness telling his or her own story, but rather "this particular, unique person was here, once lived on this earth." The task succeeds insofar as the reader is able to reconstruct his or her own picture of Carl, Edgar, and all the other now-dead loved ones. *We* may not like them as much as the narrators wish us to, and we will probably not be in love with more than a few, but the task has succeeded if we will share in the basic judgment of the narrator: the dead person should not be forgotten.

We have already discussed, under the section on truth in autobiography and in chapter 2, some of the things that can go wrong when the task of memorializing is beyond the resources of the author. Over-idealizing, repressed anger at the deceased, and self-centeredness on the part of the author/narrator are all problems we have discovered. Like tasteless, overly ornate stone monuments, some memorializing autobiographies say something unflattering about the dead protagonist and his or her family. We have, in our readings, met some truly obnoxious persons, whose manipulativeness, selfishness, and arrogance shine through in spite of all attempts on the part of the narrators to gloss over or deny these qualities. We have also met narrators who refused to move over sufficiently to let us get to know the dying protagonist well enough, who kept intruding into their storytelling in ways that we found irritating.

We have moved from the language of texts and protagonists to the language of meeting and knowing persons. This shift, which seems utterly natural to us, is itself a tribute to the success of this genre of autobiography. It is an achievement culminating in our fantasy of the support group for the newly-dead, the sense that as *persons* the memorialized protagonists continue to exist in some alternative realm, and can congregate and converse among themselves. We know that the autobiographer's art has succeeded when this picture makes imaginative sense.

Chapter Four

MEDICINE FROM
THE BOTTOM UP

THE AUTOBIOGRAPHICAL, FIRST-PERSON GENRE ITSELF PUTS the patient's perspective in the foreground, and portrays medicine from the bottom up, not from the traditional top down stance of the medical experts and specialists. This reversal is roughly analogous to the anthropologist's switch from missionaries and colonial officers to native informants when trying to learn about the cultures of tribal peoples. The human meanings of what appear to be the same events get interpreted in vastly different ways. What appears as a marvelous improvement over past practices from the perspective of medical science (or the colonial administrator), may look from the patient's (or the native's) perspective as an intrusive, senseless, and painful manipulation of the powerless at the hands of the powerful. This analogy may be loaded, but paternalistic relations between doctors and their patients are no longer an unquestioned norm, and have become a common scapegoat for many critics of established medicine. Our collection of personal narratives gives an eloquent testimony of this shift away from traditional acquiescence on the part of patients, and by telling the medical story from the patient's standpoints, our narratives inevitably raise questions about the range of doctors' knowledge and the authority that knowledge carries. Dissatisfaction with today's medical environment and ethos appears in many of these narratives, even if it developed as a major theme in relatively few.

In Western allopathic medicine, the patient's perspective is marginalized. The disease, the medically defined entity that is the subject of the doctor's concern, is what such medicine encounters. Although patients must still be able to report symptoms, the technological tests for the presence of a particular disease entity are what matter most in making a diagnosis. In contrast, the illness, the lived experience of being sick that the patient knows and brings to the doctor's office, simply does not compete with the above focus on disease. To learn if one has AIDS, cancer, or any of the other serious conditions from which our protagonists suffer, it is not enough that they start to feel sick, or even look sick. Steven Petrow, author of a collection of interviews from persons with AIDS and their families, is a case in point: he found a purplish sore on his leg, and visited a doctor who foolishly diagnosed Kaposi's sarcoma and (almost certainly) the patient's sexual orientation. Not until the blood test for HIV was given did Petrow learn that he was free of the virus. This example of medical error fueled by arrogance is not the only one in our collection.

Yet even within the practice of conventional medicine, complete discounting of the patient's perspective becomes a liability and may limit the doctor's effectiveness. Medical sociologists such as Arthur Kleinman, Arthur Frank, and Howard Brody recommend attentive listening to patients, or the study of their narratives as part of the medical school curriculum (Frank 1992). Broyard wants what we all want in a doctor, "One who is a close reader of illness, and a good critic of medicine." Someone who will treat his physical and metaphysical self as well. A doctor who can hear the story of his sickness. His ideal doctor would resemble Oliver Sacks—a doctor "who enjoyed me. I want to be a good story for him" (Broyard 1992, 45). Without good communication, the doctor's attempt to elicit symptoms will falter, and instructions about medications will be ignored or misunderstood. Obvious as this may seem, our narratives reveal how frequently communication fails, whether because doctors do not take patients' complaints seriously ("pain is what a patient feels before surgery; discomfort is what he or she feels after surgery" several narrators attest) or because patients are themselves too shy or frightened to report these honestly.

Yet autobiographers who are also patients or relatives of patients are hardly inarticulate, and usually count themselves among the most privileged and assertive sector of the population. If a writer used to describing inner states of feeling cannot be trusted to give an accurate account of her pain, for example, then what of the many inarticulate, underprivileged, and fatalistic patients who find themselves waiting passively at the clinic, and receive the doctor's information and instruction equally passively? And if a celebrity such as Gilda Radner will not find her symptoms taken seriously (so that her ovarian cancer was not diagnosed until too late), how can the ordinary patient hope to fare?

Some accounts protest directly and furiously against the exaggeration and abuse of power intrinsic to the role of healer. In their works, the patient's perspective sounds a cry for liberation, from medical authoritarianism, and from idolatrous worship of doctors and their technology. Just as liberation theologies protest religious ideas promulgated from the top down and yearn for a religious vision from the bottom up, from the perspective of the powerless, such narratives attempt to unmask the pretensions of doctors and medicine. Ironically, two of the most angry examples of this involve patients who are themselves doctors. Martha Lear's *Heartsounds* (about her physician husband) and Roni Rabin's *Six Parts Love* (her doctor father's struggle with ALS) are particularly harsh in their depiction of medical arrogance, ignorance, and inhumanity, perhaps because when a doctor becomes a patient, he or she expects to be treated as a respected colleague. Another example, Jocelyn Evan's *Living with a Man Who is Dying*, blasts the British National Health Service with essentially identical criticisms, while Lois Snow's *A Death with Dignity* finds that only the Chinese approach to health care and dying provides a humane alternative to the pathological attitudes of Western medicine.

Not all of our narrators, by any means, share this anger and outrage. Contrary to expectations fueled by publicity about malpractice, only one protagonist filed a malpractice suit and collected a substantial sum of money—and she (Barbara Rosenblum, coauthor with Sandra Butler of *Cancer in Two Voices*) makes the irony of this "blood money" only a minor theme in the narrative. Many are grateful for the fine treatment they received (Alsop 1973), the humanity of their personal physicians (Weingarten 1978), or the miraculous technologies of contemporary medicine (Maier 1991). Others, such as Alan

Paton and Betty Spohr, ignore the medical dimensions of disease altogether, concentrating either on illness as lived human experience, or on other matters entirely. Yet because almost all the narratives in our collection somehow include medicine, doctors, and illness, the manner in which these realities are portrayed is significant, and provides a fascinating glimpse into emergent attitudes and values. Medicine from the bottom up is, for the most part, neither an evil empire of power-hungry tormentors, nor a benevolent, peaceful, and healing activity. It is, like all human enterprises, an ambiguous mixture of both good and evil.

Arrogance and Bureaucracy

In our narratives, there are two related criticisms made again and again by patient-protagonists. First, doctors exaggerated regarding their expertise for purposes of self-aggrandisement, or simply because they are afraid of appearing human and fallible. At worst, doctors lie to patients, pretend to possess a knowledge that they do not really have, and are cold-hearted and selfish even when they are factually truthful and medically competent (see the above examples, as well as Rollin 1985, Schreiber 1990, and Halberstam and Lesher 1976). The second criticism is that the technological orientation of contemporary healthcare, and its bureaucratization, leads unintentionally to a dehumanizing and humiliating environment for patients. Description of hospitals, tests, and treatments abound in our literature, and few of them are reassuring. Hodgins finds hospitals to be among the world's noisiest, least restful places. Maier lies awake trying to decode the overhead-page messages he hears—a sure sign that everything now appeared ominous to him: "Paging Dr. Strong" meant that a patient needed to be physically subdued! Against the backdrop of the hospital milieu, even well-intentioned, humane doctors struggle to serve their patients. And mixed-up charts—every patient's nightmare—actually do happen, even at the world-famous Mayo Clinic (Maier 1991). In this setting, that of the classic "total institution," the patient's most healthful strategy may be to check out quickly. If that is impossible, a romance with a nurse (Heller 1986, Lund 1989, Hodgins 1964) offers a joyful antidote to this dehumanizing environment.

Now these two criticisms are hardly unique to autobiographies; they are found in Elisabeth Kübler-Ross' *On Death and Dying*, written in 1968, and indeed in Cabot and Dicks' *The Art of Ministering to the Sick*, published in 1936! Nor does our literature contain suggestions for meeting these problems that are not found elsewhere. The most frequently offered of these is hospice care, which provides a more supportive milieu. The Zorzas write their account of their daughter Jane's death, *A Way to Die*, explicitly to advocate the English model of a "free-standing hospice," while American authors mention the Shanti program for AIDS patients (Hostetler 1989), or homecare (Rubin 1982). In our next chapter, we will turn to the pictures of family and community in these narratives, and to the limits and problems even these alternatives to hospital care include. Although hospice is not magic, overall the reports of it in our collection are encouraging; to be freed of the hospital environment and ethos *can* make a difference.

In America today, as we write, the cost of health care and health care reform are other major concerns, overriding the twin critiques of medical arrogance and bureaucratization. Here, however, our narratives falter. Or rather, the autobiographical genre is a poor vehicle for an attack on the financial structure of American medicine. Almost all the authors were reticent about the exact costs of their own and their loved one's care. In contrast to medical test results, we do not find excerpts from bills in our narratives. Curiously, English, Canadian, and European authors—all of whom live and die under systems of nationalized health care—do not spend any *less* time on money issues than do their American counterparts. Why do only two contributors to our collection, Hodgins and Heller, discuss their hospital bills, while so many freely offer the most intimate details of their bodies' malfunctioning?

Does the ideology of medicine from the bottom up account in part for this reticence? This democratic, populist ideal of the patient's perspective hides the fact that many of our authors are financially well off and almost all are well insured. Joseph Heller may have been bankrupted by his illness (he had let his insurance lapse) but the reader of *No Laughing Matter* never forgets that this is a famous author with friends ready and willing to advance him tens of thousands of dollars at a time as needed, not your average uninsured member of the working poor. Hodgins wrote of his stroke at the start of the era of health insurance group plans, and mentions finances not only to protest the outrageous costs, but to explain how the insurance company actually lost money because of him: his bills came to more than they collected in premiums from his employers that year! (Hodgins 1964, 265–72).

There is, however, an alternate reason for the privacy and reticence surrounding money issues, even in narratives where details of the protagonist's bodily ills and personal fears are laid bare. The autobiographical genre itself is not the best vehicle for an exploration of an issue that clearly falls under the rubric of public policy. A thorough investigation of the health care industry and its finances requires a perspective from which individuals are citizens, elements in a public society. And this is precisely the public sphere that Americans find inimical to their quest for identity and autonomous individuality. Autobiography works well to capture the nuances of private-sphere realities, the struggle of the autonomous and ever-youthful individual to become reconciled to a reality of limitation and death. Although public and private may be far more intertwined than we care to realize, our autobiographers' preference for criticisms that relate back easily to private sphere matters—and their silence on other points—suggests how the genre itself reflects the ideology of the public/private split that Luckmann noted back in 1967.

Conventional Medicine and the Power Within

Although our narratives are unready to take on the financial and political side of health care, many of them deeply and forcefully critique another dimension of American medicine: its nearly unlimited trust in technology to triumph over disease. Recall that in 1971, the Nixon administration, with broad bipartisan support, declared a war against cancer. This national agenda consummated what historian James Patterson calls "the message of hope," (Patterson 1987, 76) the ideology that with more research, more hospital technology, and more money, a cure for cancer (or any other condition) can be found. In 1971, many assumed that the same American drive and know-how that could put a man on the moon could be applied to the conquest of cancer, the dreaded disease. And indeed, since that time, the official five-year survival rates for many types of cancer have risen dramatically. As for other illnesses, the role of the CAT scans in pinpointing the location of blood clots has dramatically altered the stroke patient's chances (compare the technology in Hodgins 1964 and DeMille 1981). Now the dreary and dangerous procedures for giving needed transfusions to hemophiliacs—described in agonizing detail by the Massies in *Journey* (published in 1975, but dealing with hemophilia in the 1950s) have been replaced by much simpler ones. (However, alas, the contamination of the blood supply by HIV has nullified this improvement, with tragic consequences for the hemophiliac population.) Most miraculously, heart and liver transplants now extend the lives of those who would be otherwise dead, and the narrators of these medical wonders (Greene 1990, Maier 1991) on the surface support the message of hope, of victory over disease through medicine and technology.

Yet in the eyes of many autobiographers, it is not the successful space voyage to the moon, but the war in Vietnam that offers the most appropriate analogy through which to gauge the true fruit of the message of hope, and an earlier era's promises. Our narratives span the late 1960s through the era of the war on cancer, the appearance of AIDS in the 1980s (Shilts, *And the Band Played On*), the recent return of tuberculosis (Sutliffe, *Grandma Cherry's Spoon*). Our narrators, even those who are grateful for their doctors' fine care and the power of medical research and diagnosis, bear witness to the distance between the hopes for a "victory" over disease, and the realities of what actually has been accomplished. Not dramatic new drugs, but a better mix of already-known ones might have saved her son *Eric*, says Doris Lund. Even the improved survival rate statistics for cancer patients are questioned (Wilber 1991); earlier detection and *not* cures account for what differences exist. In the meantime, the failure of the American public health establishment and the Center for Disease Control to take early action in the face of the AIDS epidemic, and the failure of researchers to find a "cure" in the form of a vaccine, are parallel to this nation's failure to handle the crisis concerning the Vietnam War. The authors of the best AIDS narratives express better the outrage at the arrogance and indifference of researchers and politicians alike (Shilts 1987, Monette 1988, Glaser 1991).

Medicine from the bottom up does not necessarily reflect this mood. But the patient's perspective—even of those who benefit most "miraculously" from medicine, organ transplant recipients—

reflects a message different from those 1971 hopes for a victorious war on disease. A.C. Greene in *Taking Heart* and Frank Maier in *Sweet Reprieve* tell stories of unprecedented life-saving procedures, and both are enthusiastic about the future of transplantation. Maier receives a liver transplant at the Mayo Clinic, and lives several years with it. These years, his "sweet reprieve," enabled him to get to know his grandchildren, become a public speaker on behalf of liver trans-plantees, and an advocate for donor families. Yet Maier's advocacy is not propagandizing for the message of hope in medical technology. The real outcome of transplantation is not a cure, but rather the absence of severe symptoms through stringent medical maintenance for the rest of one's life. This is a bargain he was willing to make. In fact, his whole point is that this is a decision for each and every *patient* to make, for cooperation with technological experts is a must if the transplantee would survive. Even this work, in its author's gentle and friendly way, critiques the classic assumption of the conventional allopathic disease model, which devalues the patient's own point of view and contribution to healing.

In place of a politically legislated hope through technology, one finds instead in our narratives how individuals freely place their hope in a wide range of additional possibilities. These include holistic medical practices, which we will call adjunctive therapies. Most of all, hope is to be placed in the patient's own inner resources—for strength, for deciding which methods to try, and for inward resources for healing itself. These narratives do not advocate uncritical or exclusive reliance on homeopathic, macrobiotic, or other unconven-tional therapies, but many of the protagonists try these in addition to their conventional treatments and find them helpful. A particularly striking instance is that of Dr. Anthony Sattilaro who battled the prejudices of his medical colleagues when he found—to his own amazement—that a strict macrobiotic diet sent his cancer into remis-sion (Sattilaro 1982). More typically, Ken and Treya Wilber and Max Lerner all survey and evaluate a wide range of treatment options, and make informed decisions, for which they take responsibility. It is the latter stance that protects both Wilbers from later unnecessary guilt, after Treya's visit to a special clinic in Germany for chemotherapy fails to prevent her death from aggressive breast cancer. Unlike the traditional passive patients of the allopathic model, those who de-cided their course of treatment did their best to choose, based on all the information they could gather. It is this process of seeking information and choosing that the autobiographical genre is especially adept at illustrating and modeling for readers.

Cancer, the illness in the majority of personal narratives, is one for which medicine can "do something," even if what it does is often frightening, painful, and not very effective (Treya Wilber's physical sufferings came, except at the end, not from her cancer but from the treatments for it). The patient-protagonist who suffers from an illness for which medicine can do nothing is an even more effective subverter of the message of hope and those who seek to deliver it. Yes, there may one day be a cure for Alzheimer's, or ALS; but these conditions demoralize a medical expert who has been taught that his or her role requires aggressive combat against the disease. In *Six Parts Love*, David Rabin's doctors offer him absolutely nothing when faced with ALS, not even human sympathy and support, according to his daughter. When Barbara Peabody lived through the experiences she records in *The Screaming Room*, AIDS also fell into this category of illness; she notes how differently medical personnel would have responded to her son Peter's symptoms had his diagnosis been cancer, and there would have been something they could have *done* for him. Yet within the autobiographical genre, it is finally not a matter of what doctors can *do* to or for patients, but what patients and their families can struggle to accomplish themselves.

Thus, adjunctive therapies, when they appear in these narratives, are not primarily alternatives to medicine (since most patients continue with the medical procedures suggested for their diagnosis), but as expressions of the patient's own inner resources and his or her freedom to chose. In contrast to the conventional expectation of patient passivity and silence, many of our protagonists respond to the challenge of illness by drawing upon a very different source of hope. We have already mentioned Norman Cousins, who at the very time of faith in science turned not to technology but to the Marx Brothers and Candid Camera as sources for laughter and well-being, internal as well as external. Cousin's *Anatomy of an Illness* does not promise inevitable success, but does provide a model for how taking responsibility for one's treatment salvages and restores human dignity in the face of medical dehumanization. Cousins never denies the scientific value of Western allopathic medicine, but only wishes that it was complemented with an equal acknowledgment of the patient's own role in healing. It does not, in this context, matter that Cousins' ailment was medically different from the diseases suffered by the majority of other sick protagonists. What counts is his will to live, his human power, his character.

Few patients share Norman Cousins' character (although Max Lerner certainly does!), but many explicitly recognize how an activist stance—taking responsibility for one's treatment—helped them convert the powerless role of medical patient into something more compatible with their own dignity and self-worth. Journalist Wendy Williams, in *The Power Within*, extols this method of self-direction and activist hope as the secret to surviving cancer. Her ten inspirational case histories all share some of the character traits advocated by Cousins, including a zesty sense of humor, and all avoid an identity as "cancer victim." Not all of them survive, but all prolong their lives and turn the situation of passivity and dependence upon medical expertise into one of active quest for what will work for them. An activist stance may be well on the way to becoming a norm, a response to the realities of the American health care system as bureaucratic and technologically oriented. The ethic of taking responsibility for one's treatment has by now permeated the milieu in which most of our protagonists experience patienthood. Becoming informed about the disease, questioning doctors, inviting second opinions, and intentionally selecting particular hospitals and individual doctors: all of these strategies appear frequently (at least these are options for most of our relatively well-off and insured authors). Many recognize how a patient's own passivity and denial aids and abets the medical arrogance so often criticized.

This stance has implications for gender issues, since the passivity of the traditional patient and the paternalistic model of medicine that encouraged it apply with particular force to women. In several of our narratives, the daughter represents the emergent "Cousins'-style" stance, and is appalled at her mother's docility in the face of patronizing and humiliating doctors. Rollin's *Last Wish* and LeAnne Schreiber's *Midstream* reflect this situation. Yet in the case of Frank Maier, it is his energetic activist wife, Ginny, who asks the questions, challenges the hospital personnel, and steers her husband through life-threatening illness as she had gently supported and steered him through previous decades of health.

A pitfall of the activist stance on the part of patients and their loved ones is that it can lead to an hysterical obsession with the disease, rather than a concentration on the patient's own experience of the illness. Many cancer patients become cancer experts, collectors and purveyors of information about alternative and adjunctive treatments. Frantically running after a variety of alternative therapies, some of them far-fetched, may be a form of desperation and not at all the "take charge" strategy it is intended to be. Paul Monette's role as a one-man AIDS information exchange during his friend's illness is seen by him, retrospectively, in this light. His determined quest for information could self-righteously be viewed as heroic and useful, as a way to take charge when established medical experts were helpless. But he knows that it was also a mix of hysteria, denial, and hyperactivity on his part and others in the AIDS community, which in the long run may or may not have been helpful to them and their dying loved ones:

> We were about to join a community of the stricken who would not lie down and die. . . . This network has the feel of an underground railway. It could be argued that we're out there mainly for ourselves, of course, and the ones we can't live without. But on the way we have also become traders and explorers, passing the word till hope is kindled in places so dark you can't see your hand in front of your eyes. If the government was going to continue to act as if we didn't exist, if the medical establishment was prone to gridlock over funds, if the drug companies were waiting till the curve got high enough for profit, then we would find our own way. Whistling in the dark is whistling still. (Monette 1988, 103)

Contrast this with the restraint shown by Marvin Barrett, Violet Weingarten, and a few of the others with regard to knowledge about their disease; they wish to avoid preoccupation with the medical definition of their problem, and seek an alternative orientation self-consciously, in a careful attempt to experience their intimations of mortality on their own terms.

Champions of the Power Within

During the same era when most of our narratives appeared, the activist stance received enormous support from three self-help advocates whose ideas about healing and personal responsibility appear in several accounts directly and have undoubtedly influenced many others. The works of Lawrence LeShan (*Cancer as a Turning Point*), Carl and Stephanie Simonton (*Getting Well Again*), and Bernie Siegel (*Love, Medicine and Miracles*) advocate reliance upon the spiritual and emotional resources of the patient. LeShan is a clinical psychologist with over thirty-five years of working with cancer patients and a long term interest in spiritual aspects of medicine and health. His underlying philosophy is that a cancer diagnosis can become a spiritual challenge, a turning point in one's vision of oneself—and that requires taking responsibility for integrating this insight into one's total life. This message, thoroughly congruent with the ideals of most of the narrators, is not what LeShan is often saddled with having claimed; his attempt to explore the links between cancer and coping styles was never intended to prove that we cause our own disease.

Doctors Carl and Stephanie Simonton streamline and simplify the above message. Theorizing that cancer is related to stress, their goal is to change patients' abilities to deal with stress, and to encourage an activist, positive sense of mastery in regard to one's own recovery. (According to Patterson, the popular belief that modern life and its stresses induce cancer is one of those myths not seriously supported by medical statistics [Patterson 1987, 273–76], but psycho-neuro-immunology promotes the notion that decreasing stress can have a positive effect on the immune system. Subsequent editions of the book have tried to correct the earlier impression that the Simonton's promoted the theory that patients' lifestyles and attitudes may have caused their disease to occur in the first place.) The Simonton's book, *Getting Well Again*, has an upbeat, even moralistic quality that LeShan attempted to avoid. They are perhaps best known for their ingenious imagery exercises, some of which require that the participant envision his or her cancer cells as wicked invaders, and the body's own cells as good warriors in a winning battle to oust them (more on the specific warfare imagery of this in chapter 7). The Simonton's method is tried out by Jill Ireland–who also samples all sorts of other adjunctive therapies–as well as by Gilda Radner and several of Wendy Williams' cases in *The Power Within*.

But the most relentlessly upbeat and inspirational of all is surgeon Bernie Siegel who, in *Love, Medicine and Miracles*, manages to moralize the whole activist attitude so that patients with good attitudes get better, while those with cancer personalities who hate themselves die.

Somehow, what started as medicine from the bottom up, to free patients from the external authority of paternalistic doctors, now risks purveying a new moralism about who is really to blame for terminal illness. This, at any rate, is how Arthur Frank, Ken Wilber, and (long before them) Susan Sontag (in her 1978 *Illness as Metaphor*) see such ideas as the "cancer personality" and "you made yourself sick" themes. All three protest against a moral interpretation of data between cancer and stress. Ken and Treya Wilber find that New Age belief in the power of the mind to cause and cure all conditions is destructive when turned simplistically against the cancer patient who, according to such an ideology, doesn't want to get better. It should be mentioned in favor of all three advocates of the power within that they invite patients' exploration of past and present coping strategies and of the personal meanings of illness in their lives.

Perhaps what is most problematic about the above mentioned popular therapies is their continuity with the older message of hope brought by technology. If scientific technology is no longer to be trusted to triumph quickly and inevitably, then an inner, mental technology can be made to appear as a partial replacement. However helpful an activist stance may be when facing the hospital bureaucracy, when it becomes confused with the hope that ten easy steps will win every battle, even that against death, it fails patient protagonists at a very basic human level. This, we believe, is the reason why the most thoughtful narrators, such as Frank and Barrett, finally pull back from such methods.

Ethics from the Patient's Perspective

One field in which the revolution of medicine seen from the bottom up has already had some impact is medical ethics. Traditionally, this was defined to emphasize both the special responsibilities of the doctor, and specific decisions doctors must make. "Should patients be told the truth?" is one such decision, which by today's standards betrays paternalism in its very phrasing. In this approach, the act of informing a patient—or of lying—is isolated from the total, ongoing human relationship and its social context. One particular hard decision is the subject of debate.

Recently the focus has changed, as in William F. May's superb *The Patient's Ordeal*. Medical ethics now looks at how the patient experiences the pain and challenge of severe illness. This transition is accompanied by a shift from an ethics of decision to an ethics of virtue, a concern with how one becomes the kind of person who can rise to the occasion that the agonizing decisions demand and "stand by and make good on or deal with the consequences of my original choice" (May 1982, 13). Another exponent of this approach, often referred to as "narrative ethics," is Howard Brody, whose *Stories of Sickness* includes several famous fictional examples (Mann's *Magic Mountain*, for one). Brody sees the impact of severe illness as its threat to the "life plan" of the patient, who must redefine him or herself so as to take account of a shortened, or radically derailed life span or diminished capacities. Brody, like May, wants to incorporate this point of view into an ethics less focused on isolated decisions and more narrative in its concern with the long-term identity of the patient. The study of our autobiographies would seem an obvious source of wisdom for this approach.

And yet, as noted already in chapter 3, autobiography is not the same genre as sustained systematic ethical reflection. The latter must still rely upon rational arguments, potentially generalizable to a range of similar cases. Ethical reflection, whether about decisions or character, calls for a format of argument, counter, and rebuttal. "What are the virtues that a patient ought to display? is one question May raises. Is autonomy versus paternalism really an adequate ethical framework for understanding decision-making and long-term character? An ethicist argues and reflects; an autobiographer bears witness, eloquently or ineptly. These are two different, if often overlapping, tasks.

To suggest this is to note how very few of the authors in our collection write explicitly on classical medical ethics issues, such as euthanasia or truth-telling. Why is this so, when so many narrators face the problems discussed by medical ethicists? First, they do so in the context of lives and stories which transcend these classic issues. An interesting example of this is Andrew Malcolm's *Someday*, which concludes when he orders doctors to pull the plug on his dying mother. Even though Malcolm, as a journalist, had written on just this dilemma, we don't read *Someday* as if this dilemma were "what the book was about." *Someday* is principally the story of Malcolm's relationship with his mother, a relationship where denial of death and suffering was always a hidden factor. Once more, the genre of autobiography keeps us focused upon the lives of unique, specific individuals and not ethical generalizations.

Another instance makes this distance from traditional medical ethics even more apparent. Madeleine L'Engle's husband, Hugh, knew he was dying, and he expressed in advance his desire not to be kept alive through heroic resuscitations. L'Engle finds this so unproblematic that no attention is given to the decision itself; she mentions that this matter had been decided, in the context of describing Hugh's final days. And indeed, the couple's religious value system, with its emphasis on a divine love that leaves space for suffering and death, makes any other course of action out of the question for them. There is no need to include any scene of decision-making here.

What of the far more controversial question of "active euthanasia," the decision to end a dying person's life by direct killing? Three narratives include this act. Active euthanasia ends the life of Elizabeth Cox's husband Keith, in *Thanksgiving*, but this is a minor theme of her story. In Jessamyn West's *The Woman Said Yes*, the second half of the book deals with how the narrator assisted her sister Carmen's suicide. But this follows a far more moving account in the first part of the story of how West's mother, Grace (the "woman" of the title), saved Jessamyn from a TB sanitarium and restored her to life and health. The same woman who said "yes" to life taught her daughters how to say "yes" to death; thus Grace's posthumous power, and not active euthanasia, is the subject of the story.

Of all our collection, Betty Rollin's *Last Wish* comes closest to advocacy of active euthanasia. As we become interested in Ida and Betty as persons, as unique women whose relationship is problematic long before Ida's request for her daughter's help in ending her life, we see how the work fits more into an ethics of virtue or character than an ethics of decision, using May's and Brody's categories. The autobiographer's sole responsibility is to make credible how, for *this* particular person at this time under these circumstances, no other course of action would have been in character.

In one sense, then, narrative ethics begin where autobiography leaves off. In the above example—a good one—the story relates how

Ida wishes to end her life herself, but simultaneously wishes that her daughter Betty and Betty's husband Ed do everything but take the pills. Even a neighbor is brought into the conspiracy, so that as she prepares for death, Ida is doing what she had always done best: manipulating both family and strangers, timing her requests so that before they are able to reflect on the ethics of these requests, they are already committed to a course of action mapped out by the dying woman. The anger this generates in protagonist Betty creeps between the lines of the narration, so that the mother's real legacy is a daughter compelled to mix guilt with bravado in her tale of her mother's death. In an alternative interpretation, Ida Rollin's zest for life, her energy and enthusiasm, make her death from self-induced drug overdose the act of a courageous woman who feared fading away more than she feared death. This is closer to the way Ida was portrayed by powerful, vivacious Maureen Stapleton in the made-for-TV movie (living actors are so *alive* that it is hard to avoid this shift in meaning, when a story is transformed into a drama). Yet, neither interpretation is itself a substitute for the ethical reflection May and Brody believe is needed in order to understand the issues at stake. Whether these are posed in terms of discrete, separate hard decisions or of virtue, *Last Wish* is grist for the ethicists.

Autobiography, then, although helpful for a "narrative ethics," is not medical ethics. In reality, the characters of Ida and Betty, the Malcolm family, and the L'Engles are endlessly and awesomely particular. Curiously, our autobiographies make less of a contribution to this ethical aspect of medicine from the bottom up than to the portrayal of illness as a human situation. As popularizers of alternative therapies, some of the works serve directly to enhance a patient's perspective of American medicine. Yet even in this, their very focus on individual persons and not on issues, treatments, and public policies, is both their limit and their strength.

Modern medicine has not won the war against cancer. It appears to be losing the battle against AIDS. Tuberculosis, which could have been completely eradicated a generation ago, has now returned. Yet the purpose of autobiographies is not to record the ups and downs of these medical battles. It is not to map out new strategies, therapies, or interventions. Autobiographies may advocate many specific practices, but their primary task is rarely medical education, medical ethics, or advocacy of patients' rights. Using our terms, the primary focus of such narratives of illness—medicine from the patient's point of view—will bear witness to illness as a human experience and memorialize the beloved dead. These remain the most central tasks that autobiography can accomplish.

Chapter Five

NO ONE IS AN
ISLAND

IN CHAPTER 1, THOMAS LUCKMAN WAS QUOTED AS describing back in 1967 the self of the American worldview as "the autonomous individual" who "is young and never dies." Autonomy here means that the self is free to construct and discard its own identity as if in a supermarket for the fragments of selfhood; the identity most truly ours is what we ourselves craft and create, not what we are given from birth. In that world of young, energetic, and deathless individuals, independence and autonomy are unambiguous goods. Any situation or relationship that threatens them is suspect at best, terrifying at worst. Particularly terrifying is losing one's freedom, through captivity to the institutions of the public sphere. Luckmann has no doubt that the modern belief in autonomy is illusory, given the real power of the public sphere to shape our lives.

More recently, enormous attention has been paid to issues of autonomy, isolation, and community in American society. The popularity of Robert Bellah's *Habits of the Heart* attests to a widespread sense of "dis-ease" about the consequences of American individualism and an unrestrained ethic of autonomy. Although personal freedom seems in itself an unambiguous good, the results of the style of freedom observed by Bellah (and others) are anything but unambiguous. "Too much individualism" is now perceived as a problem. Wistful or nostalgic visions of community, located back in the past and now unrecoverable, accompany this reassessment. Is the autonomy Luckmann and Bellah portray a sufficient ethic for an entire society? Is it adequate even to the experience of individuals who, eventually, do age and die? Our collection of autobiographies shows how Americans struggle over issues of autonomy versus control by institutions, isolation versus community, and search for more humanly adequate definitions of freedom and selfhood in the midst of mortality.

The relevant encroaching public-sphere institutions are, of course, hospitals and "establishment medicine." The plotline of some of the narratives constructs the drama of personal dying as a battle between the autonomous individual and the attempt by hospitals and experts to control this self, to dominate and restrict its choices. Yet, ironically, one of the criticisms now voiced against the Western scientific medical worldview is that it artificially isolates each patient, ignoring the matrix of relationships in which sickness (as opposed to disease) is best understood. Doctors, according to the normative disease model, now see patients as organisms in a vacuum, not as persons inhabiting a social space. No longer do doctors make house calls, and so the chance to see a patient in the midst of his or her family and community is gone. Thus, medicine accepts a version of the autonomous self, and in so doing ignores the potential healing power of the environment and human relationships in favor of disease-directed allopathic remedies (Kleinman 1988, 5ff.). Not too little autonomy, but too much of it may be the problem with institutionalized medicine, at least at this level.

Moreover, the same criticism is made of the Western autobiography genre, particularly by feminists. The self portrayed in autobiography is a self deliberately, artificially separated from its milieu, in order to be uniquely not "the other," and so the real web of relatedness that ties selves together is hidden or repressed. The autobiographer, like Luckmann's autonomous supermarket consumer, proudly builds an identity that focuses attention upon uniqueness and separateness from others. This criticism at least bears out contemporary partial disillusionment with a vision of an absolutely autonomous individual, attached to no one except by his or her own free and revocable choices. We do not find that it actually describes the majority of our narratives, which—as we have seen—memorialize relationships among persons, rather than promote a clear vision of a separated, unconnected self glorifying in its isolation.

Bellah and his associates avoid the easy accusation that American society is, or has become, narcissistic. In fact, they find that the real lives of the subjects they studied are filled with commitments and relationships, just as the lives of our protagonists are. What has vanished are ways to articulate these ties, to make sense of them except at the level of autonomous personal choices. The "first language" of most middle-class Americans is "expressive individualism" (Bellah 1985, 20), a way to speak of the self and its commitments that grounds these in the subjective preferences of an autonomous self. Thus, even commitment to family values is a personal preference, defended because it "feels right" at a particular time and place in life. The inability of many of their subjects to find—or feel the need to find—any further grounding for their commitments is what troubles Bellah. Once again, real relationships were maintained in spite of this failing, but their human meanings were systematically obscured and often undermined. The interconnectedness and mutual indebtedness of human life becomes invisible.

How do our autobiographies speak to this problem? The overall issue divides into three distinct forms. The first, the motif of "autonomy versus control by representatives of the public sphere," dominates some of the autobiographies and appears in most of them. Here, the worldview of "expressive individualism" finds its most enthusiastic exponents. But the other side of this celebration of autonomy is the question of "sharing versus isolation," in which a much more somber assessment is made of American society and its values. A third issue, following from the second, is the quest for community, new as well as retained from the past, which will help overcome the pathologies of unmitigated autonomy.

Autonomy versus Control by Others

What is one of the few situations in which it is permissible to treat a noncriminal adult by confining him or her? When can an adult be expected to be reduced to the status of a child? When do such ordinary courtesies as the right to bodily privacy all but vanish? As soon a you become a hospital patient, say our narrators. To be a hospital patient is to lose one's freedom, and—if one is not careful—to lose part of one's soul along with it. That all the restrictions and humiliations of hospital life are inflicted for the patient's own good, and he or she is supposed to be grateful for treatment that would otherwise be insulting and demeaning, only adds to the outrage. None of the authors have themselves spent time in concentration camps or prisons. By the standards of the other, nonbenevolent "total institutions," hospitals may be wonderful, friendly places. But then, inmates of camps or prisons do not have to pay out enormous fees in order to serve time.

For many protagonists, the helplessness and humiliating loss of control that go with being a hospital patient are the worst part of being sick. Physical pain and debilitation are bad enough, as are the aftereffects of certain treatments. But being sick in a hospital makes one vulnerable to the mercies of strangers, caretakers who are sometimes negligent or sadistic, and invariably overworked. A private room may help, but the loss of bodily privacy and mobility hurts and humiliates. A depressed or complaining roommate exacerbates this situation. Hospitals serve meals at times that suit the staff, on a schedule that may frustrate or bewilder patients. Hospitals often restrict visiting hours and decide who can or cannot visit, but teams of medical students or residents feel free to examine, question, and requestion any patient at any hour. At night, patients are routinely awakened and ordered to take assorted medications without explanation or the freedom to say "No" without a fuss. Moreover, the paperwork, the bureaucratic procedures, and the rules always seem to operate in the most arbitrary fashion, so that even those with clout—that is, doctors—are often infuriated and made helpless by the system. If you want to discover how precious personal autonomy is, check yourself into one of these total institutions and discover how much you take for granted. America is the land of the free—provided these free stay well.

The struggle of the patient and the family to gain back some degree of personal control over the dying process, which makes up the central drama of many of our narratives, occurs against this bureaucratic backdrop. This narrative of the battle between the huge bureaucracy and its autocratic experts versus the patient and family, armed only with courage and an intuitive sense of their rights as human beings, follows a pattern whose ancestry includes heroic folktales and Horatio Alger stories. A variant of this is the folk tradition of the heroic wife who fights to save her husband from prison or the gallows, traveling many miles, interceding with judges and finally triumphing over oppressive social powers through the fierce strength of her devotion. In the contemporary accounts, victory over the medical powers-that-be does not necessarily require recovery from the disease. The patient may indeed die, but he or she and the family will have triumphed if they have successfully won the war against the medical establishment, as expressed in such titles as *A Death With Dignity* or *A Death of One's Own* or *Death's Final Privacy.*

The plot of Jocelyn Evan's *Living With a Man Who is Dying* is a good example of this battle in part because the British national healthcare system over which the Evans triumph is very different in economic structure than that of American medicine. In personal terms, in the terms of the autobiography of struggle, there is virtually no difference at all. Jocelyn wants her husband Aron to die at home; she is convinced she can care for him better than the professionals in the last few months of his life. She is lied to, insulted, patronized, and ignored to an extent that is hair-raising. British medicine is portrayed as heartless, inefficient, cruel to patients, and utterly hazardous to everyone's health. When Jocelyn checks her husband out of the hospital and nurses him at home, her troubles do not end. Doctors refuse to visit, lie to her about their plans, and only a neighbor and family friend who happens to be a doctor comes through to help the young couple.

Most other protagonists do not have quite this monolithically negative an experience with the medical establishment. And one might argue that the value behind Ms. Evans' struggle is not really personal autonomy but is better described as wifely self-sacrifice for the sake of her dying husband. Or, in this context, wifely devotion and autonomy from the oppressive system go together, so that no conflict emerges between what are in other circumstances often conflicting values. This may be an important point; the plot of "individual versus the establishment" in the name of personal freedom does appear as a major theme in many of our narratives, but to the extent that it joins with the traditional motif of wifely devotion, it lacks what one might call a truly revolutionary dimension. Certainly it

mutes whatever incipient feminist motifs one can find in this literature (a topic we will examine in the next chapter). In none of our
narratives is the conflict between autonomy and wifely devotion, but
rather between private and public sphere control.

Narratives with titles such as *A Death of One's Own* (Gerda Lerner)
highlight this sense of one's dying as an act that needs to be re-
claimed from the grip of institutional domination. Key decisions in
this battle, for both Evans and Lerner, are the determination to
provide homecare. They resist attempts to return the dying man to
the hospital for a prolongation of his dying in the name of medical
management. Lois Snow nurses her husband Edgar with the help of
the Chinese medical team in *A Death with Dignity*, another work with
this plotline. Here, the Chinese are not presented as alternative
controlling "experts" who would rob the family of their freedom, but
rather as nonthreatening, friendly helpers, whose authority is never
portrayed as arrogant or oppressive: "It was not because of any
technical medical superiority or undisclosed secret knowledge that
the presence of the Chinese counted so enormously. It was mainly
because of an attitude" (Snow 1975, 6). This is ironic because the
helpful Chinese were themselves the products of, and advocates for,
the Cultural Revolution, one of the most totalitarian movements of
the twentieth century. Nevertheless, in the context of Snow's narrative, when the Chinese came, they helped free the family from the
oppressive threat of Western public-sphere medical control.

Still another, more extreme example of this plot of private versus
public-sphere control of one's own dying is Peter Noll's *In the Face of
Death*. Noll simply refused medical treatment for his cancer rather
than submit to the role of hospital patient. Sickness and an earlier
death were preferable to the surrender of freedom which hospitalization would require. This is probably the most fanatical case among
our entire collection, and one in which even a reader who admires
Noll's courage and honesty may also feel that too unbending an ethic
of absolute autonomy can become self-destructive. Had he submitted
to surgery, his life might well have been saved. On the other hand,
Martha Lear's angry *Heartsounds* shows how the promised salvation of
modern medicine can fail, and humiliate the patient as well. The
medical establishment is not only oppressive, but also, for all its high
technology, it appears inept in this work.

Must we take all this anger against the oppressive power of hospitals over their patients, this outcry in the name of dignity and autonomy, at face value? Certainly, we may find valid criticisms of hospitals as institutions, although other huge and overused public sphere institutions, such as courts and jails, are probably in much worse trouble. But it is disturbing how the problem of dying becomes, in the above examples as well as in others, reducible to the problem of autonomy versus control by others. When this happens, dying becomes a battle that is comprehensible, where the moral lines can be drawn clearly. There are "bad guys" to blame, and righteous anger deflects the narrator's attention onto the flaws and failings of the institution and its leaders and authorities. The most naive and simplistic narratives seem to promise that if the public sphere could be held off, dying would be unproblematic and nondisruptive.

It is to the great credit of the majority of our narrators that they *know* there is more to the story of dying than this. The issue of autonomy versus control by others is a real issue, but it can be used to mask the more fundamental human helplessness of every person facing death. Most of our authors recognize, some more than others, that underneath the social-control issue is another one where the moral lines are far from secure. How much of the struggle to maintain one's autonomy is a struggle not against doctors and hospitals, but against nature, time and mortality, against reality itself?

As a group, the authors who seem most aware of this issue are grown children who write of the deaths of their parents. Joan Gould (*Spirals*), Philip Roth (*Patrimony*) and Stephen Rosenfeld (*The Time of Their Dying*), not to mention Madeleine L'Engle (*The Summer of the Great-grandmother*), all write of how they watched the loss of autonomy and self-control of an aging, dying parent. For the grown children, the issue of public versus private control is eclipsed by that of role reversal. Once, fathers and mothers cared for and protected them; now they are the caretakers. The inherent sadness of seeing one's once fastidious and dignified father soil himself (Roth), or one's alert mother no longer recognize her family (L'Engle) undermines an easy allocation of blame for the loss of dignity. We know in these narratives that hospitals and doctors are not the real or the only enemies, and that anger targeted at them is irrelevant to the underlying destructive trajectory of human aging and dying. In these narratives, as well, we find that in sickness and old age, autonomy is revealed in its negative face as the possibility of isolation and bitter loneliness.

Sharing versus Isolation

Ironically, the very conditions that support and enhance the autonomous individual make life difficult and lonely for him or her in times
of sickness. The other side of personal autonomy is the lack of
community, or the restriction of intimacy and support to a tiny unit,
the beleaguered nuclear family. One minor character in Joyce
Phipps' *Death's Single Privacy* rejoices unthinkingly in the world of
Luckmann's "autonomous individual who is young and never dies."
Speaking of his parents, he says: "Am I ever glad we live in a fast-
paced, highly mobile society. I can visit them. They can all visit me.
But I'm not stuck with living with them" (112). As all the grown sons
and daughters of elderly and sick parents would tell such a man: just
wait until one of them gets sick! The individual that gets sick most
often will be the elderly parents themselves; we have many narratives
dealing with just these situations. But it can also be the son or
daughter, no longer able to care for himself or herself, and forced to
abandon a life of independence for a return to home, and homecare.
This is the situation in Barbara Peabody's *The Screaming Room*, of the
Hostetlers in *A Time for Love* (both of which concern grown sons with
AIDS), and of the Zorzas in *A Way to Die* (in which their young adult
daughter dies of cancer). Suddenly, instead of visits, the family is
once again established as a fulltime intense living unit—or is it now a
dying unit?

Loneliness and isolation are experienced at two levels: of the sick
person himself or herself, and of the family or single person, mo-
bilized around caretaking. In both cases, a wall or veil separates the
sufferers from normality, from the world of the well. In an enormous
number of narratives, a similar episode occurs: after months of immersion in sickness or caretaking, the protagonist gets some free time.
He or she goes on a brief vacation, or takes an afternoon walk in the
park. Expecting to enjoy the freedom of the experience, the actual
event is marred by a veil or invisible wall sensed everywhere and in all
interactions. The protagonist wanders through public space, and observes strangers walking or shopping. Instead of a glorious anticipated
day of freedom, the protagonist experiences how illness and isolation
cast their long shadows over even the most innocent outings. For
LeAnne Schreiber, even a fleeting attempt to find herself, a creature

among creatures, on an outing to a nature preserve, ends in demoralization: "I just wanted to stroll and smoke and think, all activities that made me feel criminal in the eyes of the right-minded Minnesota joggers who clogged the trail . . . I was determined to find some sanctuary for my troubled soul, but there was no pleasure in the search" (Schreiber 1990, 203). For many, unrefreshed, and depressed, no real escape appears possible. In Evan's words, living with a man who was dying was "living in a world that didn't and couldn't exist for other people" (Evans 1971, 62).

We should stress here that only a tiny number of our narrators have no families, and so the isolation of the dying person does not—in these tales—take the form of out-and-out neglect. No one is literally left alone to die, although in a few cases the fortuitous and compassionate intervention of a nonrelative may have been what saved the sufferer's life (as in Eric Hodgins' *Episode: Report of an Accident Inside My Skull*, Joseph Heller's *No Laughing Matter*). Instead, the isolation of the dying person lies in his or her lack of communication, even with those on whom survival depends. Joan Gould's mother, for example, alienated her family all her life, and continues to reject and try to destroy relationships, even, and especially, as she is dying. LeAnne Schreiber reports: "Mom is in hiding now, too ashamed of being sick to allow herself to be seen by anyone but the family" (Schreiber 1990, 199). The father in Carole Konek's *Daddyboy: A Memoir* long concealed his creeping Alzheimer's Disease from everyone, and neither acknowledged nor communicated that anything might be wrong with him. The Robinsons, Joan and Eric (*One Dark Mile: A Widower's Story*), had a precarious marriage that depended upon a mutual pose of heroism and martyrdom. When this collapsed, shortly before Joan's death, both seemed to have accepted separation and welcomed it. In contrast, May Sarton, writing *After the Stroke*, had clearly craved a life of solitude all along, and built a life for herself that made a necessary dependence upon others a torment. In all these cases, although the exact meaning of the isolation varies, there is a sense in which isolation is the half-chosen fate of the dying protagonist. Sarton's solitude had been for her a creative opportunity to live as a poet, while Gould's mother consciously blamed others for her isolation, interpreting her life in terms of a series of betrayals by others.

What narratives of failure and dysfunctionality may reveal is the

extent to which the wider community, the larger network of relationships, has vanished for the protagonists of these tales. The Koneks
and the Robinsons seem to implode upon one another, as do the
Rubins in *Caring: A Daughter's Story* and the young family in Cox's
Thanksgiving: An AIDS Journal. Elizabeth Cox laments: "I can no
longer do this alone. I need more help. The circle of support is too
small" (195). Locked together in sickness, they must depend upon
each other for nearly all physical, emotional, financial, and spiritual
support, and they are well aware that their own resources are
stretched thin. If home is where, when you return there, they *have* to
take you in, then these narratives also testify to the continuing need
for home, however emotionally unsatisfactory it may be. In two cases
of husbands dying of AIDS, it was the estranged wife who provided
final caretaking (Perry and Pearson); isolated from all other ties, the
dying men had no other place to go except back home, to the
remnants of the nuclear family they had left behind earlier.

The special problems of families previously broken who must return to some semblance of unity for the sake of the dying, appears in
a variety of these narratives. Rose Levitt's estranged husband returns
home to share in the task of nursing their adolescent daughter Ellen
until her death. As healing as the experience may have been for their
relationship, the Levitts remain separated. Barbara Peabody's ex-
husband lets her take over the primary care-taking for their son Peter
as he dies of AIDS, but he is at least present at certain key scenes in
the saga of Peter's illness and dying. In the earliest example of our
collection, John Gunther's *Death Be Not Proud,* mother and ex-wife
Frances writes her own final chapter that contradicts many of the
assertions in the main text. Against a background of isolation and the
disappearance of all wider networks of support, many of these caretaking families are compelled to take account of their ties to others—
ties fragile and fractured, but the only ones they have.

In other narratives, the portrait of family solidarity and support is
far more celebratory. Even though the nonfamily world of medicine
and public sphere activities are portrayed by Ronni Rabin as ugly and
hostile, the family she describes in *Six Parts Love* more than compen-
sates. The Rabins win against the hostile world, even if father David
dies slowly from Lou Gehrigs Disease (ALS). An even more upbeat
account of family solidarity as a bulwark against the twin threats of
cancer and modern medicine is Jill Ireland's *Life Wish.* Although

Ireland has all sorts of extrafamilial satisfactions in life—including a glamorous film career and enormous wealth—she finds her truest joy in her family. She describes in detail their enormous, yet somehow intimate, Christmas celebration following a harrowing course of chemotherapy:

> I was fortunate to share Christmas with my family and friends. For the rest of the day, the disease was far from my mind. I felt whole and happy. With thoughts of cancer slipping farther and farther in the distance, I could hardly believe I had been ill . . . Well, maybe this was my most special Christmas gift." (295–296)

Miles away socially and economically from Jill Ireland, Sandra Albertson in *Endings and Beginnings* records how as a young widow she could return with her small children to her mother's house for the summer, regaining strength through temporarily pretending that she had never left home. Both of Madeleine's narratives, *The Summer of the Great-Grandmother* and *Two Part Invention*, beautifully portray familial bonds and point to a sense of larger community.

What all of these examples reveal is the flaw in a straightforward, enthusiastic endorsement of autonomy as a sole and ultimate value. Sickness is one situation that simply and inevitably encompasses human dependency. The public sphere is not well-suited to meet this need without enforcing a humiliating loss of personal control. The private sphere—home—must do this job, whatever its resources and limits. This in turn burdens the family unit with a tremendous sense of isolation, throwing members back upon each other for love, support, and consolation no longer available from outside. Or is there hope for outside aid? We turn now to the quest for community, for a unit of support larger than the family, as this appears in our narratives.

Communities: Natural and Artificial

Stephen Rosenfeld in *The Time of Their Dying*, devotes an entire chapter to the city of Pittsfield, Massachusetts (57–70). Why? Because, as he explains, the lives of his parents were intimately bound up to their community. Pittsfield was exactly the kind of place, he tells us, that most American intellectuals have scorned, and from which they have departed as soon as possible. A conventional town, with a Jewish as well as a Gentile elite and a set of institutions (chamber of commerce, synagogue, local newspaper) that provided identity, stability, and community for long-term residents. Pittsfield is home in a different, more inclusive sense than the isolated households described in the previous section. The senior Rosenfelds were well-known there: several generations of Pittsfield men had bought their suits from the Rosenfeld family haberdashery; the father's one-time ambition to become a musician had been converted into the Pittsfield-scale activity of writing a music column for the newspaper. And, so, it is only expected that the Rosenfeld's doctor should make house calls in the form of friendly family visits, dropping by when there was no medical emergency, and fully prepared to tend the family when there was. This scene—of the doctor chatting with the long-time neighbor and patient—is memorable for its contrast with the more normative portrait of doctors and hospitals given earlier—and also because the narrator, the elderly couple's grown son, fully realizes that he is describing a "sense of place and family centrality" (119) foreign to his readers. This Pittsfield is no longer a reality to son Stephen, to most of the families in the narratives, and to the reader.

At one level one may ask: Is Pittsfield really like this? Was it really like this for all its citizens, not just for the relatively wealthy, civic-minded and respectable Rosenfelds? If we had more—or indeed—*any* narratives from Italian-American families living in traditionally ethnic neighborhoods such as South Philadelphia, would we find similar stories of multigenerational structured communities? The fact is, we do not find such narratives, and in the ones we do have, there is a dearth of "Pittsfields." "Heading home" means, for almost everyone, heading to the immediate nuclear family or its less traditional substitute; the wider *where* of home is not taken into account. Significantly, the majority of our narrators live in either New York or California, two archetypal destinations of refugees from Pittsfield.

If the Rosenfeld's Pittsfield represents the lost community mourned nostalgically by many Americans, including Robert Bellah and associates, its disappearance as a natural human environment is one of the most noticeable features of these narratives. All of the authors do live somewhere, but the majority of the narratives could take place *anywhere*. New York, Milwaukee, Chicago, Los Angeles: the settings are interchangeably huge and anonymous. Mobile protagonists such as the Wilbers, the Glasers, and the Spohrs all identify not with intergenerational hometowns, but with more self-selected interest groups. Bellah and others call these "lifestyle enclaves," and contrast them with natural, "authentic" communities (Bellah 1985, 71ff.). A lifestyle enclave is made up of a narrower cross-section of humanity, who choose to live and/or associate with those who share (self-selected) values or activities. The Spohrs (*To Hold a Falling Star*), for example, live in a retirement village and take their vacations with other peppy and adventurous retirees, as well as with family members. The Glasers (*In the Absence of Angels*) live in Los Angeles and associate with others in the entertainment industry. The Wilbers (*Grace and Grit*) move back and forth between California and Colorado, but their world is actually that of transpersonal psychology and the New Age. Other examples of lifestyle enclaves would include the world of gay New York, before and after AIDS, as described so vividly in Andrew Holleran's *Ground Zero*, and the world of 1970s style "radical Christianity" in which JoAnn Kelley Smith's dying is described in *Free Fall*. Not all of our authors inhabit such clear lifestyle enclaves, but the major point of Bellah's label is to differentiate these artificial and self-chosen communities from the more fundamental, and in his eyes, more authentic form.

From the testimony of our narratives, one would never come to share Bellah's antipathy for lifestyle enclaves. Narrators and protagonists secure in such wider networks (wider, that is, than their family units) find in these much that is helpful and positive. Even when these human support systems do not share an understanding of the deeper problems of the dying individual and his or her family, they can offer neighborly support such as cooked meals, transportation, and financial assistance. As Carol Pearson says of the Mormons: "People who won't even drink coffee have a hard time understanding homosexuality and AIDS, but they don't have a hard time understanding suffering and need" (Pearson 1988, 218). The same appears true of the Mennonite congregation in Hostetler's *A Time for Love*. At this level, religion works to continue what the entire community of Pittsfield once accomplished. These same tasks are picked up by the far-more-specialized support and self-help groups soon to be described. Even Joyce Phipps (*Death's Single Privacy*), who has serious grievances against the church and clergy, praises the faithful performance of neighborly tasks by members of her congregation after her husband's death. Other lifestyle enclaves do not appear to be so well equipped for this role, perhaps because they are more loosely organized. What matters, though, is that neighbors in some form are there to help.

Having stated this, it must also be made clear that many of these neighbors were present and helpful long before the specific crisis recorded in the narratives. One can easily imagine the Hostetlers, for example, cooking, ferrying, and raising money for the other families in their congregation; Carol Pearson tells us of her extensive work as a Mormon community visitor and helper. JoAnn Smith took children into foster care, took care of a large extended household, and assumed a lifestyle that made caring for others in trouble a central value. Religious groups less centrally concerned with this value, or less organized around such activities, will be less successful in mobilizing when the crises come. For example, LeAnne Schreiber describes her mother's church trying rather feebly to assist, but after being rebuffed once or twice, they retreat from the picture. Schreiber's mother had been described as devout, a regular churchgoer, but her religious experience had not included this dimension of neighborliness one finds in other accounts.

Neighbors can help, but the level of help provided may not be deep enough, or in tune with the sufferer's distress. Those protagonists without such neighborly support are clearly at a disadvantage, more likely to be physically and emotionally exhausted by caretaking and housekeeping basics without a respite. But the presence of the minister's wife with a Jell-O salad—however real an example of neighborliness and support—will not guarantee that the deeper isolation and terror of the sufferer's plight will be ameliorated. The very special circumstances of long-term, life-threatening illness have brought forth far more specialized, and even more artificial communities of support.

The Wellness Community, visited and joined by Gilda Radner (*It's Always Something*), is one such very specialized self-help support group. This is a group explicitly for people with cancer. Gilda's first reaction is anxiety:

I was afraid to be around people who had cancer, I guess because I wanted to pretend that I didn't have it. And I didn't want to get depressed, more depressed than I already was, something I was sure would happen if I went to the Wellness Community. (138)

In contrast, Radner finds the group health-giving, tolerant, and a place where she can maintain her identity as a comedienne without denying her illness. The Wellness Community sponsors joke nights, where the group members help each other put the misery of chemotherapy, for example, into a positive context, as those who have "survived" it push those in the midst to complete their course of treatments. Above all, it provides role models for what courageous and successful living with cancer can mean: "The same people in gangs can do things that the individual could never do alone, the gang of us fighting cancer makes us all stronger" (148). This is the kind of group that plays an important role in many of the life-histories collected by Wendy Williams in *The Power Within.*

Another example of such specialized, recently invented communities is the workshop attended by Marvin Barrett at Pendle Hill (a Quaker community in Pennsylvania), a workshop just for cancer patients and their relatives. Barrett, a more critical observer than Radner, notes the way some participants have grasped on to "cancer patient" as a new identity, or have become fanatical advocates for the alternative medicines discussed in the previous chapter. In this case, it is the chance to come together briefly and share stories that provides the focus of the community; it has no continuity over time, and performs none of the neighborly tasks mentioned earlier. Here, however, participants can experience, even if temporarily, a lifestyle enclave even more selective than those mentioned by Bellah.

> I feel normal, healthy even. Not because so many here are worse off than I, though they may well be, but just because I now qualify for membership in an interesting, congenial group. I belong. . . . (Bellah 1985, 160)

The same group of sick persons meeting in hospital waiting rooms and clinics do not a community make; there they are isolated and frightened individuals in the clutches of public sphere medicine.

The widespread popularity of such support groups and workshops transcends their particular appeal to many of our sick and dying narrators. These structures, coming into vogue during the 1970s, appear to provide a refuge from both the public sphere institutions and from too much enclosedness in the tiny family units. Their ideology of suspicion toward professional expertise ("only those with cancer know how to deal with it") and their spiritual affinity with twelve-step programs is interesting. These groups focus intensively on taking responsibility for one's situation, but also on mutual help. They are all voluntary, and so their participants are a self-selected group who may well be used to talking about themselves with a bunch of strangers.

Mutual help, however, can turn into mutual depression. When a long-term member of the Wellness Community dies, everyone suffers discouragement. This is a problem leaders of such groups must learn to deal with. The outcome of cancer being chancy, it is still possible to maintain an atmosphere of overall hopefulness even in the face of unexpected and unwished-for deaths. This also explains why the many special communities and sources of support described in the narratives dealing with AIDS do not have the same atmosphere. There are buddies (Whitmore), hospices for the dying (Hostetler) and outpatient support groups for patients and their families (Peabody). There are organizations (Glaser) and information networks (Monette). All of these must supply support and care, against a background knowledge that AIDS is a disease from which no one has yet recovered. Indeed, Peabody comments how much of a contrast she saw between the AIDS groups she and Peter attended, and any parallel group for cancer patients. This does not mean that no community exists—far from it. But the upbeat ideology of the self-help revolution is not always clearly represented here, as it seems to be in Radner's and others' descriptions of groups like the Wellness Community; which is not to say that many of their practices (visualizations, affirmations, and so on) are not to be found in AIDS support groups.

The prevalence of these new and specialized forms of community (using the term much more inclusively than Bellah would allow) lets us reflect on the limits of autonomy as a value. In a sense, such groups are absolutely congruent with the model of autonomous individualism described by Luckmann: they are self-chosen, and one joins them as a way to integrate "cancer patient" or "cancer survivor" into one's previously chosen identity. They can be joined and dropped out of at will. Even more specialized than the lifestyle enclaves and traditional voluntary associations such as churches, they do not replace Pittsfield, Massachusetts or the local congregation in all ways and at all levels. However, their very presence in the American scene is a testimony to the inadequacy of the isolated individual, however strong, wealthy, or well-supported by a family to cope with illness and death alone. It is exactly the most mobile, affluent, and unencumbered members of that society who seem most at ease in such groups—those who have had the chance to live out most completely the vision of the autonomous individual who is young and never dies, and have found this vision wanting at the time of illness and dying.

Chapter Six

WOMEN, MEN, AND DYING

IT IS DIFFICULT TO WRITE ABOUT GENDER. Today, gender—and the gendering of experience—is a sensitive topic, and one of the factors uppermost on the minds of many who study any area of experience. There exist a host of preconceptions that written works by men and women will be different, and that the experiences of illness, dying, and mourning by each gender will also be different. In fact, a new set of stereotypes about masculine and feminine styles of experiencing have emerged to overlay, and in some cases, confirm an older set about the natural roles of men and women. But are there indeed obvious and consistent differences between the way women authors and men authors of first person mortal narratives tell their stories? And are illness, dying, and mourning indeed so differently experienced that gender becomes the major factor in interpreting these events? In this context, a central paradox is that although experiences may indeed be gendered, death itself happens to everyone, male and female.

Narrators: Male and Female

We find that women are indeed far more often the narrators of our Type III stories, tales of the death of a beloved. The majority of our examples concern the death of the husband or of the mother. But the second fact is that most of the clichés about gender—including some proposed by the authors themselves—are simply not borne out in our collection of narratives. The man or woman who sits down to write a first person mortal story is already unusual, one of a self-selected group. Often she or he is a writer already, used to examining private feelings and intensely curious about his or her own experiences. Even if the author is an amateur, the act of going public with readers about very private experiences already selects out from the ordinary run those individuals with courage, or a sense of mission about the importance of their story for others.

Thus, the genre itself requires certain capacities that function across gender. Take, for instance, one of the themes popularized by Carol Gilligan, and a prominent part of the "new" view of women's style of experiencing: that women are more relational in their knowing, in their interpretation of situations. Women's knowledge is less of abstract conceptions ("universal justice") and more of the concrete, person-centered mutual responsibilities of each of us to care for the other (Gilligan 1983, 73). This perspective is not really new since it is indeed a view very close to a much older view of women as naturally at home in the private realm of personal, familial relationships and unsuited for the public realm of work, laws, and politics (a view expressed by no less a psychological authority than Carl Jung!). Does our collection of narratives support Gilligan's generalizations about women's relational approach to reality?

Put simply, they do not. Try writing a tale of "How I grew very sick, and needed caretaking from family members," or "How I myself took care of a dying loved one": such stories are relational at their core, no matter *who* tells them. Everyone who is very sick must be taken care of by others, and no adult in American society finds this experience easy. What interests the readers is not the medical details of the illness, but the struggle of human beings to suffer it, including how their relationships are transformed or renewed by the struggle. It is true that women are the traditional caretakers, and this hardly seems to have changed in the twenty years or more since the start of the Women's Movement. But the stories told by male caretakers are similar enough in basic plot and in the relational focus (such as in narratives by Roth; Wilber) to put Gilligan's generalization in jeopardy. A person focused on universal abstract concepts such as justice would not write narratives such as the ones we have surveyed.

Or, take another generalization, this one supplied by one of the widows writing her story. Xenia Rose repeats, without too much criticism, the slogan: "Women mourn, men replace" (Rose 1990, 123). Her assumption is that because there are so many more unattached women than men, men are free to find replacements for their dead partners, while women must learn to grieve and live alone. Yet her narrative includes episodes where she herself frantically tries to replace her dead husband. More important, a man who does not need to mourn would never write a memoir of his dead wife's last illness (such as Meryman did in *Hope*), nor a tribute to her life of companionship (Paton, *To You, Departed*), nor an anguished journal of his grief (Lewis, *A Grief Observed*). The entire memorializing function of such narratives expresses the work of mourning, and so all of the authors can be said to truly mourn. The generalization appears invalidated by the nature of the genre itself.

When we remember how self-selected our group of narrators are, and how the demands of writing such intensely feeling-oriented, private accounts require all authors to become both introspective and highly focused on intimate relationships, we will not expect that these writings can be used to confirm bifurcated portraits of how each gender experiences. Real differences do emerge, especially given the continuing social role of caretaker for women, but these are at the level of the protagonists, not at the level of the narrator's style, or his or her decision to write at all. A writer who followed Gilligan's masculine pattern, or who was indifferent to feelings, or who replaced rather than mourned, would never become part of our collection.

We find ourselves, then, in dispute with those who genderize autobiography to such an extent that no generalizations about selfhood and storytelling can be applied to women's writings and men's writings simultaneously. Moreover, characterizing male autobiography in terms of dualism, abstraction, hierarchy, and isolation of the self (as in Henking; Jagger and Bordo) is itself too dualistic and counterproductive to an adequate understanding of the first person mortal narrative. The variety of narratives written by women, the historical possibilities available to any narrator of a certain period, and the range of other factors (religious background, class, and so on) all need to be considered real and relevant. We find it particularly disheartening when feminist analysis of autobiography yields such pronouncements as the one declaring [masculine] autobiography impossible for women, for the former demands a view of a unified self inimicable to women's experience (Henking 19, 522–23). Even if these ideas should have validity for some personal writings by women, there is no trace of evidence for them in the works we examine in this study. Or, as in Jagger and Bordo's anthology, generalizations are proposed that equate masculine with Cartesian dualism, antiecology, and everything else philosophically undesirable and politically incorrect.

Having said that most of the clichés about men and women and about their storytelling styles do not apply to the narrators and protagonists in our literature in the obvious and simplistic ways one would expect from contemporary claims about gender, does that make gender entirely irrelevant? Certainly not. In the rest of this chapter, we will examine the ways in which gender does play some role in the experiences of protagonists, as well as the ways in which it does not.

Women as Caretakers

"Don't say 'children,' say 'daughters,' " goes one response to the question "Who will care for elderly parents?" Overwhelmingly, women remain the primary caretakers for the sick and the elderly. Certainly since the nineteenth century, an ideology of the home as women's sphere reinforces the link between women and care for the sick. Although mid-nineteenth century women nurses fought for the role of caretakers to nonfamily members (as in the case of army nurses Florence Nightingale and Clara Barton), no such battle was ever needed in order to demonstrate the superiority of women nurses to their own family members. Today, this role remains firmly in place. The difference, now, may be that, as in the case of Gerda Lerner, the wife can insist that she keep her professional job outside the home while she cares for her sick husband.

> I soon learned that working was essential to my own mental health. I
> gained strength for the long pull by being away from the hospital a few
> hours each day. . . . There was some social pressure on me to make an
> opposite decision. The worst conversation of this kind I can remember
> was with my own physician, a woman doctor whose opinion I greatly
> respected. (Lerner 1974, 78)

Lerner remarks of her husband, Carl, "Obviously, it would not occur
to him, nor would anyone urge him, to give up his work in order to
devote himself to nursing me" (79). The expectation remains that
women's professional lives come second to their care for their family
members, no matter what the ages or the circumstances of the latter
may be.

For the most part, women are the primary, or even sole, caretakers
of infants and small children in our society. Women are practiced,
then, in dealing with bodies and the messiness of bodies, as men
rarely are. This, at least, remains a strong cultural expectation, with
which all protagonists, female and male, must contend. Even a childless woman will, it is assumed, be more at home in dealing with the
ailing, incontinent body of another than any man would be. Women
are in tune with the physical realities of bodies, and are also trained
to be more gentle in touching, more responsive to others' pain, more
patient to others' complaints—or so goes the very powerful social
stereotype.

Our collection of narratives in one sense provides a tribute to this
belief. Works such as Diane Rubin's *Caring: A Daughter's Story* reveal
that even in an unhappy and conflicted family, the daughter's obligation to care for her mother lets her relatively healthy father remain
unhelpfully preoccupied with his own needs. In a more extreme case,
an ex-husband who lives a gay lifestyle in San Francisco during the
1970s contracts AIDS and comes home to his divorced Mormon wife,
who lovingly takes care of him until his death (Pearson, *Good-Bye, I
Love You*). Only death, and not divorce or deep conflict over values,
can separate the woman from her caretaker role. In Carole Konek's
Daddyboy, the grown daughter screams at her mother's martyr-like
caretaking for her father with Alzheimer's Disease, yet this pattern is
in complete continuity with the mother's permanent identity as the
one who takes care of *Daddyboy*. Narratives of dying teenagers are far
more likely to be written by their mothers, depicting her driving the

child to and from the hospital just as she had carpooled him or her to all the rounds of suburban activities in earlier days of health. Nor does a mother's responsibilities for caretaking ever end. Helen Hostetler (*A Time for Love*) and Barbara Peabody (*The Screaming Room*) nurse their grown sons dying of AIDS, while other mothers practice their caretaking skills upon their own aging parents (L'Engle, *Summer of the Great-Grandmother*; Williams, *Refuge*).

But the flaws in the uniform portrait of female caretaking as a natural role, an extension of motherhood, are quite apparent. First is the presence, in our collection, of a small, but memorable, number of male caretakers. Eric Robinson (*One Dark Mile*) is the most dismal, Ken Wilber (*Grace and Grit*) and Richard Meryman (*Hope*) the most devoted, and Philip Roth (*Patrimony*) the most eloquent. All perform just those tasks traditionally and stereotypically assigned to women: nurse, companion, driver, housekeeper, and cook. All must face the deterioration and loss over bodily control of their loved ones. Roth, writing of the illness and dying of his father, takes on these responsibilities as a patrimony. Part of what his father has to give his son is the opportunity for care, the return of the debt each member of the younger generation owes its elders. Roth recognizes this, amid the mutual shame of having to clean up after his father "beshat himself":

> You clean up your father's shit because it has to be cleaned up, everything that's there is felt as it never was before ... once you sidestep disgust and ignore nausea and plunge past those phobias that are fortified like taboos, there's an awful lot of life to cherish. (175)

Caretaking binds together generations, and a sense of this all but overrides the gender division so obvious in most presentations of caretaking.

Caretaking is, or ought to be, intrinsic to marriage, and an obligation laid equally on both partners. The day after Ken Wilber marries his wife Treya, she is found to have breast cancer; they spend their honeymoon in the hospital. *Grace and Grit*, the story of their marriage, is also the story of her gradual dying. In some ways this story mirrors that of Shireen Perry, who loves her husband *In Sickness and in Health*, although he develops AIDS almost immediately after the wedding takes place. The difference is that Wilber, as a male caretaker, is in what he and others recognize as an anomalous position. As a writer and researcher into philosophical and spiritual systems, he has the freedom (and the money, one assumes) to devote all of his time and energy to supporting and taking care of Treya, but recognizes how unhealthy and how isolating this role can be:

> What is more difficult for the support person . . . is the inner turmoil that starts to build on the emotional and psychological levels. The turmoil has two sides, one private and one public. On the private side, you start to realize that no matter how many problems you might have, they all pale in comparison to the loved one who has cancer. . . . So for weeks and months you simply stop talking about your problems . . . now you have *two* problems: the original problem plus the fact that you can't voice the original problem and thus find a solution for it. (361)

Although LeAnne Schreiber is the narrator of *Midstream*, her dying mother's principle caretaker is the father, whose isolation and self-immersion in the task infuriates his middle-aged daughter, as did the same behavior on the part of Carole Konek's mother in *Daddyboy*.

What happens when caretakers fail—or believe they fail to live up to their own and society's expectations of care? For instance, why should a young and childless woman have any special love for nursing tasks, or skill at tending the sick body of even the most beloved husband? Rebecca Rice, in *A Time to Mourn*, primarily describes her first year of widowhood after the death of her much older husband Len. She avoided the basic caretaking tasks by hiring a full time nurse and refusing to set foot in Len's room during the final weeks of his illness. She is aware that she has failed, is filled with guilt—but does not seem quite aware that this failure may be tied to the peculiarities of their marriage. It is clear that Len was the one who took care of *her* in health; she is not prepared, or willing, apparently, to alter the relationship at the end. Nevertheless, she as well as Gerda Lerner and Carol Ann Pearson, knows the roles and rules that go with marriage, and she suffers, in part, from having violated the role of wifely caretaker.

Another aspect of women as caretakers is the overwhelmingly female staffing of nurses and nurses aides in most American hospitals. Both men and women patients expect to find women as caregivers in hospitals. As Frank Maier notes, when he enters the hospital, he enters a world of women; this is the other, less official face of

American healthcare. Maier is honest enough to comment how, as a journalist, he had never been surrounded by women, and his serious illness was the first occasion in his life that he had the experience of being befriended by women. Yes, he notes, some women make terrible caregivers, and some men were terrific and tender, but on the whole, his relations with nurses, social workers, and a woman chaplain open up a realm of relationships he had hitherto ignored: "For someone like me who had spent his adult life playing a self-centered game in which points are awarded for aggressiveness and ambition, this was indeed a strange new world" (Maier 1991, 74). And what about AIDS, gender, and caretaking? AIDS, of course, is a disease that initially struck men, and continues to do so in overwhelming proportion. Moreover, AIDS among gay men struck a group who had broken in some ways with American gender patterns, and who rarely had devoted Mormon ex-wives to take care of them. We see it as significant that of the AIDS narratives we surveyed, almost all were written by mothers and wives: Elizabeth Cox, Shireen Perry, Elizabeth Glaser, and most of the others bear the same relationship of caretaker to the deceased, and fill the role in exactly the same manner that they would, had the death been by some other cause. Even Glaser, who herself has since died of AIDS, buried her small daughter Ariel, and then went on to establish a foundation for research of pediatric AIDS, did what other mothers of dying children do.

This pattern probably does not reflect the reality of demography of AIDS so much as the way narratives are selected for publication and marketing. Perry, Pearson, and Hostetler write directly for religiously conservative readers, with a message of compassion for AIDS sufferers. Glaser writes as a bereaved mother, and one who herself is infected with the AIDS virus. A caretaking wife or mother is not only a figure for whom we feel compassion, but is also one who does not challenge gender stereotypes, or any other beliefs about sexual behavior. Such writers must know that the last thing they need is to alienate prospective readers by introducing such features into their stories—readers who may be already repulsed by AIDS and the behavior with which it is associated.

To be honest, such potential readers would not be reassured by the works on AIDS written by journalists, or others who are members of the gay subculture. For example, Andrew Holleran's eloquent *Ground Zero* contains no episodes of caretaking, and no references to this—although it is concerned with the effect of the epidemic on the gay community of New York City. Friends vanish while one is out of town on business, and the narrator discovers later that they have died. Not even the limited caretaking of the "buddy" who appears in Whitmore's *Someone Was Here* is present in Holleran's vivid portrayal of mass death. Money's *To All the Girls I've Loved Before* and Dreuihle's *Mortal Embrace*, accounts of their own sufferings with the disease, omit both scenes of caring for others, and of being cared for. Nor does Petrow's *Dancing Against the Darkness* focus on those, except in the cases of a woman caring for her infected husband, and a couple caring for their dying son. These cases replicate the patterns in our collection: they follow the gender lines of conventional family relationships, and conventional gender roles. The one magnificent exception to this is Paul Monette's *Borrowed Time*, about which we will have more to say later in this chapter. Monette's story focuses precisely on his caretaking for his dying friend/lover, and on the relationship between the two men as death approached.

Gender, Bodies, and Control

Many of the current theories about gender differences are not fundamentally theories about social roles. An earlier phase of feminism decried the way social roles were legitimated by the supposed natural inclinations and capacities of women and men; the agenda at that time was to break through barriers so that women who wanted to drive trucks, train as astronauts, or serve on the Supreme Court were given the opportunity to do so. But while the contemporary theories mentioned earlier in this chapter do not want to return to the previous, more restrictive arrangements, they share a renewed concern with the differences—whether innate or acquired—that men and women bring to their respective tasks and experiences. Sometimes, as we have already indicated, we find the intersection of this topic leads directly into a reheated set of leftover stereotypes, served up as a fresh and original view of gender differences.

Among these is the very pervasive belief that women are more in tune with their emotions and their bodies. Women are less likely to be control freaks, less likely to *repress* emotions (*suppress*—consciously decide it is too risky to express them—is another story). Women do not accept a Platonic or Cartesian dichotomy between body and spirit; they are thus more able to live with their embodiment, and within their bodies; they befriend the physical realm, a belief that lies at the heart of what is now called "eco-feminism." It is worth stating that a few of our authors share and advocate these ideas; Terry Tempest Williams, in *Refuge*, is the most eloquent, along with Joan Gould's *Spirals* and Mary Trautmann's *The Absence of the Dead is Their Way of Appearing*. How valid is this cluster of ideas, when applied to the protagonists and narrators of our stories? How much of a role does gender, as opposed to other factors, play in distinguishing who is a controller and what imagery is used about bodies and nature?

Recall that for many authors, the issue of control by self versus control by the hospital staff is a preoccupation. Loss of control is devastating for all sick protagonists, including sick children who can no longer go to school. The massive loss of control over one's own body is felt as a blow by all. There is, at this level, absolutely no evidence that women are less threatened than men. Even if women are less used to control in other spheres of life, the loss of control over one's bowels or bladder is so basic and so humiliating that it overwhelms every adult (Blumberg in *Headstrong* is just as devastated by this as is Philip Roth's ailing father in *Patrimony*).

But do men and women differ significantly in how they respond to this loss, and how they attempt to compensate for it? Are isolation, repression of feelings, and imposing a military model of struggle more typically male strategies? Do women, being more attuned to their bodies, feel more acceptance of their bodies' limits? Our answer is a cautious no. There are many cases where this pattern holds, but many others where it does not. We have mentioned Peter Noll, who seems to be our clearest example of a control freak, atypically absolutist and rigid in his definition of freedom. Any hospitalization makes him the victim of others, and so he lives in the face of death rather than undergo the corrective surgery that might have saved his life. Yet in this example, its very extremeness marks it as atypical. The vast majority of male protagonists and narrators renegotiate the meaning of control, of freedom, and of dignity as they progress through the trajectory of their illnesses.

An example of a woman who apparently did not adapt, progress, or wish to relinquish or redefine control is LeAnne Schreiber's mother (*Midstream*). Denial, refusal to have others see her helpless, and pervasive silence and isolation over the nature of her illness, makes her dying one of the saddest recorded. Likewise, Joan Robinson, wife of Eric in *One Dark Mile: A Widower's Story*, dying of ovarian cancer, is another example of a woman who takes control to extremes. It would be hard to find anyone more manipulative than Joan, and everyone lets her get away with it. Eric writes, "She insists on going to her death in her own way. I believe that she will even interview the Angel of Death before she lets him over the threshold" (103). Both of these women are described as "elegant" and "fastidious"; to us, both appear frightened, selfish, and narcissistic.

But then, some husbands and fathers described by their widows and daughters certainly seem to have become this way: Xenia Rose's (*Widow's Journey*) famous musician husband shut her out as his illness progressed. Carole Konek's *Daddyboy* with Alzheimer's Disease was in some ways tragically an exaggerated version of who he had been when healthy: he controlled the family whether sick or well, leaving a legacy of resentment and mutual accusation. It is a measure of how good a storyteller Joan Gould is that her narrative of her mother's death (one of the deaths in *Spirals*) is free from this legacy, although her mother was as difficult and controlling and embittered as any of the persons mentioned already. What do all these accounts share? The sadness, anger, and guilt left behind when someone who was difficult in life dies, and this, rather than gender differences emerges to mark such narratives.

Difficult, dysfunctional, neurotic: perhaps although American society is willing to give a very sick person some leeway to behave in peevish, childish, or selfish fashion, we have trouble acknowledging this, or setting limits to it. Although women as caretakers are overwhelmingly the recipients of this behavior, both men and women exhibit it. The cases we have cited are those where an obviously narcissistic, over-controlling, or rejecting stance dominates the dying person's last months, making life miserable for caretakers and others who survived. There is from our narratives no general evidence that women take being sick "better," or are less likely to fall into this unhappy pattern.

The second half of the eco-feminist claim is that women, being less inclined to Cartesian dualism, are generally far more in tune with their bodies than are men. An alternative way to state this is that, traditionally, women were associated with "nature" in contrast to male "spirit," and, hence, reduced to being bodies whether they wished to be or not. The ancient Church "Fathers," psychoanalysis, and a wide variety of other sources are used to support this view. But whether in the positive or negative framing, the idea suggests that women will be less ignorant and less likely to be at war with their bodies. Does our literature in any way bear this out?

Recall that the opening chapters of many of the narratives deal with the onset of illness, and how the protagonist responded or failed to respond to the first symptoms. Many of the narrators look back at this period and marvel at how ignorant they were about their own bodies, or how blithely they dismissed obviously ominous symptoms. Based on the frequency of these retrospective judgments, we cannot say that "in tune with one's body" is a verdict most of our narrators would be willing to pass on to themselves. A very few were inwardly certain they had cancer before their diagnosis was confirmed. Many more report postponing medical care, or confidently staying with some less threatening diagnosis. Because early detection is one of the surest ways to treat cancer, this behavior, this "out of tune" stance toward one's own body, can even be fatal. On the other hand, both Gilda Radner (*It's Always Something*) and Barbara Rosenblum (*Cancer in Two Voices*) felt certain that something was wrong—but their complaints were not diagnosed until too late. (Patriarchal male physicians' demeaning treatment of female patients is a different issue, which we will not take up here.)

In our next chapter, on imagery and associations of death, we will discuss more fully the theme of bodily destruction and mutilation. Here, however, we will note that at least three of the illnesses mentioned in our narratives are not only gender specific, but have clearly palpable and almost visible warning signs. Breast cancer, prostrate cancer, and testicular cancer are more easy to spot, if not to self-diagnose. One can feel a lump, a mass, something hard, or become aware of atypical functioning in a place that already has major emotional associations with gender identity. Will women be more adept at noting such sinister abnormalities? Will women's traditional link with nature and body stand them in good stead, alerting them to the fact that something feels wrong? *Feels* in all of these cases is meant literally. We are no longer thinking of amorphous intuitive "being in tune" with one's body, but "hands-on" reality.

The answers provided by our narratives do not support the eco-feminist claim about a positive awareness of one's own body, nor do all the traditionally negative associations between women and embodiment translate into better preventive health care. We have come across narratives where intelligent, introspective, and activist women felt breast masses and postponed any medical attention (Blumberg), and others where one suspects that even self-examination may have been omitted. Women, as well as men, are likely to plead a busy schedule, and think that social obligations, work responsibilities, and family vacations justify postponement of medical treatment. It is often the doctor who must correct this. Men are not necessarily better in this regard; Arthur Frank (*At the Will of the Body*) struggles to avoid the reality of his testicular cancer. He takes his symptoms to two doctors, both of whom misdiagnose the problem: "At that point two physicians were telling me that nothing was wrong. I wanted to believe them, but my body insisted otherwise. . . . If I had not doctor shopped for a *third* opinion, I would probably be dead" (25–26). The power of denial is underestimated by those who believe that "being in tune with one's body" is a basic characteristic of any group in American society, when what the body has to reveal is frightening.

But there is another aspect to this same question, one that deals more with social role aspects of gender identity, and less with alleged innate psychological differences. Breasts are visible; the loss of a breast is a publicly visible bodily mutilation in a way the loss of a testicle is not. Moreover, it is true that women, much more than men, are likely to be concerned with their physical appearance and the deterioration of their bodies. Recall that LeAnne Schreiber's mother refused to see her friends (and her priest) for this reason. Yet, typically, Joan Gould's husband continued going to work although grotesquely bloated from his cancer and its treatment (*Spirals*); so long as he could continue to work, his identity remained intact, and he could joke about appearing pregnant. Thus, to some if not all women, socially visible changes in their appearance, such as the loss of hair or a breast, are major issues, but not in themselves ultimate issues.

Although in a real way, these mutilations are prefigurations of death, they are also surmountable as social obstacles. Ireland, Lorde, Blumberg, Wilber, Schwerin, and Rosenblum all lose breasts to cancer. Many of these narratives deal explicitly with changes in lovemaking, the adjustment in clothing, and problems with prostheses that the protagonists experience. These are real problems, but not—for any of the women writing—the most fundamental ones. Especially for Lorde, Schwerin, Wilber, and Williams, these problems only point to the more ultimate issues of spiritual vulnerability, and social injustice.

Yet appearance counts; it is not *nothing* for the women mentioned above, or for others who suffer from baldness and the other side-effects of chemotherapy and radiation. Treya Wilber was supported by having a totally bald (by choice) husband, who was himself often mistaken for the cancer patient! Gilda Radner and husband Gene Wilder took "bald pictures" and sent them out as Christmas cards. But this particular visible change is not truly gender-linked, either. Arthur Frank protests the way children are not supported by adults in an honest response to the question from strangers, "What happened to that man's hair?":

> Every attempt to hide cancer, every euphemism, every concealment, reconfirms that the stigma is real and deserved. When I heard that woman explaining my shaved head to a child, it was a personal victory for me to smile. [The woman had suggested to her child that perhaps Frank was in the army.] It would have been a social victory if I had walked over and said, "No, actually I'm recovering from cancer, but it's all right; cancer's only another disease and diseases are only human." That would have broken the cycle of stigma. (97–98)

As we will see, a fundamental threat to one's own body is a threat to one's identity and self-esteem, one's very being. The inner impact of lost body parts, or even lost hair, is a real impact; Frank, Lorde and others bear witness to this. But illness cuts through certain of the ideologies of gender. Although culturally, women may indeed be more closely linked to body and nature, in reality, all of us are equally embodied. Even if it were clearly demonstrated elsewhere that women are more in tune with their bodies, in the face of the threat of terminal illness such a distinction crumbles. Women and men both fly from whatever intuitive awareness they possess about their bodies. Denial is not, we believe, gender specific in this context.

Gender-Identity: Fusion and Separation

There is one other topic related to the contemporary psychological theorizing about gender; this is the manner in which, allegedly, gender is differently established for boys and girls. In a widely quoted work, Nancy Chodorow's *The Reproduction of Mothering*, it is claimed that babies are from birth treated differently by their mothers. The little boy is "other," he is to be defined as over against his mother. The little girl, on the other hand, is not; she remains "fused" in the mother's unconscious, and in her own, with the maternal presence. Gradually, of course, girls do develop separate identities, but they are never so separated from mother or from others as are boys. Chodorow is quoted by Gilligan, and some version of this thesis has made its way into feminist writings. The aforementioned views of women and autobiography seem based upon this account that women lack a separated, atomistic, individualized self. Chodorow's account explains women's preference for a relational mode of knowledge, for an ethic that does not pit one agent against another, and for a concern with mutuality and the nuances of others' feelings. So long as women alone have responsibility for the care of infants, they will reproduce this pattern of gender difference. As a thesis about early infant development, this lies completely outside our sphere of interest here. However, as a belief about how women and men continue to relate as adults to each other and to the other generally, it is worth examining critically.

Fantasies of fusion appear sporadically in the best of our literature. As highly as autonomy, personal uniqueness, and individuality are valued in America, at another level, that of unconscious emotional yearning, the hope or fear of fusion with another person is not completely banished. In telling the story of the death of the other, of the beloved, this theme *does* emerge. For example, LeAnne Schreiber feels herself fused with her mother as she gazes at a photograph—even though their lives have been radically different and in her work she self-identifies with her journalist father. Joan Gould and Simone deBeauvoir also report such fleeting feelings that, in spite of differences in lives, conscious values, and personal choices, something fundamental bound them to their mothers so that the borders between self and other potentially could become fuzzy.

These confessions of fusion fantasied between grown daughters and their mothers do indeed follow the pattern set forth by Chodorow. They also occur in cases where the mother/daughter relationships were filled with conflict, where the daughter's chosen lifestyle had been an explicit rejection of the mother's. The stories of these relationships, culminating in the mothers' deaths—as in *Midstream, Spirals,* and *A Very Easy Death*—are clearly stories of a final phase in the mother/daughter relationship, and in the daughter's own self-definition.

> Death is, without doubt, a dazzling white light, as I said before. In a bed immaculately made, the pillow puffed up, the sheet and blanket tucked under her chin, my mother rested, not the mother I knew but the mother I'd always wanted to know, her head tilted to one side in sweet, good, girlish compliance, sweet as a good child put to bed, stripped of her quarrels as she was stripped of her clothes, the bruises and tobacco stains hidden beneath the covers. Looking at her the way I looked at her now, I could easily have told her that I loved her. I could easily have called her Mother to her face.
>
> But she was always like this, I heard her tell me. Death is transformation. She was transformed back to what she was meant to be in the first place. (Gould 1988, 294)

The death of the mother is, in a sense, the death of the last possibility of fusion, the final chance for the unconscious infantile situation to flicker into awareness. Fusion-fantasy does not, by itself, resolve the problematic relationship. But it is part of coming to terms with the mother's death, to re-endow the tie with the merged selfhood of its earliest phase.

But, once again, is this phenomenon gender specific? Amazingly enough, Philip Roth reports the same fleeting, but deeply real, sense of fusion with his dying father in *Patrimony.* When Roth himself suffers a heart attack, shortly before his father's death, he joins with his father in fantasy, as they had never been joined in their lifelong relationship of never quite understanding one another.

> I had come to feeling myself *transposed*, interchangeable with—even a sacrificial proxy for—my failing father. . . . I was never a heart patient alone in that bed: I was a family of four. (226)

Roth becomes his father in the same way that Gould becomes her mother. Yet, both, in contrast to the correlates of Chodorow's theory, are intensely individualized persons who had a passionate sense of their own separateness from others. It is this, perhaps, that gives them strength to accept into consciousness the fantasy of fusion that may indeed be leftover from childhood. But which, in the case of Roth, is inexplicable by the terms of Chodorow's theory (fathers never provide an experience of merger with either their sons or daughters; such a sense of fusion is linked exclusively to mothering). If we want to argue that other authors must feel similar fantasies, but be unable or unwilling to express them, we are in the realm of pure speculation. Once again, gender may be less of a key factor than the theory presupposes, and a fine writer's sensitivity and introspectiveness can match or outweigh its alleged effect.

All of the above examples of fusion pale when set beside the one spectacular case of this: Paul Monette's strong and unshakable conviction that he and his lover/friend Roger were really "the same person" (Monette 1988, 13). Monette's powerful and moving tale of Roger's death from AIDS begins with this claim, although the unfolding story makes clear that, at the ordinary level of character, Monette and his friend were indeed two very different persons. Nevertheless, the fusion motif is repeatedly stated (84); each man is really only half of one joint person, "Roger/Paul." In a curious detail that confirms this vision as part of their ongoing life together, Monette mentions that the two dressed from a common stock of underwear; as one person, even the most intimate garments did not need to be separated into two piles. Thus Roger's death is not just the death of the other, the beloved, but the death of the self. What remains is not one lonely person, but a mutilated half of a once-fused couple. We are not even hearing the language of soulmates, which appears sporadically in some of the accounts of married narrators (Wilber, for example), but of fusion.

Is this a test case for Chodorow's theory of gender identity? Is it the exception that proves the rule to be valid; after all, Monette as a gay man is someone who had already broken with many of the rules of gender identity (although not the basic one; he is always clearly a man and not a woman, throughout this book and his subsequent autobiography, *Becoming a Man*). Perhaps we should forget altogether about theories such as Chodorow's, which claim to deal with elusive infantile experience, and concentrate instead on the question of how adults mourning losses construct and reconstruct their relationships in the light of these losses. We could also suggest that Monette, writing a book for readers who might not necessarily approve of, or understand, his relationship with Roger, must stress and overstress how permanent and fundamental it was to his life, as the label "lover" will not permit. He himself writes how this term distorts what Roger was to him; he is explicitly preoccupied with this as a problem of communication with readers. Yet these explanations alone seem inadequate; Monette and his lover were fused before mourning, and the message to readers is secondary to the need to clarify to himself who Roger had been. Roger had been himself.

On this weird note, the discussion of gender should close. If a reader supposes that gender is irrelevant to the experiences of illness, dying, and caretaking, she or he is mistaken. Nevertheless, it is equally mistaken to be guided by contemporary popular generalizations about gender differences, and to mine our collection of narratives for confirmation. The basic reason is that our narrators, however diverse, are not representative of the population at large, which is the population for which psychological theories such as Chodorow's and Gilligan's, or other theories such as eco-feminism, are intended. Within the limits of this genre, male and female writers both share certain qualities, such as introspection and interest in their own private experiences, which make them atypical anyway. What differences we have found exist clearly at the level of social roles, particularly the caretaking role, and not at all clearly at the level of intrapsychic experiencing, valuing, and awareness.

Chapter Seven

DEATH AS DESTRUCTION AND LOSS

THE ACCOUNTS WE EXAMINE TOUCH ON A VARIETY of topics. We have already seen how they offer a new portrayal of medicine, of human relationships, of isolation, and community. But one thing that they all share is that they are, fundamentally, tales of death. Although the events of the story concern illness, dying, and mourning, death is present throughout. It appears as dreaded threat, as future certainty, and as inner presence within the narrative. All of these stories are fueled by this presence of death and the protagonists' and narrators' encounter with it. All have been touched by death. In this chapter, we will look beneath the surface of the plots, of the events retold, and examine the ways that death is present in the narratives.

As Mary Winfrey Trautmann stated in the title of her book, "the absence of the dead is their way of appearing" (Trautmann 1984). Death is very present within these stories, even as the book jackets proclaim "this is a story of life, not death!" If it were still the case that American's response to death is no more than denial, repression, and silence, these stories would never have been published. Yet what is indeed absent, and glaringly so, is a universally shared vision of how death is present in the midst of life, and of its way of appearing to us. This is precisely what *each* author must construct, deliberately or unconsciously, forging a vision at an individual, personal level. Even those authors whose journals catalogue just the facts of day-to-day caretaking (such as Barbara Peabody's *The Screaming Room*) are simultaneously engaged in this task.

How, then does death become present in these narratives? What images, what cluster of ideas and associations, help to encounter it? How do narrators symbolize death's reality? What events prefigure death for their protagonists? These questions naturally assume that indeed death *can* be acknowledged, *can* be made present through symbols, *is* imaginable. This is itself a view that some psychological and especially psychoanalytic theories deny. According to such a perspective, fear of death itself lies outside the bounds of what the unconscious can ever accept or envision. Sick persons may fear abandonment, separation, mutilation, and castration, but they do not truly fear death.

Our perspective will be just the opposite: by linking death with abandonment, mutilation, and so on, humans are able to symbolize death into becoming a presence within the totality of their experience. Certain experiences innately suggest such linkages. (This is the perspective of Robert J. Lifton in *The Broken Connection*, which we find very helpful). Yet we also assume that human beings have a certain amount of freedom in the choice of how to construe death, what symbolic linkages to notice, and which to disregard. For example, is death symbolized as annihilation, extinction, or as a transition to an afterlife realm? Is death portrayed as a quasipersonal enemy, a hostile power come to get us and defeat us? Or is death a peaceful return to nonaction, Freud's own "death instinct" or Nirvana principle? In the three Semitic religious traditions, imagery for death has been linked heavily with that of judgment. To die was to see and be judged by God; in Christianity, death as a universal human fate was construed as a punishment for original sin. We find that however powerful these thoughts were in the past, this entire cluster of ideas is notable by its complete absence from all of our narratives. Not even the most orthodox of Christian writers invoke such motifs today when writing in the autobiographical vein. Whatever makes death fearful for contemporary Americans, it is not because it leads immediately to an encounter with a wrathful judge, or can become a gateway to Hell.

By contrast, some motifs of our narratives are so pervasive, so taken for granted by all of our narrators and by us, their readers, that to raise them to explicit consciousness as symbolism seems hardly necessary. Throughout our narratives, there appear to be two principal strands of imagery and associations: death as destruction, and death as loss. These are the simple facts of death, around which our protagonists' fears cluster. But most of our narrators know that these simple facts of death permeate all their experiences of life, of their bodies and their entire identities as living persons. We are not speaking of individual discrete items of furniture, so to speak, but of the room within which the human dramas are played out. In this death-space, then, the diseases that destroy the protagonists' bodies are harbingers of death; every small change in physical appearance brought about by disease will remind the protagonist of the approach and nearness of death. Death as destructive force may claustrophobically close down possibilities; it can even be construed as a personified enemy, against whom the sick person must mobilize an attack. In contrast, death as loss is so pervasive an American theme, and dominates so many of the narratives, that it is simply assumed to be the natural and universal mode of construing death's meaning. Even those narrators who refuse to accept in the sense of eventual accommodation, for whom the loss is beyond the power of any consolation or coping, emphasize this imagery, this constellation of associations. That it is imagery and associations, rather than simply unmediated natural fact, is what we will want to remind readers in this chapter.

Those narrators who eventually recover from illness or mourning have been touched by death, carry its destruction, its losses, and its nearness within them ever after. Death as destruction and loss is with them wherever they go, no longer safely banished from the universe and yet not fully and publicly acknowledged by society, either. It is to this ongoing presence that many of our narrators bear witness to consciously, and to which all of them indirectly point.

Death as Destruction

Death is the destruction of the body, its mutilation, and eventual disintegration. To the extent that we are our bodies, death is *our* destruction, mutilation, and disintegration. Within the context of these narratives, partial destructions such as amputation of a breast, or emaciation, become stand-ins for the total destruction impending on the horizon. As we will see, although losing a breast or a leg is not the same rationally as losing one's life, it serves symbolically as a vehicle for the latter (in rhetoric, this is called synecdoche). As embodied selves, then, we fear the destruction of the part because it opens up the horror of the possible destruction of the whole, of ourselves as total entities.

But there has been, in the West and elsewhere, a classic response to this threat. To the extent that we can imagine ourselves as severed from our bodies—as souls, spirits, minds—we can separate our hopes for ourselves from the destiny of the body, from its final and total destruction. As our flesh grows weaker, our spirits within may glow and grow stronger and purer. The real self is not only in the breast or the hair, but is an enduring, transtemporal and transspatial being, whose tenancy in the house of the body may come to a close without true trauma, and without true mutilation of its own being. In the meantime, it lives in its decaying dwelling, no longer identified with the desires and urges of the latter, but able to let go and move on. The traditional, philosophical term for such a split identity is *dualism,* its classic exponents Plato and Descartes.

Classic dualism allows the sick and dying person to be fully alive as soul, even in the midst of the moribund body. In its most strident form, dualism refuses to portray death as destruction or loss at all. The soul rejoices at its release from the unwanted encumbrance of the body, its unsuitable partner during life; at death, the freed soul may now return to its own element, the eternal and nonmaterial realm of forms, God, the ultimate reality. More muted or nuanced dualism allows that the soul may survive, but does not endure the body's death without suffering some rupture in its own being. In these versions of dualism, soul and body belong together; at the final resurrection of the dead, the soul and its recreated body joyfully embrace and reunite (a well-known drawing by William Blake conveys this image of lovers' reunion, for the soul is traditionally feminine).

Both forms of dualism benefit the dying person. Not just the imagery of a life after death, but also in the insistence that the destruction of death upon and within the body is *not* to be confused with the negation of the true core of the person. Unfashionable as dualism may be philosophically, we find several striking examples of dualistic death scenes in out narratives. Treya Wilber, for instance, becomes more herself and more a purely enlightened being as she approaches death (at least in her husband Ken's account). As her body deteriorates, the more "real" and "truer" Treya emerges more sharply. The accidental woman in her thirties burns away: the pure spark of the eternal ageless and timeless Treya, "the Star Dakini," becomes visible to those around her. Dying children, such as little Alex Deford, become more enspirited as they reach the point of death. From this perspective, dualism remains a desirable option for the very sick, and those who care for them.

But there is a price for dualism, and for many of our narrators the price is far too high. To be a strict and strident dualist is to declare the body an "other," a "not-me," and even an "enemy of the true me." And this is simply not the way most Americans in the late-twentieth century want to live with their bodies; we value our sense of ourselves as embodied beings. Perhaps, indeed, we have gone too far in this direction, and—as several thoughtful narrators such as Audre Lorde and Arthur Frank insist—we worship a falsely perfect ideal body and cannot cope with the imperfections of the real ones. Certainly, we support a huge advertising and health and beauty industry that would fold up were the dualist position to be universally adopted. Classic dualist metaphors of the body as house or clothing (and therefore exchangeable or discardable) appear very rarely in our narratives, precisely because for the vast majority of narrators and readers, our bodies are our selves. Dualism has so often been blamed for alienating persons from their bodies that although it may make dying more bearable, in our culture that is not a sufficient reason to accept it.

Philosophically, "holism" or "monism" is by far the preferred twentieth-century vision of personhood. In this view, the person is intrinsically a unit, functionally and ontologically. Not only do we experience life as a totality, but we are metaphysically "one stuff," all bound together. Some may say that we are most ourselves in experiences that are irrevocably and joyfully embodied, such as in sex and in physical sports. The catch is that then we are also to be most ourselves in illness and dying, in the destruction of the body/self. The mutilation of the body is, automatically and unavoidably, the mutilation of the "I" whose identity is constituted by this particular body. And this process, for the holist, unlike for the dualist, is the destruction of the *entire* unit. Death's destruction is thorough, total. Nothing beyond the body/self can escape to tell the tale of miraculous survival.

When philosophers and theologians argue these positions, the alternatives are reasonably clear-cut and mutually exclusive. When narrators of first-person accounts of illness and dying explore the ways in which the protagonist's body is and is not the soul or true core of the person, the results are much murkier. First, even those narrators whose religious faith includes a classic dualist assertion of survival after death in some fashion (such as David Watson, Shireen Perry, Helen Hostetler, as well as the Wilbers) they do not primarily pitch their stories into testimonies for this belief. Other religious authors (JoAnn Kelley Smith, Sandra Albertson) deliberately deny any belief in the survival of souls after death, and reject that element in their religious traditions without much debate over it. We will spend more time on this curious pattern in chapter 8.

One thing that does survive death's destruction, however, is the narrative itself, the (disembodied) voice telling the story. This is particularly poignant for the Type II narratives, for the voices now exist only in texts, and no longer in the flesh. The voices of David Watson, Violet Weingarten, and Stewart Alsop continue to speak, although the bodies of all three are long since decayed or burned. Thus, the process of writing is inherently an expression of dualism, albeit at a different level than that of the philosophical-theological. To write a journal of one's dying, as Peter Noll and the above authors did, is to proclaim the writing soul's transcendence over the destruction of the body, and so a kind of victory over death. From the narrator's perspective, then, one does not have to become a self-conscious philosophical dualist to advocate that the true self is the disembodied soul; one's continued writing in the setting of bodily destruction demonstrates a severance of identity, and denies the holistic fantasy that selves and bodies are one and the same.

Yet from the stance of the ailing and dying protagonist, things usually do not look this way. Typically, when the previously healthy adult protagonist starts to get sick, he or she feels betrayed. The body had previously been taken for granted as oneself; it had been innately trusted to bend to one's will. Now the body may become a trap, a stranger, or even an enemy, suddenly noticed as "other"—as nonself—if not for the first time, then in a manner that breaks through prior unconscious holism. The body has a life and a death trajectory of its own, and one must learn to live as Arthur Frank's title suggests, "at the will of the body." The initial "betrayals" may be minor, or frightening and painful: headaches, dizzy spells, lumps, moles that bleed, chest pains. After a while, the protagonist begins to watch for these, to turn to his or her body and read it for reassurances that it is still the same as always. But the signals come back mixed. By now, the body is a source of messages, dispatches from an alien country.

This is the way the trajectory of death as destruction often begins. What first gets destroyed is the unconscious identification of body and self. Although the focus of many of the narratives is on what are clearly major mutilations, such as the loss of a breast or a limb, the real work of mutilation may be this earlier and internal one. Something is disrupted, torn apart; a radically new relationship between self and body is beginning: the body as the sender of messages, and the self as the decoder. This new relationship rests on an incipient dualism: the protagonist becomes the observer and monitor of his or her own body, even if he or she is by philosophical conviction a holist. It seems possible that the inclusion of so many medical statistics, such as blood counts and biopsy results, is a sign of this new and estranged relationship between protagonist and body. The former now knows his or her body in a radically new fashion, as the object of medical investigation, as the sender of messages the protagonist can transcribe but only doctors can interpret. Since otherwise there is little interest in such information for others (as Alsop wryly admits) we the readers must accept this information against a backdrop of our own unconscious and ill-formed, naive identification with our bodies as healthy.

The signs and messages of our narratives are decodable as cancer, AIDS, cystic fibrosis, ALS, and so forth; they are not ever just intimations of sickness, but intimations of mortality. Moreover, whatever the protagonist may have hoped at the time, when the narrative is written, he or she knows what these prefigure. Audre Lorde reflects this in *The Cancer Journals*:

> This event called upon me to re-examine the quality and texture of my life, its priorities and commitments, as well as the possible alterations that might be required in light of that re-examination. I had already faced my own death, whether or not I acknowledged it, and I needed now to develop that strength which survival had given me. (61)

Retrospectively, these signs were pointers toward death's hidden presence, had the protagonist cared to look in that direction. Sometimes, they have been long-term markers, going back years before the critical phase of the illness, as in Robert Murphy's deadly creeping paralysis, the first manifestation of which appeared in a temporary movement disorder at age ten, falsely and fatally misdiagnosed as rheumatism. These reported signs are markers along a corridor toward a closed door, and the narrators, if not the protagonists, know that each step brings that door ever nearer.

As mentioned, it is the next level of destruction that overtly preoccupies many of the protagonists. Removal of a breast or a limb, even the loss of hair due to chemotherapy, are bodily mutilations extensively discussed in these narratives. These are true, visible mutilations, changes in one's public as well as private self-image that require massive social coping by those who suffer them. They are also dramatic symbols for the work of death as destruction. Again and again, protagonists report feeling mutilated, unwhole, permanently damaged. Yet even the loss of hair, which usually does grow back after chemotherapy, is also a sign of destruction, of a self no longer untouched by death. The experience of seeing clumps of one's own hair lying at the bottom of the shower can convey with dramatic horror this sense of becoming a ruined, mutilated self. All of these changes carry with them, in our narratives, the possibility of that total destruction of the body that will come at death.

It is important to note that, in our narratives, bodily mutilations are not due to accidents, but diseases whose progression is terrifying, mysterious, and often unstoppable. Patti Trull, writing *On With My Life* at age thirty, about her cancer and resulting leg amputation fifteen years earlier, knows this. She notes that even for an adolescent, losing one's leg is *real*, while dying of cancer is barely imaginable; the one-time presence of bone cancer haunts her subsequent life and career choice. Her adventures often focus on activities as a one-legged woman, such as riding a bicycle and downhill skiing. Nevertheless, she maintains an identification as one who lost her leg to cancer, and her first career was as a physical therapist for children with cancer.

The most often discussed and highly charged of these specific bodily mutilations is the mastectomy in breast cancer. It is common, it is gendered (although men *can* have breast cancer), it is very likely to be seen as destruction of the self, not just the body; no matter that a breast is not as "useful" as a leg. Three years after her breast surgery, Doris Schwerin (*Diary of a Pigeon Watcher*) secretly continues to feel mutilated and attacked, angry at nature and herself. Perhaps because she had no warning and was not consulted at all about the surgery, this response persists. Grief, anger and fear cluster together in this experience. She knows, as she watches the pigeon family outside her New York apartment, that what she truly fears is still the cancer; that what she truly mourns is still the loss of part of herself.

> I must not mince words. I am as frightened of my cancer as I was that Bozo wouldn't fly. The claustrophobia of being caught. That was it. Events over which I have no control. Having a dreadful disease is walking into the mysterious climes of Fate. My joyful journal of the birds is really a notebook about Death. I am still, three years after the operation, traumatized. (Schwerin 1976, 188)

It is not an option for her to become the kind of Platonic dualist who serenely rises above the woes of the body, secure in identification with the soul and the soul alone.

Those who underwent similar surgery more recently—among them Jill Ireland, Audre Lorde, Terry Tempest Williams' mother Diane, Barbara Rosenblum, Betty Rollin, and Treya Wilber—were given more information and more warning, but still must respond to the threat of mutilation of the self. All of the above authors acknowledge that something in themselves has been cut away; they are unbalanced not just physically, but in themselves as selves. More-over, refusal to admit that something has been cut away is itself a target of a few authors. Why, Audre Lorde complains, does Israeli General Moishe Dayan get to wear an eye-patch and get treated as a war hero, while a one-breasted woman is viewed as repulsive and disgusting?

> Yet there still appears to be a conspiracy . . . to insist to every woman who has lost a breast that she is no different from before, if with a little skillful pretense and a few ounces of silicone gel she can pretend to herself and the watching world—the only orientation toward the world that women are supposed to have—that nothing has happened to challenge her. With this orientation a woman after surgery is allowed no time or space within which to weep, rage, internalize and transcend her loss. (Lorde 1980, 62–63)

Is a woman's struggle against death not considered valid? Is her courage not as real as a man's?

Lorde particularly attacks the wearing of prostheses, artificial breasts that are, apparently, marketed with slogans that claim that these products are true replacements for the amputated breasts. Does a woman's own body exist to be viewed by the world, real only insofar as others can perceive her? Or does she exist as an embodied self, her own being, mutilated but real? To pretend that one exists as one did before is a lie, a denial of what the survivor of this kind of surgery knows to be true in her own body. And in this context, it is a denial of death, of death's potential to destroy totally what remains. Jill Ireland, politically a million miles away from Lorde, shares some of this reaction against prostheses; she wears one, but it is *not* a replacement, merely a cosmetic device useful for her career. In *Spence + Lila,* a novel by Bobbie Ann Mason, a middle-aged farmer's wife responds in an earthier and yet just as vigorous fashion; she takes the "fake breast" and laughingly plays catch with it along with her daughters, ridiculing the social norms blasted by Lorde, and triumphing over mutilation through humor.

The point of these authors and other authors who experienced radical mastectomy is not to claim that this inevitably overwhelms the self, or that the sense of mutilation is catastrophic and irrevocable. But they wish it acknowledged as real, and so to base any subsequent identity on awareness that death has been at work in them; they have survived, but not unscathed. Lorde's seemingly fanciful comparison with Moishe Dayan is not so far-fetched after all. In one case, that of Terry Tempest Williams, it becomes even more apt. At the age of thirty-four, after the deaths of mother and grandmother, she is the eldest survivor of what has become a "clan of one-breasted women;" her family in Western Utah was exposed to above-ground nuclear testing in the 1950s, with catastrophic and cancerous consequences.

But these mutilations and destructions are visible; what is destroyed is a piece of the woman's social body, a piece which serves as a powerful symbol of the whole. The corresponding sexually charged mutilation for a man is not publicly visible, but the examples from our narratives show us an even greater sense of death as destruction surrounding surgery for testicular or prostatic cancer than that which mastectomy evoked. The mildest of three examples is that of Arthur Frank, who suffered the removal of one testicle without, he claims, experiencing a major disruption in his identity as a man or a husband. As an alternative to death from cancer, this operation seemed to him a reasonable and beneficial choice. "If I had been in my late teens . . . the operation would have had a different meaning. At my age, I was more interested in being able to pull on a pair of pants without wincing" (Frank 1991, 37).

This balanced assessment is, however, belied by the testimony of two other male protagonists, Max Lerner and Peter Noll. In his eighties, Lerner is threatened with the possibility of a similar operation as Frank had endured in his late thirties (albeit for a different kind of cancer). "Don't let them do an Abelard on you!" a friend warns him (Lerner 1990, 98). He concurs, and refuses the surgery. To be mutilated as a male was a needless outrage, an additional and intolerable attack against his identity, although he is willing to go through with several other demanding and heroic treatments. Noll, even more extreme, wills himself to a perhaps needless or premature death because he refuses to consider undergoing similar surgery. In this case, his "freedom," his refusal to submit to the passive status of hospital patient, and his masculinity are all tied together. Some mutilations, then, are seen as truly a fate worse than death. Or rather, the symbolic linking between mutilation and death is revisioned so that the total destruction of an intact, whole body is preferred to the destruction of the sexually charged part. The cases of Lerner and Noll might actually support the Freudian claim that death is less of a real fear than castration.

In facing destruction of the body, we have noted how few protagonists turn to classic Platonic dualism, the claim for a transcendence of the body's end through identification with the soul who endures. There is, however, another mode of dualism that operates in some of the accounts, which seems to deserve the label "Cartesian." Here, the body becomes object, and the mind takes charge over it, refusing to be a victim of either disease or the destructive power of death at work in the body. Here, too, ironically, military imagery appears— but in a fashion very different from Lorde's reference to mutilated but heroic General Dayan. The method of imagery therapy developed and popularized by the Simontons requires that the cancer experience be revisioned as the invasion of "enemy" bad cells into one's vulnerable body. The mind is then to call up the troops, the army of "good cells" which will fight the cancerous ones and totally destroy them. The body itself become the site of a bloody battle; not a civil war, as in the apostle Paul's famous passage of a struggle within the body/self (Romans 7:15–24), but an invasion. Yet the mind, transcending and in control, has the power to command the body's own resources. Any heroic and ruthlessly determined leader of a war campaign becomes the ideal for the self-as-controller. Alsop, who lived and died before the Simontons entered the arena of cancer care, discovers dynamic military imagery on his own, paraphrasing Sir Winston Churchill:

> We will fight amongst the platelets. We will fight in the bone marrow. We will fight in the peripheral blood. We will never surrender. (Alsop 1973, 68)

Yet for Alsop, this is a humorous fantasy, while the Simonton's therapy is promoted in dead earnest. In fact, as we saw in chapter 4, the major appeal of this form of therapy appears in its ethic of autonomy, of taking control over one's own healing.

Whether or not this form of therapy is effective against cancer cells, its heavy reliance upon a military Cartesianism raises questions for the more thoughtful narrators. Arthur Frank, for example, finds the shrill claim of "victory over victimhood" a shallow approach to the real meaning of illness. To be ill is to learn the limits of one's control, and part of the lesson of illness is how to live within a body that *is* limited, imperfect, and invariably vulnerable. To turn one's body into enemy-held territory is to let the illness further estrange one from oneself-as-body, by identifying with the triumphant, manipulative, and curiously disembodied mind who runs the show. Frank is in favor of active and informed participation in one's treatment, and all the other agendas of the Simonton-type therapies, insofar as these relate to the social authority of medicine. But the role of the sick or dying person is to bear witness to his or her own suffering, not necessarily to attempt a military defeat of what is, after all, still oneself.

Yet are the viruses and cancer cells "oneself," or are they alien forces, evil presences which are comparable to enemy agents or Nazi panzer divisions? Demonizing the disease is a frequent strategy in our narrative; the destruction of "bad cells" by mental power is only a particularly vivid development of this imagery. Death as destruction is not to be accepted when the battle is being waged. In fact, one might wonder if the resurgence of this imagery, and the popularity of the Simonton's work, is a reaction against the simple endorsement of acceptance of death as an ideal found in some of the earlier autobiographies from the 1970s (such as those by Sandra Albertson and JoAnn Kelley Smith). To fight against death, not to go gentle into that good night, appeals not just to Max Lerner but to Jill Ireland, Gilda Radner, Elizabeth Glaser, and Frank Deford. It certainly appeals in *The Power Within* to Wendy Williams, journalist-chronicler of those who heroically "beat" cancer and survived or dramatically outlived their prognoses.

But the most thorough and extensive example of military imagery is also a fine illustration of its sinister potential. For Emmanuel Dreuilhe, dying of AIDS, the battle against the virus requires a strange flood of military metaphors. AIDS is the Nazi war machine; he is the French Resistance movement and so on. Yet somewhere in the middle of his *Mortal Embrace: Living with AIDS,* he admits that he has forgotten what cause he is fighting for; the battle for life has become itself a substitute for living. At the very end, this process has indeed consumed him; he has fallen in love with his enemy the virus, for it alone gives his life any meaning. In one last apocalyptic military image, he predicts that he will follow Hitler's example of self-chosen death amid the ruin of war: "If I ever come to resemble Berlin in May 1945, it will perhaps be time for me to poison us both, AIDS and me, in our bunker" (158). In this instance, the sheerly destructive power of death is so evident, so unmitigated, and so total that the self is buried under the rubble even before the virus wins the war. And this is precisely what most of our authors fear most deeply: that the presence of death as destruction will engulf the self, even the writing self, so that not just the body and mind, but the disembodied voice of the narrator will be silenced and destroyed.

No example could be less typical of our collection of narratives than Dreuihle's. In almost all other cases, the power of death to destroy is somehow integrated into the power of the self to incorporate destruction into enduring, if imperfect and vulnerable life (as in the image of "the clan of one-breasted women"). Or, the imagery of death and destruction is supplemented by the theme of death as loss, giving rise to different constellations of imagery and a different emotional tone than Dreuihle's work reveals. Through this imagery narrators find the solution to Dreuihle's dilemma of no longer knowing for what cause he fights so hard against death's destruction. Those for whom death is loss do not share Dreuihle's particular problem. They are all too well aware of what and whom they have loved.

Death as Loss

Although death as destruction plays a real and significant role in these autobiographies of late twentieth-century persons, death as loss is the overwhelmingly dominant motif. Death is loss for the beloved who watches his or her loved one dying; death is equally loss for the dying protagonist. The absence of the dead is their loss from our lives; our mourning is our adaptation over time to the absence. Trying to convey the full devastation and sorrow of their loss is one of our writers' major tasks. Even some of the mutilations and destructions discussed already can take on the shape of loss: mourning for a lost breast, or lost sense of the body's wholeness, is one way that narrators try to master the threat of bodily destruction.

Death as loss is a motif shared by both the dying and the bereaved. Thus, it is no surprise that contemporary theories on the process of dying resemble theories of bereavement as a process. Both bereavement experts and those who counsel the dying assume the loss paradigm, although all acknowledge that there are obvious differences (out-and-out denial, for example, is not the major experience for the bereaved as it can often be for the dying). Popularization of

Elisabeth Kübler-Ross' "five stages of dying" model greatly furthered this merging of the two experiences, since the model can easily be made to fit any major loss. Those among our narrators who use it or criticize it apply it to both situations indiscriminately. Almost always, the criticisms we find in the autobiographies mirror those found elsewhere: the model is too schematized, too prescriptive, everyone faces death (or mourning) in a unique way, and so on. Beneath these frequently voiced criticisms is the awareness that even this basic and seemingly uncontroversial motif of death and loss does not yet, not quite, have the status of a universally normative, socially mandated meaning for the encounter with death. How to face loss, how to integrate one's losses into one's total life experience, remains a private-sphere, very personal and individual task. To the extent that a five stage model seems to deny this, to force everyone into a mold, narrators find it oppressive.

Death as loss, however pervasive and taken for granted as a model for encountering death, is not one stressed in the Christian religious tradition. In fact, it is noticeable by its absence; traditional Christian funeral rites included no prayers specifically directed at comforting those who mourn, and contemporary revisions of those rites often focus so heavily on resurrection hope that little room is left for acknowledging grief, for attending to death as a loss. In Judaism, highly structured traditional mourning rites did, and do, exist, but the prolonged and intense agony of bereavement is not encompassed by these, especially in the abbreviated form in which they are practiced in American Judaism. (We will say more about the positive contributions and gaps in both Christianity and Judaism in chapter 8, but it is highly significant that the theme of death as loss, which is so central to our narratives' response to death, is not adequately met by existing religious sources.)

Moreover, the question about destruction, and what if anything of the person can survive death is—however philosophically and spiritually interesting—beside the point when it comes to the experience of death as loss. The dying person loses his or her life on earth, with its rich texture of relationships, memories, connections to nature and history. The relatives or friends of the dying person lose that individual's presence in their midst; they must rearrange their lives so as to be able to function without him or her. For the mourners, indeed, "the absence of the dead is their way of appearing." For

neither the dying nor the bereaved is the continued existence of the
dead elsewhere, in another more spiritualized eternal existence, a
mitigation of the reality of the loss *here*. Nothing could more eloquently express the "this-worldly" character of even the most spiritual of these narratives, than this insistence. Even existence in an
afterlife-realm is no consolation against the present reality of death
as loss.

Given this overwhelming construction of the experience of death
as loss, we must ask the question, "What, exactly, is it that will be lost
at death, or that the bereaved find most gone after death?" Curiously, this is not a question which gets asked explicitly very often; the
answers seem so obvious: "the future"; "one's life-plan" (this is
Howard Brody's answer; see *Stories of Sickness*); "relationships." These
obvious answers are also the least adequate, and, given what we find
in the autobiographies, perhaps the least truthful. What does it mean
to lose one's future? Why, if this is the focus of loss, should so many of
the protagonists mourn their pasts, and remain relatively silent about
their lost futures? As for the notion of "life-plan," the encounter with
death very often shatters careers; but it almost inevitably shatters
careerism. Whether or not the protagonist recovers, his or her interest in job success, in the pursuit of more money, promotions, or fame
has itself been put to death. In Paul Tsongas' autobiography (*Heading Home*), we find this truth summarized succinctly: "No one on his
deathbed ever said, 'I wish I'd spent more time on my business.'"

> My bright political career now seems irrelevant. I am leaving the Senate
> more qualified than I have ever been, but others will take my place. As
> an ordinary citizen, I can partake fully of the joys and responsibilities of
> family, and give thanks. (165)

The only career that does not seem shattered through this encounter
is that of writer: for the writer, serious life-threatening illness is the
stuff of his or her vocation (Broyard, Weingarten, Sarton). Hence,
the "life-plan" answer is doubly inadequate.

We may use Tsongas to illustrate another obvious inaccurate answer. No one regrets that he spent inadequate time on his business
because, today, money and material possessions do not, by themselves, bring an interior sense of fulfillment or happiness. According
to historian Philippe Aries, Renaissance men used to weep at death for

the impending loss of their villas, their gold, and other possessions. In America today, the world's wealthiest and most materialistic culture, do we find this phenomenon? Not at all. At least, nowhere in these narratives do material possessions play this role. Impending financial ruin may have prompted a few of our authors to write for publication (Lesher and Halberstam come to mind), but this is very much a concern of those who know they will survive. Death brings an end to crushing medical expenses, but the dying in our narratives do not mourn the loss of their stocks and bonds, their IRAs, and so on. Nor do houses, cars, fine clothes, the new VCR or camcorder figure at all as *possessions*: items that will be lost and so must be mourned. An expression of grief over the impending loss of relation with a beloved pet is much more likely than mourning any material object, however expensive. We hesitate to claim that this proves that Americans are not truly materialists, truly greedy for possessions. But the complete absence from all our narratives of the "weeping for possessions" documented by Aries suggests that our standards of appropriate attachments have certainly changed since the Renaissance.

If not over possessions, then over what or whom do the dying weep? In raising this question in the context of autobiographical texts, we ask over which aspects of loss do narrators persuade their readers to weep? Houses, and even occasionally cars come to symbolize a life lived, a set of relationships and memories, a family's history. As real estate, as something to own, they are beside the point. So to answer the question, "What is lost at death?" we turn not to possessions but to their human associations: the relationships and shared past of family life. Once again, an answer that the future will be lost may seem more reasonable, but it is the past which can be genuinely mourned, and the past that is evoked in all its richness, beauty and tragedy, which is subjectively real to the protagonists, and with which our narrators fill their pages; the past that although already past, is still available but soon to be lost forever.

Here, houses play a special role, visible as seemingly enduring monuments of relationships which are slipping away. Stewart Alsop vividly describes the family's dilapidated, but beloved, country home. Stephen Rosenfeld, Madeleine L'Engle, May Sarton, and Agnes DeMille do likewise. Nan Shin, in *Diary of a Zen Nun*, gives an equally meticulous and loving description of her monastery in France. The places will endure, as physical places; what will soon be gone forever are the persons who inhabited them. In a different use of the house in permanence/change imagery, Laurie Graham describes rebuilding the house as she mourns for her husband George after his death. The turn-of-the-century farmhouse had belonged to them, and so can symbolize their relationship. But only she ever lives there— which she does in spite of her continuing fear that it will collapse around her. Graham's husband had also collected antique cars, and as she fires up the 1909 Stanley Steamer he gave to her and goes for her first solo drive, we find ourselves as readers linked through her attachment to this object, beloved possession of the absent George, and also to our own (pervasively American) fantasies about cars as extensions of selves.

Houses and cars, then, become symbols of the family and its history. Not the future but the past must be recaptured because it will soon be gone, or one's relationship to it will dramatically change. "I suppose I took a new interest in my ancestors when I learned that I was statistically likely to become an ancestor myself," (Alsop 1973, 94) Alsop states. To start to see oneself as an ancestor, is to see oneself as the most recent of a lineage of those from whom one has received a patrimony (as in Philip Roth's title) or, in many cases, a matriarchal legacy. Alsop and L'Engle know and trace their ancestry for us, filled with the awareness that an impending loss brings. In L'Engle's case, it is her aged, senile mother who is about to become an ancestor, and whose personality now exists principally in her daughter's memory, where she may be evoked alongside her own mother, grandmother, and great-grandmother. Ancestors also play a role for Jessamyn West, whose Quaker mother's stories helped save her from TB (*The Woman Said Yes*). Terry Tempest Williams also evokes her Utah ancestors, in the sense that her Mormon family going back to the nineteenth century becomes an abiding force in the story of *Refuge*. One may rationalize this heightening awareness of ancestors; after all, with the collapse of the future for the protagonist, the past then becomes all the more burdened with meaning. Curiously, although narrators often tell us that they grieve for a lost future, we find very few examples of protagonists who extensively and emotionally share with us a specific string of future possibilities that they now realize will never arrive. Even those with children, while grieving that they will never see their children grow up, fail to offer elaborate imaginary scenarios of how their future lives might unfold.

Ancestors, not descendants, are more to the core of what protago-nists genuinely have and know they will soon lose.

But ancestors beyond the generation of one's grandparents are a rarity in American narratives. The childhood home, the immediate family of one's youth, and remembrances of grandparents visited during the summer: this is the milieu of Andrew Malcolm's *Someday*, and this is the degree to which the family as past imagery is real for the majority of narrators. These family memories can be vivid, evok-ing a realm as "gone" as the world of Alsop's Revolutionary War forebears, or as in Marjorie Sutliffe's *Grandma Cherry's Spoon*, whose narrator does a marvelous job of recreating scenes of the dirt-poor Ozarks farmers circa 1920. What this tells us is that, on the whole, for Americans, the relevant past is one's own past plus one generation back; no further.

Even here, we should not let the proud and loving attention of Alsop and L'Engle to ancestors be mistaken for the universal norm as to how the past, which will soon be lost, is apprehended. For some narrators, the past is a minefield, and the relationships from the past so tragic and painful that to return to them is to enter a dreaded terrain. And yet, because the past will soon be lost, it must be re-gained and revisited while there is still time. The dying, or very sick, protagonist knows this, as does the protagonist who serves as care-taker. We are not now speaking of the relationships between the narrator and the memorialized beloved (although a few of these works might well be subtitled "I'm so miserable without you it's almost like having you here"), but of the past of one's immediate ancestors whom one is about to join, or whose lost presence is evoked by the impending death.

Take, for example, Marvin Barrett (*Spare Days*) and Mary Kay Blakely (*Wake Me When it's Over*), two narrators who suffered life-threatening illnesses, and who share only one other experience: the traumatic, tragic death of a brother. For Barrett, this is an ancient wound, for his brother had been killed by a runaway car when both were small children, and he has forever after blamed himself. The guilt he carries with him, and his sense of the inexplicable quality of fate—he still wonders how he could have let go of his brother's hand—must be systematically revisited, mined by him as protagonist for any possible spiritually redemptive potential (Barrett 1988, 19). As narrator, he knows that there is no answer to the questions of guilt and responsibility; he will never know why and how he "permitted" his brother to die. But it is important that he, as protagonist, learn this finally and fully before he himself dies. At a less sophisticated level of awareness and analysis, Mary Kay Blakely believes that she let herself fall into a nine-day coma brought on by stress and untreated illnesses, in part to atone for the suicide of her depressed, beloved brother Frank. She had never been able to help Frank, and (she realizes as narrator) no one could have. In both these cases, to recapture the past of a lost relationship is not necessarily liberating or healing, but it is an important step in facing death as the loss of all family relationships.

This theme, in fact, dominates a few of the narratives. Once again, it touches those who mourn or take care of the dying, as well as the dying themselves. Unmourned or partially mourned deaths from the past pervade Gerda Lerner's account of her husband Carl's slow death from a brain tumor; many of these occurred in the context of the Holocaust, and indeed the Holocaust accounts for why she has, by now, no living family beyond her immediate household—her children who deliberately ask not to be included in this narrative. Another instance of this is clumsily told by the Zorzas (*A Way to Die*) in which father Victor discovers that the only way he can accept his daughter's impending death is again to mourn his own family's deaths in the Holocaust, and his partial betrayal of them. It is significant that although there are many Jewish authors in our collection, the mass death and mourning of the Holocaust appear in only two of the narratives.

More typical is the account by Doris Schwerin of her unhappy relationship as a child to her cold and rejecting mother, culminating in the mother's sudden and surprising death when Doris was fifteen. In facing her own mortality, Doris finally is able to recollect her mother, and connect her own life and survival to the lives of her long-dead parents: "I'm standing here with one breast, I'm different and yet strangely whole, more whole than I've ever been, I was on my own, yet theirs" (Schwerin 1976, 287). Here we have a real sense of what the recollection of "ancestors," even if only one generation back, can mean. Paradoxically, the "wholeness" experienced can be felt most fully just as the impending loss of one's own life draws nearer, becoming an undeniable fact of one's living identity.

With the death of any individual comes the loss of that person's memories, role in a family, and private history. But this history is part, albeit a small part, of the wider, more public history of American life and people. Philip Roth mourns not just his father, but the moment of sociological time his father occupied. This was a time when Jewish men were discriminated against by the insurance industry, he reminds us bitterly; not bitterly because of discrimination, but because it has been so quickly forgotten, Even his father no longer remembers it properly. But remembering is important for Roth.

> "I must remember accurately," I told myself, "remember everything accurately so that when he is gone I can recreate the father who created me." *You must not forget anything.* (Roth 1991, 177)

Another middle-aged male narrator, Rosenfeld, mourns not only the deaths of his parents, but of their way of life and the small urban community of Pittsfield, Massachusetts, which nurtured and supported both his parents and, secretly, himself, who left Pittsfield for cosmopolitan Washington where he writes for *The Washington Post.* The Pittsfield of his parents, like the lost middle-America of Malcolm's *Someday,* is as mournable as its elderly inhabitants.

Women narrators seem less concerned with the relationship of individual to the wider community. Yet we find the equivalent to Roth's and Rosenfeld's sense of a lost social world in the manner that Madeleine L'Engle and Terry Tempest Williams both mourn mothers who managed to be strong and charming individuals yet never broke with the conventional social roles for women. To evoke these mothers is, for their daughters, to reflect on the ambivalent legacy of womanhood, the triumph of character over social role. Far from being weak and "victims," these women lived their lives joyously and richly, albeit within boundaries that their daughters find oppressive. In contrast, LeAnne Schreiber, Joan Gould, and Diane Rubin all had mothers who had *not* successfully managed to integrate strength and charm, whose own lives had been constricted and whose response to social powerlessness was to focus on manipulation of those within their family circle.

While the death of a family member is often connected by these narrators to the loss of a part of one's experience, in none of these cases is the death of an individual a strong symbol of the death of an entire way of life or a community. In order to find this variant of "death as loss," one must turn to the AIDS narratives. We note, however, that the works by Peabody, Hostetler, Perry, and Pearson were all written by persons outside the AIDS community (the phrase itself is a powerful and exclusive one). Monette, Dreuihle, and especially Andrew Holleran's *Ground Zero* are "insider" reports, and offer a vivid account of how each individual's death became part of the demise of a whole way of life. The portrait of gay New York City drawn by Holleran is divided into before and after. Not before and after the virus, which must have been present in some of the men's bodies from the early 1970s, but before and after the illness was present as a conscious factor for Holleran's protagonists. He and his friends must now mourn not only their lost companions, but lost parties, lost extravagances, lost sexual practices.

> AIDS has been massive form of aversion therapy. For if you finally equate sex with death, you don't have to worry about observing safe-sex techniques: sex itself will eventually become unappetizing. And the male body will turn into an object of dread—not joy—an object whose touch makes you lie awake afterward with the suspicion that you have just thrown your life away for a bit of pleasure. (25)

And these, in turn, all symbolize a lost freedom, and a lost life to both narrator and protagonists. In the book's final scene, the narrator stands not in New York but on the shores of the Caribbean:

> The swimmer is trying, in some peculiar way, to swim enough in this gorgeous sea to cleanse himself—though he knows the thing that must be cleansed floats in an interior sea, and no amount of sea water over the skin can wash it away. (226)

Remembering, he grieves, and yearns for an impossible healing from the ocean outside of himself. Not only gay New York, but the world as a totality will soon be lost to him. Gone is gone is gone. Although other AIDS narratives would clearly want to challenge this message (Paul Monette does not accept it in *Borrowed Time,* nor in his more recent *Becoming a Man*), Holleran's dramatic merger of total loss and total destruction (represented by the title of his book) are further evidence of why AIDS is not—by the witness of these narratives— merely another disease.

Yet even here, the final scene is not of a community engaged in collective mourning, but of the isolated, individual self, standing at the edge of the vast unknown and grasping its very private mortality. For it is in this encounter with death as loss that the heart of what is truly lost emerges. It is not the future or the past, not possessions or ancestors, or even the reality of other persons in the external world. It is the experiencing, feeling, remembering self who will be gone. It is this self, with its intuitively felt connection to life in this world, to the lives of others past and present, who will be gone is gone is gone. It is the self who writes the journal, the disembodied voice, who expects to become lost. Every self has a story, and the story will end. The experiencing self tries to cram together every thing, every experience, every memory: platelet counts, walks in the woods with grandchildren, quotes from favorite authors, detailed retellings of quiet dinners with friends—*everything*. For everything becomes precious precisely as it is the experience of the experiencing self. The living enjoyment of even the most fleeting moment of experience, such as Arthur Frank's view of the moon through his window one night, is relevant, is crucial, is vital. Never will that particular piece of experience be repeated in the story of this experiencing self again, ever, in the whole history of the universe. Though the moon shines many nights, although the flowers bloom year after year in May Sarton's garden, although the cycles of nature small and large repeat (like the flooding of the Great Salt Lake in *Refuge*), from the standpoint of the experiencing self these cycles are unique, one of a kind moments.

There are many, many such moments in our narratives. The protagonist sees himself or herself as the locus of experience, as the one within whom oceans, people, flowers, and memories come into a unity and a continuity. The protagonist in the midst of the flow of the story is brought to a halt by this recognition; what will soon be lost is himself or herself as the center of experiencing. In those Type III stories where it is the death of the beloved that constitutes the narrative, there is often a double moment of recognition of loss: when the dying person becomes aware of how as experiencing self he or she will soon be gone, and when the caretaker-protagonist who is also the narrator acknowledges this, takes note that the beloved is mourning the impending loss of his or her experiencing. And then for the caretaker-protagonist comes a third moment: recognition that after the death, all her or his future experiencing will be alone, without the beloved. This focus on the experiencing self as the "essence" of loss does not mean that the external world or other persons are not genuinely treasured, or genuinely mourned. But in these, as in other autobiographies, the self, with its story to tell, is at the core. The self with its connectedness, fragile and soon to be broken, is what will be lost. It is here that death as destruction and loss are fundamentally epitomized. It is in this sense that death comes as the end of everything for our protagonists. Not all of them accept death as extinction theologically. Rationally, they know, too, that others will survive, that nature will not end, that their houses and their pets may live on. But as selves who can experience and connect with life, they sense the impending loss of everything and everyone, the destruction of that unique being who can gaze at the moon from his or her window.

It is with this insight that we open the door to how religion and spirituality appear within these narratives. If wider frameworks of meaning—some traditionally religious, others a contemporary equivalent—sometimes become a resource for these autobiographers of death and dying, these frameworks must leave room for the centrality of the experiencing self. They must speak not only to death as the destruction of the body, or of the loss of the person's past history of relationships, but to this most basic threat to the self as locus of experience. In chapter 8, we will see the possible roles for religion, in the landscape of first person mortal narratives.

Chapter Eight

SPIRITUALITY AND RELIGION

The Concept of Spirituality

Over the past decade or more, the term *spirituality* has enjoyed a renaissance, as many persons wish to identify and describe how one relates to that which he or she finds most ultimate, a source of personal grounding and meaning in the universe. To use the term *spirituality* in this fashion points toward a sense of one's links with the deepest level of reality, and highest truth. Although these links may be elusive, barely articulated; nevertheless, they lie at the heart of an individual's life. Spirituality, when defined this way is easy to contrast with religion. The latter almost always involves the idea of a tradition, something handed down; it also generally assumes a community. Religion is not meant to isolate itself into one, marked-off holy corner of life, but for many persons that is how it has come to function. Spirituality, as a concept, intends to overcome this sense of a "sacred precinct" and encompass whatever one finds true and meaningful and even holy, including that which lies far from the sphere of the religious. Some definitions of spirituality are tied more explicitly with a sense of "spirit," as distinct from mind or soul

(May 1982). In our view, this is less necessary, especially since it reintroduces potential divisions that the term itself, in its contemporary flowering, seems intended to bypass.

What strikes us as significant is not how many persons have recently offered definitions of spirituality, but how important the phenomena covered by such definitions now seem. It is simply not enough to speak of religious versus secular narrators, for example, and analyze our collection of first person mortal accounts using that dichotomy. We seek a term that allows us to probe for deeper, more idiosyncratic frameworks of meaning, and grapplings with ultimacy, than what religion suggests. Moreover, some of the secular authors—the ones who inform us that they aren't churchgoers, don't have any faith, and so on, have touched this level of engagement with reality and meaning, and are able to tell us about it. While such dimensions may be noticeably lacking in some of the stories of the religious ones.

Yet if we introduce and rely on the term *spirituality*, we will need to clarify its relation to religion. For the purposes of this study, religion is marked by four components: creed, cult, code (ethics), and community. Belief, some form of worship or ritual, an ethical system, and a group: these are the necessary ingredients to religion. We may then say that *spirituality* will always refer to how an *individual* lives meaningfully with ultimacy, his or her response to the deepest truths of the universe as he or she apprehends these. By these definitions, some persons have a religious mode of spirituality; their religious involvement lives not on the surface of their lives as external practice or habit, but as interior truth, shaping their vision of themselves and their world. Madeleine L'Engle's Christian faith fits this model well, as does Elizabeth Gee's Mormon faith in *The Light Around the Dark*. Another clear example of this is Nan Shin, whose *Diary of a Zen Nun* reveals Buddhism not as creed or cult, but primarily as a way of being-in-the-world, a very personal way of seeing and attending.

But there are those whose spirituality is more eclectic, private, idiosyncratic, and fragile. Being a member of those whose worship, for example, does not place one within any public community. Mary Winfrey Trautmann involves herself with several Christian churches during her daughter Carol's long battle with leukemia. But by the end of her story (*The Absence of the Dead is Their Way of Appearing*) she has migrated spiritually, so that her tie to the divine is no longer to the Christian Trinity, but to a supernatural feminine figure she calls

"The Companion." It is to this figure that she pays a (visionary) visit at the end of her narrative, and discovers her dead daughter side by side with this powerful, numinous, and supportive presence. There is no reason at all to label such a story "secular," for the narrator's spiritual journey lies at the heart of how she responds to her daughter's dying. In fact, for such accounts, Carl Jung's term *personal myth* might well be best. These narratives tell of a journey which indeed is shaped by myth—but no longer the shared Christian myth of Trautmann's (and Jung's) origins. Terry Tempest Williams' *Refuge* is an equally clear example of an author whose spirituality can no longer be contained by her family's traditional Mormon faith, yet whose intense involvement with nature and ecology serves to guide her vision of change, death, and renewal.

Others are less explicitly mythic about their spirituality, yet it remains an important element in their stories. We find, for example, that Audre Lorde and Violet Weingarten can both be depicted in terms of spirituality as we define it here. Lorde's vision joins sexual, spiritual, and political energy, so as to confront and incorporate death into her being. Weingarten approaches her own mortality not so much through formal prayer, but through listening and attention to intimations of both death and life. So, as well, can Elizabeth Glaser be construed in terms of our definition of spirituality, in her book *In the Absence of Angels*. Glaser's ancestral religion was Judaism, but her spirituality is a mesh of Judaism's prophetic passion for justice with an awareness of natural forces and powers within the universe and herself, which lies close to that of Trautmann, although less clearly articulated.

It is not the case that every human, by definition, possesses spirituality, not, at least, in our usage of the term. For a substantial minority of our narrators, the idea of a framework of meaning, of a total response to the deepest level of truth is unacceptable. To expect great lucid meanings, or to search behind the particularities of events for their ultimate dimensions and transempirical truth would be futile. Only the facts count. Transcendent references, even of the most private and personally empowering variety, betray these facts by holding out a promise of a "Beyond" or "Beneath" or "Above." For these authors, as for Terrence Des Pres (who in *The Survivor* examined narratives of the Holocaust), "Life, the earth in its silence, is all there is." (Des Pres 1977, 208). For those who hold this point of view, spirituality is a phantasm, an illusion they must renounce.

This last point of view must not be minimized, dismissed, or lost sight of in the discussion that follows. Just as it is easy to contrast the homemade and idiosyncratic spirituality of a Trautmann or Weingarten with the seemingly more formulated and articulated versions of L'Engle and Nan Shin, so it is even easier to dismiss the rejection of spirituality as a sign of the loss of depth. But this is a mistake. The moral refusal to accept ultimate frameworks cannot be equated with superficiality, even if the positivist principle of "just the facts" is inadequate on philosophical grounds. One is reminded of Albert Camus' narrator Dr. Rieux in *The Plague*, although in this case the novel itself becomes a philosophical framework for defending the thesis that there is no adequate framework of meaning for human suffering.

Our collection contains a few Rieux-like storytellers. Gerda Lerner and, in a different way, Barbara Peabody both are narrators who deliberately eschew the quest for any larger, more explicitly ideological sacred canopy for the events they describe. For Lerner, to be secular means to tell the story of her husband Carl's illness, their coping as a couple with his increasing disability, and her remembering of her family's sufferings and many deaths (see chapter 7). To be humanistic is to stick resolutely to the *human events*, and not try to puff them up into transhuman or transhistorical truths. To remember her aunt and uncle is, for her, a real and necessary task; to link their survival or deaths to any explicit ideational frameworks from Judaism, the Enlightenment, or Marxism would be to destroy the real memories, to betray those persons who are now known through memory.

Lerner just about says this explicitly, while for Peabody it is inferred. *The Screaming Room* contains one agonizing scene after another of her son's dying of AIDS. Her task is to be there, to nurse Peter, and to record "just the facts" of his dying. The message behind the words is that it is wrong to look for a message, a meaning written like flaming letters in the sky, which will make any sense of the nightmare. The very project of searching for sense, order or meaning is a moral flight from the reality of "just the facts," a position that, in fact, approaches Camus' outlook. Because we respect the freedom of our narrators to maintain this stance, we find it wrong to label it a spiritual outlook or a form of spirituality in spite of itself. We take their disagreement, and its serious challenge to the underlying promise of meaningfulness, as part of our interpretive task.

Autobiography, Spirituality and Religion

Our first generalization about the roles of spirituality and religion in our collection of narratives is that autobiography appears to be an ideal vehicle for the expression of spiritualities. The process of writing the narrative may also become the process of articulating, synthesizing, and reconfiguring these elements in a personal myth. No well-structured framework may have previously existed; these expressions of spirituality emerge in the telling. Disparate practices may now be connected together into an overarching, even though idiosyncratic, vision of "how the world means." In one's journal, the only accusatory voice is one's own. This voice may be cruel, harsh, embittered, but it is not usually a voice that insists upon a standard of orthodoxy, or scans every sentence for false doctrine. Even a theological writer or an evangelist, whose interests clearly do include doctrine or creed, does not let this concern dominate the autobiographical storytelling (Watson, Stringfellow, and Lewis; see below).

For many narrators who long ago rejected the standards and role models of their childhood, including their childhood's religiousness, this freedom from worry over heresy will be a taken-for-granted one; the external presence of religion is no longer a constituent in their experience at all. For a few, it is important to retain these memories of religion as oppressive norm or as negative ideal. They may not yet know who they will be, but they know that they do not want to return to the faith, whatever that faith may have been. LeAnne Schreiber and her brother go to church as a family and receive communion to please their mother, who seems to confuse this act with the return of genuine faith.

> When the priest started to deliver communion, I decided to receive. I wanted to spare Mom any pangs my staying behind might give her, and I also thought the church had probably changed enough for me to receive communion without the pretense of being a good Catholic. . . .

I decided to risk my soul for my mother's sake and hope that God, in whom I didn't believe, would forgive me. . . . Mom, who had continued to cry throughout Mass, turned to Mike and me and explained that her tears were tears of happiness at having us with her at Mass. (Schreiber 1990, 36–38)

Whatever precarious individual spiritual awareness LeAnne finds, she finds alone (*Midstream*) while fly fishing for trout, and it is a far cry from her mother's Catholicism. In the end, in an ironic development, her mother, too, drops out of the church, isolating herself from her priest, as well as all but her closest family, because her vanity won't allow her to be seen as a sick woman. But we are left not with the picture of a loss of faith, but with a recognition that even the mother's piety had been on the surface, a matter of show in the life of a woman who relied upon denial and appearances more than almost any of our other protagonists.

Although the Schreiber situation is not so unusual, only a few narrators bother to remain overtly hostile or rebellious against a traditional religious outlook. In the case of the Zorzas (*A Way to Die*) or the Rabin family (*Six Parts Love*) this hostility adds a petulant and adolescent tone. In *Ellen,* the adolescent protagonist hates a God in whom she doesn't believe, but this fits with the portrait of a sixteen-year-old in the 1960s. The hospice movement in England (which the Zorzas write their book to promote) was founded under religious influences and auspices, and it continues to enjoy a more explicitly religious reputation than in this country. Hence, the Zorza's active acceptance of hospice in spite of its (to them) ridiculous entanglement with religion, might be considered part of their story. The Rabins, who had left America to live in Israel but returned disillusioned several years before father David's fatal illness, feel morally superior to religious people of all faiths (Zorza 1980, 33, 163) and make sure to tell us this in the same tone in which they list by name the friends whom they feel avoided and ignored them during their ordeal with David's ALS. In the case of Paul Monette (*Borrowed Time,* and later *Becoming a Man*), it *is* necessary to the first story, and, in the second narrative, to his political stance as a gay activist, that Western religion be present as the chief force for oppression. But Monette, unlike the Zorzas or the Rabins, can write a story in which this theme is integrated into his and his friend's quest for a spiritual

alternative—the ancient Greece epitomized in the end by Socrates—
which celebrated homosexual love and the quest for truth in the face
of death.

With all these diverse examples in mind, we may say that autobiographies reveal the process of identity formation as a private
sphere matter; they mark off a social world which validates this by
turning religion itself into a private matter. An autobiography will
work best when it portrays one person's search for a way to be a self,
to become a self, one person's spirituality-in-progress, in the making.
This is richly illustrated in Elizabeth Gee's *The Light Around the Dark*—
her journals from her five year struggle with breast cancer. Gee writes
about her full life as scholar-ethicist, mother, wife of a university
president, and includes her deep Mormon faith. Her writings show
us a woman whose personal philosophy is extraordinarily deep and
wide. Throughout the course of her disease process, Gee works on
issues of her own mortality. This was written two years before her
death, when her original cancer had been "cured."

> These days I think more about the theology of my religion, what it says
> about birth, death, immortality, and divinity, and I see more and more
> how it fits with other psychological and philosophical frameworks—
> even physics. Right now I am reading a few works by Joseph Campbell,
> and I am struck, as was he, by the repeating themes that underlie
> mythological symbols and metaphors, how ideas go different ways to
> the same end, toward a suggestion of awakening, a turning both inward
> and outward at the same time to what Campbell calls "the horrendous
> power that is of all creation." I don't think my beliefs are a mere coping
> mechanism, but rather a gift of truth in which I am enlightened by a
> wondrous story of what it means to be human. (97)

What will not fit the genre is any attempt to make an individual's life
exemplify a universal pattern, a norm or ideal that will then be
imposed upon that person's story. A tale that shows a man or woman
who happens to be Christian struggle with illness and death will
sound right; a story that uses a first-person narrative to exemplify
"the good Christian death" will not. The latter will sound stilted, like
an advertisement for Christianity, or like a "proof text" for doctrine;
it will not work as autobiography. For *Christianity* here one may
substitute any *creed*, any *ism* or religious/political agenda. The more
the narrator squeezes his or her story into such a "proof text" mode,

the more the contemporary reader rebels, suspecting that the real story has been covered up in the interest of marketing a belief system.

Yet if the narrators' spirituality is of the kind where religion plays a formative, positive, and interiorized role, the results can be powerful and persuasive testimonies to the continuing vigor of religious traditions within the midst of contemporary culture. Alan Paton, Madeleine L'Engle, Max Lerner, and Nan Shin give their traditions voices who are prophetic, authentic, and deeply aware of the ambiguities of faith in a complex world. The religious faiths involved—Christianity for Paton and L'Engle, Judaism for Lerner, and Zen Buddhism for Shin—become recast as living spiritual perspectives within the narratives of all four. But in all of them the tradition is almost inseparable from whom they are as persons; it has become for them an interiorized personal truth to which they bear witness. Here we meet persons, not "Christianity" or "the Jewish tradition." All of these work as autobiographies and are not to be confused with testimonials or religious propaganda.

Now an interesting test case of this affinity of autobiography for spirituality and not necessarily religion is the very famous narrative of *A Grief Observed*, a journal written after his wife's death by the Christian apologist C. S. Lewis. Lewis first published this under a pseudonym, N. W. Clerk; he recognized how the painful account of his private battle with God conflicted with his confident public theological voice of *The Problem of Pain* and other apologetic writings. The narrator of *A Grief Observed* is a widower furious at God's seeming abandonment of him, hurling invectives ("cosmic sadist") at a God who is now absent just when He is needed most. The tale the reader constructs based on this text alone is that after a short and very happy marriage between two middle-aged people, the wife (H.) becomes ill, and although she goes into remission, she eventually dies of cancer. She dies at peace with God; it is her mourning husband who is alienated and angry. Within the journal, eventually the door that has been slammed shut reopens, and God is present once again, although in a new way. God is not foolish enough to restore a lost situation exactly to what it had been before, the protagonist learns. Moreover, it is in the nature of human relationships to be finite, and so point beyond themselves. After courtship, marriage; after marriage, bereavement. Our eternal destiny is not to be found in such relationships, however valuable they may be. The protagonist must learn this, although in one sense he knew it all before. It is, after all, standard Christian doctrine. At the very end, he quotes form Dante's *Paradiso*: "She turned back to the Eternal Fountain," and in identifying H. with Beatrice and himself with the poet of *Divine Comedy*, the narrator's grief is healed and his search for God consummated.

What makes *A Grief Observed* such an interesting test case of the thesis that autobiography and spirituality go together is that the above summary is not what contemporary American readers receive when they buy the current Bantam edition of this book. In fact, the effect of *A Grief Observed* is quite different than what we may infer was Lewis' original intention. The first reason is that the book has his name on it, and so is marketed alongside *The Problem of Pain, Mere Christianity*, and so on, as one more item in the Lewis corpus. It adds greatly to the impact of the story to know that even the great C. S. Lewis—"Mr. Christianity" himself—could get so angry with God, could be so miserable after a death. The book has often been recommended to devout mourners on just this ground; it grants those in grief permission to experience "unreligious" emotions such as anger at God. But in this fashion it becomes theology in a way possibly not intended.

The other alteration is an even stranger one, separating the voice of the bereaved husband from the reader's expectations. An afterword by Chad Walsh provided in the current edition retells the "true" story of Lewis' marriage to Joy. Instead of an everyman-type sequence of love, marriage, then cancer, we learn that the cancer came first! Lewis married Joy when she was already dying, and apparently (if we can believe Walsh) the marriage began as one of convenience, not love; only later did a genuine romance flower. Lewis never actually *lies* about this in the text; it is hard to judge this as an example of untruth in autobiography. The only parallel instance of "first cancer, then marriage" in our sample, Eric Robinson's *One Dark Mile*, focuses so directly and intensely on the abnormality of the whole relationship that Lewis' revision of his own story is understandable. Yet it is clear that Lewis did *not* intend *A Grief Observed* to be a book about himself, as was his earlier *Surprised by Joy*. On the other hand, the spirituality of the work is real; it is not the great C. S. Lewis as "Mr. Christianity," but a particular widower struggling with God. He knows that there is a Christian ideal of facing death and of mourning; his own experiences cannot be made to fit this, and he does not wish to distort or betray these, however unpleasant and shameful they may be.

What happens when the narrator believes his or her experiences do provide testimony for the truth of Christianity, or of any religious perspective? In a few works, the protagonist becomes caught in the struggle to present "Christianity" as well as tell the story of the "I" suffering illness and death. A conflict ensues; the didactic dimension expands, and the narrator of a story loses out to the would-be theologian. A clear instance of this is Ken Wilber's *Grace and Grit*: the story of his wife Treya's illness and death is interrupted by chapter 11, an overview of Wilber's transpersonal metaphysical system of levels and stages. Wilber tells his readers in an introductory note that religion and psychology were among Treya's most abiding passions, and because he seems sure that Treya's experiences provide proof of his model, the reader needs to be taught the system. Alas, in this case, what we learn from Treya herself remains at a tangent with the goals of her husband as spiritual instructor.

When this process takes over, the life events will then be used almost allegorically to symbolize truths that can be stated completely independently of the narrative. For instance, the theological point may be to teach that God heals in ways that defy human expectations, and that God's true healing is compatible with medical failure. David Watson's *Fear No Evil* teaches this message. Watson, a leading English evangelist whose affiliations with the Charismatic movement led him to reject any simple equation of illness with God's will, trusted God for healing from his terminal cancer. God never fails him, and yet it is clear by the end of the book that the narrator will never recover. Once again, this is the kind of book which is useful to the devout who share Watson's theology of healing, without his nuanced appreciation of what this can include. But is it a successful autobiography? Not entirely. (Note that the rejection of an earlier standard theological interpretation of illness as God's will is shared by many religious authors, conservative and liberal alike; because of this, Watson's work may be very useful as a theological teaching to correct for the misinterpretation that physical healing is *always* God's will.)

JoAnn Kelley Smith, the dying protagonist/narrator of *Free Fall*, is also vulnerable to this problem of becoming a didactic theologian instead of a storyteller. She and her husband state their faith-position early on in her illness; it is important to her to affirm that she does *not* expect healing in the manner Watson does; nor does she believe in a traditional afterlife. These theological positions remain unchanged and indeed are affirmed throughout the narrative. Yet her real agony is that she becomes fearful of not being "a good witness" as she dies a long, lingering death.

> All through my illness I have been haunted with an overwhelming fear that my faith will not stand the final test.
>
> I feel this responsibility so strongly that the possibility of failure creates the deepest of all my fears. . . .
>
> It has been so important to me to demonstrate the reality of Christ in my life that I will do almost anything to preserve that witness. . . .
>
> This fear has virtually immobilized me. (45)

What will happen if she fails to measure up to the Christian ideal of dying, an ideal that seems to leave no room for either anger or hope? When she finds that God lets her abandon this expectation, and remain herself in all her muddled and manipulative imperfection, this is indeed a liberation, bringing life and realism to her narrative. Her task is not to die "perfectly" but to find something real within her suffering, just as Samson found honey in the carcass of a dead lion (Judges 14:5–9). This freedom is the free fall of her title:

> The first leap I made was to give my life to God in this present life. . . .
> When you decide you are going to be God's person and not your own, you really don't know where that is going to take you or what you are going to do or where you are going to be. . . .
>   Dying, in my best understanding after these many months, is that when I take my second leap of faith is when I take my last conscious breath. In faith, I believe that God will reach out and catch me. (57)

As with Lewis, one meets a person here, and the didactic emphasis that lurks all around her story is somewhat mitigated.

In these examples, the tension between religion and spirituality is clearly present, but in a fashion that works at one level (or task), if not at both. A work that fails to be even good religious propaganda is Shireen Perry's *In Sickness and in Health*, which attempts to tell the story of a husband dying of AIDS as a testimony to the power of faith in Christ, and as a message of compassion for AIDS sufferers. One sees lots of religion here: Mark and Shireen are active in church, their friends pray and sing scripture songs with them. Unfortunately, these religious activities are described in the same tone that Perry uses to tell readers about her home decor. We never find out much about Mark's interior life, and his desertion of her for a six-month period is explained away rather than acknowledged by the narrator. Nor does the book provide any realistic information about AIDS as a disease. In short, *In Sickness and in Health* is problematic because it encourages the idea that a spiritual perspective means denial of the realities of human experience, of anger, suffering, and defeat, in favor of a simple set of externally based formulas. Fortunately, few of our authors, whether religious or not, come close to this degree of inauthenticity and evasion.

However, it is also a minority of our narrators for whom religion plays anywhere near the central, articulated role it does for Watson, Smith, Wilber, or Lewis. We now turn to the process of spirituality-in-the-making as it appears in far more of these stories of death and dying.

Eclectic Spirituality

The autobiographical genre is ideal as a vehicle for presenting, and, indeed, formulating in words the shape of one's spirituality. But this is in part because a process similar to that which Luckmann, back in 1967, labeled "the supermarket model" of identity formation holds true, and is visible within these narratives. According to Luckmann, modern postindustrial societies leave identity to the private sphere, where it is actively and energetically constructed out of fragments, self-selected and assembled in highly idiosyncratic fashion by "consumers." A less derogatory image, one closer to the style of our narrators, is that of a quilt: a quilt may be sewn from scraps, but if sewn skillfully, it will have an aesthetic unity and usefulness quite beyond that of any of the individual pieces. For either of these images to work, one needs to recognize the prior existence of a large range of available "scraps," or "products," from which the sewer/shopper may chose.

The quilt image is helpful because it avoids a bias often shown by researchers and commentators toward contemporary nontraditional spiritualities. The identity fragments or quilt pieces may not, from another more scholarly or historically informed perspective, be *isolated* at all; they are instead genuine elements of a larger system that has been ignored or repressed—torn into bits and pieces or discarded. In short, they are meaningful in relation to this larger system, and lose their meaning when put "on the shelf" for "purchase" as independent items. This point of view privileges the religious system out of which individual practices, beliefs, and physical artifacts came, and denigrates the value of their reassembling in a hodgepodge for purposes of contemporary identity formation. To use examples from our texts, mantra-based meditation exercise, chants, and Tibetan temple bells all existed, and still belong, within their various religious systems. A visit to Lourdes is part of Roman Catholic devotional piety. The poem often quoted in our collection,

There is a time for everything,
and a season for every activity under heaven:
a time to be born and a time to die. . . . (Ecclesiates 3:1–2)

is found in the Bible, which in turn is an important constituent of what are now two separate religious traditions. Yet each and every one of these items has become quilt scraps, separate fragments that get sewn together in what a religious purist would call *syncretism*. This term is not just descriptive; it connotes the illegitimate mish-mash of elements whose meanings are twisted when they are forced into a phony compatibility. American society has taken syncretism and made it into an art form, a norm of how to pursue one's individual, private-sphere spirituality. Even if in the past all religions have taken bits and pieces of older traditions and reconstructed these (Ecclesiastes' somber meditations on life and death were at one time part of a trans-Near Eastern tradition of wisdom incorporated by Judaism), by the twentieth century this syncretizing process has become pervasive and very rapid. Tibetan bells, a Hindu mantra, and a quote from the Bible may all make sense to the same protagonist, who will find meaning, or at least try for meaning, through all of these. But the end result will be to turn these into products, all but interchangeable, and no longer filled with the resonances of their particular religious traditions.

In our autobiographies, supermarket, or quilt spirituality, is, if not the rule, at least very frequently encountered. The first and foremost legitimation given is that the protagonists who are deathly sick are more than ready to try *anything* if it will heal them. "If it will help to heal my cancer, I will meditate, hold crystals, visit Lourdes, and eat macrobiotic food," they maintain, just as many will endure chemotherapy, surgery, and radiation while also employing adjunctive therapies. Since health is not a state of full bodily freedom from disease, but a stance of attunement toward, and within, the world and themselves, spiritualities that promise health are worthy of trial even if they never promise cures. Shopping for adjunctive therapies, protagonists enter a true supermarket, and must suspend disbelief in the religious frameworks proposed by some practitioners of such therapies. Anthony Sattilaro simply never believed the macrobiotic worldview, but ate the food and—miraculously—got well. Many, although far from all, adjunctive and alternative therapies come with worldviews, or philosophies that rely upon a quilt-like conglomerate of ancient and modern belief fragments (Ireland's *Life Wish*, and Radner's *It's Always Something*). Human extremity may be God's—and any other force or power's—opportunity. Rather than seeing this as a sinister testimony to the gullibility of the desperately ill, we may find in this stance an American version of the traditional link between spiritual concern and the nearness of death. Whereas the dignified and conventional Paul Tsongas finds in the Episcopal Church a place to renew his links with God and his family (*Heading Home*), other questing protagonists are more adventurous.

Here, the sheer availability of alternatives and the general ethos of California as a haven for such options may be a factor in determining how much of a "supermarket" the protagonist can experience. But to focus on California misrepresents how pervasive this stance of receptive eclecticism has become among the well educated and spiritually concerned population today. When Terry Tempest Williams and her Mormon grandmother attend a Jungian workshop on dreams (appearing in nightgowns for effect!) they do so in Salt Lake City, not known as a bastion of New Age spiritual opportunities. When our narrators or their families become sick, they attend workshops such as those of Stephen Levine (reported by Butler and Rosenblum in *Cancer in Two Voices*), or become involved with support groups whose members participate in and swap stories about a variety of practices (Radner in *It's Always Something*). Some, like Tsongas, are propelled toward seeking on their own a new level of involvement with whatever is easily available as a spiritual resource. Marvin Barrett (*Spare Days*) attends a workshop for cancer patients at Pendel Hill (a Quaker retreat center near Philadelphia) and documents for us the variety of participants, and their stories of adjunctive, alternative, spiritual, and medical quests. The participants share a cancer diagnosis, a certain spiritual openness, and the money to attend such an event. Barrett also notes, with regret, that for some, the openness of "I'll try anything" had been transformed into a fanatical zeal to push *their* choices exclusively and intolerantly. Scare stories of those who died because they resorted to conventional medicine rather than rely solely on the adjunctive/alternative spiritual therapy fill their conversations. Barrett, sensitive and spiritually mature, finds it sad that the quest for alternatives can turn as shrill and as dogmatic as the least appealing forms of traditional religion.

But the "I'll try anything" approach does not generally result in dogmatism, at least not in our narratives. Moreover, the spur of terminal or life-threatening illness only adds urgency to the supermarket model Luckmann believed was already the norm in American society. Alienated from overarching, universal, and intergenerational patterns of meaning, these consumers shop; less for cures, they hope, than for a world, a cosmos, a universe that will feel true and yet reflect some basic sense of order and purpose. The original sources of any of the products on the shelves—whether Asian, Western religious, pagan and nature-oriented, or what-have-you—are barely glimpsed.

And the shopping metaphor in some cases may be less metaphorical than literal. Not only does the protagonist visit a series of experts, all of whom are paid for services, but he or she supplements "shopping" for spiritual meanings with some actual trips to Neiman Marcus. In Jill Ireland's *Life Wish*, for example, the consolation of both kinds of shopping is vividly portrayed. She endures chemotherapy by resorting to visits to adjunctive therapists, several of whose philosophies might be contradictory and all of whom are nevertheless quite helpful to her. Yet her truest satisfaction is found in the celebration of a lavish family Christmas, where who gives what to whom is exquisitely detailed for the reader. Is Ireland's spirituality of the supermarket variety? Or are her trips to what she refers to as "Needless Mark-up" themselves a spiritual practice, an attempt to create a framework of order and meaning, blending consumerism and family values?

The quilt metaphor may be more appropriate to the spiritual eclecticism of an Arthur Frank or a Terry Tempest Williams. They both construct, evaluate, and test possibilities against their own experiences rather than simply "buy." Even Carol Pearson, no longer a model Mormon wife of Utah but a divorced Los Angeles woman whose gay ex-husband needs nursing, blends her remaining loyalty to her tradition with feminist neopaganism (Mary Daly particularly impresses her). She is not so much "shopping" as constructing something that can be used, that will really work in a world where the categories of order and meaning she had previously learned and interiorized no longer fit. Mary Kay Blakely (*Wake Me When It's Over*) sought in political feminism a strong and enduring identity. Under pressures both internal and external (the changed political climate of the 1980s) this identity cracks. Her own healing from a nine-day coma comes, she believes, from the inspired meditation of a feminist New Age "healing circle," which meets back in Indiana while she lies desperately sick in New York City. In this kind of quilt-making process of spiritual formation, it is less necessary to name the exact forces and powers at work, and more important to sew them all into a pattern that makes sense of one's own past and present. This is no longer frantic shopping, but it is a construction out of fragments. It is not heading home, for these protagonist do not want or need a return *back*, yet it requires some use, however oblique, of ingredients from the past.

Judaism as a Religion of Life, not Death?

So far we have looked at the process far more than the content of our narrator's spirituality. It is very easy to emphasize how detached the majority of them are from the mainstream religious traditions of the West, and how the process of supermarket or quilt-making eclectic spirituality complements this detachment. Yet to ignore the abiding role of particular religious motifs, beliefs, and other content is to dramatically overestimate how secular these accounts, and these people, really are. Moreover, in generic discussions of religion such as that which opens this chapter, it is very often Christianity that is being treated as the norm, the standard for what religion is like. Even—or especially—when Christianity is not named, and one hears only about religion, this can well be the case. It is particularly true when the roles of religion in regard to death are so narrowed that the standard function of religion is reassurance that you and your loved ones will not be annihilated at physical death. The majority of theories about, or measures of, religiousness work best for Christianity— not because it is the ideal among religions, but because it subtly guides the expectations of researchers who formulate the theories in the first place. How does this bias affect our evaluation of the religious component of narrators' own spiritual perspectives? Are there influences from religion which are all too easy to overlook? More specifically, given the religious backgrounds of our authors, how do Christian/Jewish differences affect their understandings of spirituality and death?

In order to answer these questions, we should stress that in the past, Christianity in both its Protestant and Roman Catholic branches included elaborate and explicit portraits of the fate(s) of the soul after death. Long before Dante in the fourteenth century, and continuing through the Reformation, specific and vivid expectations about Heaven flourished. (Carol Zaleski's *Otherworld Journeys* and Jean LeGoff's *The Birth of Purgatory* are good sources for how these images structured the hopes and fears of ordinary persons.) Their exact contents changed, so that the theme of a family reunion in heaven emerges as a main concern only with the rise of the modern nuclear family; Protestant piety of the nineteenth century was absolutely cluttered with these hopes. One may say that Christianity not only taught a belief in an afterlife, but depended upon articulating and imaging this for ordinary persons. Challenges to particular beliefs, such as the doctrine of Hell (Daniel Walker, *The Decline of Hell*) were just that: challenges to specifics, not to the very basic idea that an after-death existence was important.

Moreover, in many other ways, Christianity is a religion where concern with death plays an enormous role. Its central rites, particularly the Lord's Supper, with its imagery of the murdered body and shed blood, asks those who share it to "remember Christ's death until he comes." Baptism as well is baptism "into Christ's death," according to Paul (Romans 6:3–11). Devotional practices as well, such as the Stations of the Cross, intensify this concern. The spectacular death-scenes of St. Stephen (Acts 7) and, of course, Jesus himself, paved the way for an entire tradition of martyrdom tales, of a fascination with the violent deaths of the faithful. Christianity was always in the business of confronting death, and dealing explicitly with it (Bregman, *Death in the Midst of Life*).

What often gets overlooked is that the same was not necessarily true of Judaism. Jewish beliefs about an afterlife were always rather shadowy and understated by comparison. Judaism leaves room for death by stipulating an extended period of mourning, but the "theological" significance of all the specific practices of mourning is not stressed. All in all, Judaism's comparative disinterest in death and afterlife has been summed up by the frequently cited generalization: Judaism is a religion of life, not death. This implies that birth, marriage, how to work, love, eat, worship, and study are all religious topics, and far more central religious topics than how to die. Historically, how to lead a Jewish life has been the principle focus—not how to emulate a founder who died, nor how to prepare for an afterdeath existence. Traditional Jews accepted that there would be a world to come in which the righteous would share. Today, liberal Reform Jews frequently claim that Judaism never supported a belief in an afterlife; this may be inaccurate historically, but serves to validate the theme that Judaism is a religion of life, not death. Certainly the idea that this life exists only to prepare one to enter the world to come is quite foreign to Jewish thought.

These widely accepted generalizations about both religions have some important implications, even when one is dealing with the worldviews of comparatively secularized persons. When we acknowledge that death has been a high-profile, central topic in Christianity but not in Judaism, we may wonder how it is that a large proportion of our collection of personal narratives are written by persons of Jewish background. In contrast, we have found exactly *two* narratives of any types from authors of Mediterranean Christian background; one of these is by Paul Tsongas, writing not as a Greek-American but as a U.S. Senator. Even if it is misleading to assume that our collection in any way reflects demographics (see chapter 1), the fact that so many Jewish authors write within this genre is interesting. What is really important to ask, then, is how Judaism's traditional lack of concern with death (relative to traditional Christianity) affects what they have to say.

We note that tales of Jewish background are not distributed equally by category. While six of twenty-five tales of the narrator's near-death and recovery (Type I) fit under this rubric, an astonishing one out of every three examples of Type III ("How I watched a loved one die") do; twelve of thirty-six stories of nursing a loved one through a terminal illness are authored by persons who come from Jewish backgrounds. By contrast, Jewish authors are relatively underrepresented in Type IV works, tales of mourning by widows and widowers. How can we interpret this, in the light of the claim that Judaism is a religion of life, not death, and also in the light of what the narrators themselves do and do not tell us?

A first step in any interpretation is to note how little a role Judaism *as a religion* plays in our collection of narratives. "Of Jewish background" is the best way to characterize the authors, precisely because for so many of them no other living connection with Judaism appears explicitly in the stories. Based on these, one could never reconstruct anything of the ritual practices of Jewish mourning, including the family's sitting Shiva for a week after the death. One could never learn a thing about Kosher food laws, Jewish marriage and divorce laws, or ritual bathing. Almost none of these appear in our narratives. By these obvious and explicit criteria of religion, then, we have narratives by secular Jews who lack both knowledge of and involvement with their religious tradition. For instance, Martha Lear tells the story of her husband's death from heart disease—angry at the medical establishment and affirming an ethic of control and autonomy. One learns that the Lears are Jewish, just as one learns that Joan Gould—whose temperament and ethical vision is very different—is Jewish. But the Gould family party occurs on Christmas; this is a taken for granted fact of their lives. No Jewish festivals, religious scenes either positive or negative, appear in either book. This is the norm for the majority of examples in our collection.

In some cases, we do find references to Judaism as a religion. These, however, tell an ambivalent story. Particularly revealing is the account by Stephen Rosenfeld of his parents' deaths. The parents, living in the small city of Pittsfield, Massachusetts, had helped found and support the local synagogue. It would have been completely out of character to have held the funeral service anywhere else. But Rosenfeld recalls how, at his father's funeral, the traditional readings were replaced by ones from Emerson, Dunne, and Goethe, especially selected in advance by his father:

Steadily, tranquilly, cheerfully
He finished the voyage of life. (Rosenfeld 1977, 124–26)

Rosenfeld, the son/narrator, finds this especially appropriate. Although his father's loyalty to the synagogue and the Jewish community of his hometown was unquestionable, an inspiring passage from Emerson best conveyed what his father's real faith—his *spirituality* in our use of the term—had really been. All along it was not Judaism as a religion, but a version of personal reflection and civic loyalty that made his father the person he was.

Yet once again, if Judaism is a religion of life, not death, there is something fitting in Rosenfeld's father's life and funeral celebration. Not the intense preoccupation with God, death, and the soul's destiny—the characteristic focus of Christianity—but a sense of community, personal uprightness, and faith in the value and goodness of human beings permeate the legacy of both the father and the views of his son. What counts is not interior salvation, but a life lived in solid relationships with people, in whose memory one may hope to live on just as one lives on in one's children. Rosenfeld shares this ethos with Joan Gould, especially as she paints her portrait of her dead husband, Martin. It is certainly very congruent with Philip Roth's more emotionally complex tribute to his own father in *Patrimony*.

What other Jewish authors would take issue with in this account is not its lack of "God-talk," but its social complacency. Max Lerner and Elizabeth Glaser, along with Barbara Rosenblum and Sandra Butler (joint authors of *Cancer in Two Voices*) are moved by a passion for justice, a prophetic sense of distance from the status quo and the traditional centers of power. For Rosenblum and Butler, taking up unpopular causes, and living an alternative lifestyle as a lesbian couple, seem to come naturally. This is what being Jewish meant; not a religion but "Always understand we live on the margins. Always" (7). For both women, this was a fundamental element in their identity, "a sense of urgency of a principled life" (6). Glaser, by temperament neither feisty nor subversive, takes up the unpopular and controversial cause of pediatric AIDS research, for it is the only *just* response to the injustice of being stricken with the AIDS virus. To struggle against social prejudice, the indifference of the Reagan administration, and the persecution of the *National Enquirer* is her spirituality, and it is an appropriation of the prophetic strand of the Jewish tradition.

He has shown you, O man, what is good.
And what does the Lord require of you?
To act justly and to love mercy
and to walk humbly with your God. (Micah 6:8)

In the light of her enactment of this theme, one might even return to
the case of Martha Lear, and revision her critique of the medical
establishment as a parallel, if much less successful example of the
battle for social justice.

Nevertheless, of all of these figures, only Lerner invokes any of the
explicit religious content of Judaism to interpret his own personal
plight. In his reading of the Bible, one struggles and contends with
God, rather than submits or surrenders. Thus his attempt to voice his
experiences facing death is titled *Wrestling with the Angel*, referring to
the story of Jacob in Genesis 32. A more revealing title might be
Glaser's: *In the Absence of Angels*. Neither God nor angels come to her
assistance. Elizabeth and her husband Paul depend on friends, political allies, and her own courage and sense of outrage. She senses no
cosmic wrestling partner, only Senator Jesse Helms as her opponent
(who, along with *The National Enquirer*, she finds beyond her capacity
for forgiveness). Although it may be superficial to label such a narrative "secular" and entirely dismiss the residual presence of Jewish
tradition in it, the absence of God, of a transcendent framework for
meaning, or a religious interpretation of death and suffering is a
somber testimony to the world of American Judaism as Glaser experiences and embodies it.

Why, then, are so many narratives of death and dying written by
Jewish authors? Does the very fact that Judaism's traditions about
death remained underdeveloped, in contrast to Christianity's, free
Jewish authors to explore concerns in a personal rather than theologically determined fashion? Not only the erosion of the tradition,
but even its disinterest in the topic when in full strength makes new
approaches to dying and grief a real possibility for Jewish authors.
Perhaps the very generalization that Judaism is a religion of life, not
of death can be turned on its head: because Judaism as a religion is so
depleted or absent or muted in our narratives, their authors may
focus on death in a new mode. This suggestion becomes plausible if
one considers writing an autobiography as a task appropriate for
spirituality but not so fitting for religion (as we defined and discussed

these two terms earlier in this chapter). Whether or not that spirituality can be discerned as Jewish, the very gap left by religious disinterest in death leaves a door open to personal, idiosyncratic explorations of meaning. If this is the case, then, secular Jewish narratives arise out of a slightly different process than do secular Christian narratives. The latter know the tradition in its articulated, massive, and unambiguous form, and dismiss or reject it (as in LeAnne Schreiber's visit to church with her mother). The Jewish authors, dimly aware that Judaism has always been a religion of life, not of death, may write of death secularly, knowing that it has not been a Jewish topic. In contrast, mourning *has* been a Jewish topic, and so, significantly, there are nowhere near the proportion of accounts by persons of Jewish background focused upon grief and bereavement.

Although we speculate that what fuels the accounts by persons of Jewish background is the need to say something about death and dying, using a genre that encourages personal rather than traditional or communal visions of what is real, we must balance this by stating how clearly the preoccupations of Gould, Glaser, and Lear are matched and mirrored by authors of Christian backgrounds. Even the devout Madeleine L'Engle writes of family relationships, ancestors, and places she and her husband Hugh had lived, not of the after-death destiny of his soul. L'Engle, along with almost all of our contemporary Christian authors, would take strong exception to the claim that Christianity is a religion of death, or one preoccupied with a life beyond death. If the statement about Judaism as a religion of life implies the obverse of Christianity, they would reject this entirely. Alan Paton's account of his wife's death and of their life together reveals not an interiorized, other-worldly link between God and the soul, but a life of loving mutuality, and an everyday spirituality generated within their marriage that propelled both of them to break with their conventional backgrounds and oppose the South African government's racial politics.

As for the majority of authors from Christian backgrounds for whom religion no longer plays any substantive role in their lives or spiritual vision, the same focus on family intimacy, memorializing, and human community can be found here as in the works by Gould and Rosenfeld, for instance. Richard Meryman's wife Hope is remembered and mourned just as Gould remembers and mourns her husband; neither Hope Meryman's loss of religious faith during the course of her illness, nor her husband's indifference to such matters, influences the real story he wants to tell. The Massies, facing their son Bobby's hemophilia (*Journey*), struggle with the disease, their own despair, and society's indifference just as energetically and prophetically as does Elizabeth Glaser. Jocelyn Evans, of Scottish background, living and writing in London, is as angry at the British medical establishment in her account of *Living with a Man Who Is Dying* as is Martha Lear in New York City. One might agree that her Presbyterian ancestry included the same prophetic strand as does Lear's Judaism—but a far more probably influence on Evans is husband Aron's Marxism.

To fill in this picture, we must also remind ourselves that all of these authors write in a context in which saying anything about death is difficult. Although Christianity traditionally says a lot and Judaism traditionally says little, it is generally agreed that contemporary society's refusal to say anything, its utter denial of death, is unhealthy and unrealistic. Neither religious tradition can be invoked to support or justify it. In fact, the very same generalization that Judaism is a religion of life, not of death has probably been used in other contexts to abet American avoidance of death. A religion focused exclusively on life will leave death to doctors, to a medical model, and remain silent about its meaning. Yet neither Judaism nor Christianity opted for the silence and denial many of our authors protest against. Whether being of Jewish background restricts one's religious resources in developing personal spiritualities of death and dying, or— for the very reason we have given—may actually free authors to engage in a distinctly contemporary style of encountering death, the real lesson of our collection may be that a life or faith that excludes death completely is impossible to live.

The Wisdom of Surrender

What should be apparent from our treatment so far is that just as "Americans deny death" is an oversimplification, so "Americans are secularized" is also a half-truth. For all the distance of our authors from the traditional eschatological preoccupations of Christianity, or from any of the religious aspects of Judaism, we find it inadequate to speak of their spiritualities only in terms of distance and absence. If the medical model of illness, dying, and death is the truly secular discourse of our society, all of our authors are in some degree of protest against its tyranny. If religious traditions no longer enjoy a monopoly of meanings in this area of human experience—and this would be one definition of secularization as a process—that does not mean that the frameworks of ultimate meaning have vanished. They clearly have not. What we have discovered in our narratives is a space where such meanings can be created, however elusive, evanescent, and severed from major institutional settings these may be. *Spirituality* is the contemporary term that best captures these meanings, although as indicated, a clear and easy split between *spiritual* and *religious* may obscure some deep connections.

If there exists an emergent spirituality of dying, of facing death, what does it look like? Are there generalizations, patterns of insight that run through many, although not all, of our narratives? Since autobiography focuses so heavily on the unique individual, on this particular set of events and persons, the whole idea of searching for generalizations may seem to threaten the integrity of each individual case to be and remain itself. But, as in our discussion of death as destruction and loss (chapter 7), it is possible to state something about what introspective and articulate Americans, writing in the autobiographical mode, discern and discover when they enter the special spiritual state of "being dying." Facing death, whether or not one eventually recovers, brings a certain knowledge to many of our narrators.

> In an important sense cancer is a calling, a calling to adventure that if accepted culminates in the passage to a new humanity and an even greater understanding of the wonder of life. The other response, the other view of cancer or any crisis—that rejects the call, that refuses to look for meanings, other sorts of wellness and possibilities— transforms the potential adventure into a disaster, a void, a state where promise and hope are relinquished, and where the protagonist is a victim. (Gee 1992, 71)

We will call this the wisdom of surrender. It comes after the massive effort to buttress and advance the self's autonomy, its freedom to will and to remain an active living presence even in the midst of death. As we saw in chapters 4 and 5, when face-to-face with the medical establishment, our authors unquestionably opt for an active and autonomous stance. Becoming sick should not diminish one as a moral agent, a decisionmaker—yet it clearly does, given the nature of contemporary Western medicine. The only alternative to reasserting one's autonomy, one's control over one's life and medical treatment, is to become a victim, a passive recipient of others' manipulative decisions. In the joint account by the heart patient Lesher and his doctor Halberstam (*A Coronary Event*), we see the archetype or even caricature of this battle between two controlling egos both determined to "do it my way," who can join forces only because they are dedicated to a similar value system, one that touts a ruthlessly selfish autonomy at the expense of all else.

Moreover, as we saw in chapter 7, military models of battle against the disease, the "bad cells" of cancer, encourage an extension of this ethic into one's deepest experience of illness. Within the hospital bureaucracy, to stay in control is a must for a patient who wants to retain his or her humanity. Within one's own body, cancer represents a threat to self-determination, to one's ego-strength and ability to remain an agent rather than a victim. According to Wendy Williams, the power within is what made it possible for her ten cancer survivors to win their battle; they never saw themselves as victims. Feisty persons do well; those who lose are the ones who let themselves be bossed around by their doctors, and perhaps others in their lives before that.

Max Lerner, for whom the adjective *feisty* is an understatement, expresses this idea magnificently. "My triumph over illness" is the subtitle of his account. Cancer and death are enemies, but against old Max (who at age seventy-eight begins his encounters with two cancers and a heart attack) they really do not have a fighting chance. Lerner exerts autonomy and self-determination on a scale worthy of a mythic hero. Ironically, one of the experts whose advice he weighs and rejects is his own son Michael, who pioneered research of adjunctive and alternative cancer therapies and founded the Commonweal Cancer Help Program in Bolinas, California. He consults Michael and all his children, as he consults with others, but he makes his own choices. He remains in control of his own fate.

And so it is no surprise that at the deepest level of religious imagery, Lerner selects from all of Jewish tradition one particular story that exemplifies struggle, activity, and even contending as the proper stance in relation to the divine. Jacob wrestles with "a man" throughout one night by the ford of Jabbok. The physical contest was a draw; the spiritual one, a victory for Jacob. At dawn, his opponent is forced to bless him, and says "Your name will no longer be Jacob, but Israel, because you have struggled with God and with men and have overcome." (Genesis 32:28). Later, Jewish tradition substituted "an angel" for "God," but in Lerner's account this change is irrelevant. To wrestle with God and with men is more noble, more excellent, and more worthy of a blessing than to submit. As Lerner himself puts it, "In life-threatening crises the task is to fight death without denying its reality and the preciousness it lends to life, while at the same time asserting life" (Lerner 1990, 168).

Well, we can't all be Jacob, and we certainly can't all be Max Lerner. What we find significant in our accounts is how many of our protagonists reach a point where they cease to want to follow this model. A turning point in their lives comes as they recognize how an alternative path opens up an even deeper kind of blessing. Not in relation to doctors and hospitals, but in relation to a universe where surrender is wiser and truer than a never-ending struggle. This is a difficult lesson for anyone to learn, and it is particularly vulnerable to becoming distorted into a plea for overall passivity, dependency— and so colluding in one's own dehumanization at the hands of medicine. For some who object to any idealizing of submission or surrender, this ideal is also suspiciously gendered, women are *supposed* to submit to their husbands as to God. Why legitimate an obsolete sexism in the name of some supposed cosmic wisdom?

Agnes DeMille is the match for Max Lerner—by any standards of character, feistiness, creativity, and intelligence. Her enormous energy and self-discipline, plus her years of training as a dancer, help her overcome much of the damage from a major stroke. She has a long history of taking control of her body and her movements, and so in her own eyes has a distinct advantage when it comes to physical rehabilitation. Moreover, like Lerner, by the time she suffers her stroke (at about age sixty-eight) she has already produced a body of creative work and knows herself as firmly established in her chosen field. She does not rest on past accomplishments, however; she is rehearsing for a special performance, with her own dance company, when she becomes ill.

In *Reprieve: A Memoir*, DeMille tells how "the insult" to her body led to a new life, a life to which she had been forcibly reborn. What happens to her is that she recovers the freshness and vividness of sounds and sights, remembered from childhood. And then something else follows:

> And I suddenly was aware that I was happy, happy in a way that I had not been before. Happy in the moment, contented, trusting. It was enough somehow. I had stopped sweating after the moment. Great ideas are not promoted from this nerveless state, nor great art, nor in truth anything at all, except possibly wisdom. (201–202)

In her rebirth, she experiences awareness and "awakeness" which has nothing to do with career or achievement. "I had reached the state of the coral polyp and 'simply was' and that was enough" (202). Although she knows that this experience could be linked to Christian faith, the same faith her sister, dying of cancer, holds, she refrains from building up such a connection. It is enough that this wisdom came to her, and that she receives it. In its light, she reevaluates her career, her contribution to dance, recognizing and perhaps, overemphasizing its limits. Such detachment and objectivity flows from the wisdom of that nerveless moment.

Agnes Demille is not alone. Again and again, at the very heart of our narrators' encounters with death and their own existence, we hear of such moments. Doris Lund, mother of dying teenaged son Eric recognizes in such moments not salvation or triumph over death, but a rockbed of truth of existence no longer controlled by "sweating after the moment." Arthur Frank, who as a sociologist of medicine is aware of the philosophical and ethical issues surrounding illness, comes to a vivid apprehension of what life at the will of the body can bring, when he gazes out his window at the moon. This moment teaches him something; not didactic propositions about God or fate or death, but something more real. Elizabeth Gee tells of a similar experience watching the early morning sun play on the Colorado mountains:

> Suddenly, I felt a release from my fear, from my fixation on biopsies, surgeries, and procedures. . . . Now I feel no heaviness of mind. . . . The storm is behind me. Instead of despairing. I look out on the long expanse of my life to fine threads of light coming from all sides,

to traveling through dark spaces but passing through to clearings. (136–37)

Oliver Sacks injures his leg while mountain climbing alone, and as he attempts to crawl back down, he is vividly aware of how absolutely special every moment, every tiny perception has become. He does not expect to survive the night on the mountain and recognizes how this very enhancement of his vitality is itself a surrender to the certainty of impending death. "All of these thoughts and images . . . were essentially happy and essentially grateful." He quotes Auden: "Let your last thinks all be thanks." (Sacks 1984, 34).

In all of these examples, as in DeMille's, the experience of sudden, grateful immersion in life's moment, in the bare "isness" of being, is presented in terms free from "overbelief," or indeed from any consolidated and articulated belief system. These moments happen; they are graced in some way. But protagonists do not meet God, nor do they enter Nirvana, and they have no interest in building up from this fleeting, but lasting, touch of wisdom, any comprehensive philosophy or religious worldview. Yet these moments happen to them.

Other protagonists, filled with the same sense that they have been graced not by great ideas or great actions, but by some hitherto-hidden wisdom, do frame this experience within a spiritual vision of a more communicable kind. Frank Maier had been a conventional Roman Catholic, a *Newsweek* journalist, and a member in good standing of "the old boys' network"—or so he paints himself. Terminally ill with liver failure, he begins to read the Bible late at night in his hospital bed. He learns, among other things, of his own great denial. What he had mistaken for acceptance of death was actually a macho-religious version of "I'll do it my way." And the easy faith he had always taken for granted is gone. What he receives instead is a new and immediate awareness of God's nearness, a state tied to his reading of Isaiah 49:15–16:

Can a mother forget her infant, be without tenderness for the child of her womb? Even if she should forget, I will never forget you. See, upon the palms of my hand I have carved your name.

"These three sentences . . . were to become the mantra for my dying. On nights when I could not sleep, I repeated them over and over"

(Maier 1991, 98–99). And so, Maier, too, experiences epiphanies, "so fresh, so simple and so self-evident that I wondered why I had never thought of them before ... jolted into a state that I can describe as both enlightening and somehow holy" (132–133).

Somehow holy: this is what one senses when one acknowledges that powers are at work in the universe that transcend wills. To surrender to this holiness is not defeat. It is certainly not a surrender to death or disease in themselves, directly. These epiphanies brings wisdom, a striking clarity about what really matters, and a recognition of how falsehood, denial, and egocentricity had previously ruled one's life. Protagonists who receive this wisdom bear witness not only to suffering and illness, but to a "how" for encountering both holiness and death. The power is not necessarily within and it is certainly far from the titanic ego-strength exhibited by Max Lerner—and by some of the other protagonists in their own moments. And even to these protagonists themselves, it matters less whether they recover medically, and more whether they live, awake and in the full presence of what is somehow holy in life.

This holy wisdom of surrender is, as well, a wisdom in the presence of death. Last thoughts and spare days are its proper time-markers. In some sense, it may be what human beings can learn as practice for their own deaths, as these loom close. One of Wendy Williams' cancer fighters actually comes to this conclusion, almost in spite of the theme of her journalist-narrator. Finding a dying gull on the beach, Julie tells how

> Terrified and hypnotized I watched. . . . I expected a long wait. Death must take time. It must be an immense and monumental process requiring many hours. The bird circled its long neck round and round several times, hid its head under a wing, drew three long breaths—and died. Death was startlingly simple, the surrendering a natural culmination of life. Surrender is appropriate and timely, it is not capitulation. (Williams 1990, 108)

If we remain true to accounts such as these, we may find how both God and nature can become the object of one's surrender. But this is a terrible phrasing for what DeMille, Maier, and Julie experience. In this wisdom, one ceases to exist in a realm of clearly designated objects. One is grasped, graced, awakened, and reborn in the same moment of nearness to death. Yet we also note these same narrators' own reservations and silences. Out-of-body experiences, reincarnation, and glimpses of a blessed afterdeath condition are thoroughly foreign to them. All of the eschatological concerns of the New Age spiritualities as well as of traditional Christianity remain outside the vision of what the protagonists experience, and narrators convey. The wisdom of surrender is not information about death, or God, or possible universes outside this one. It lies, instead, close to the bone of the everyday, yet a million miles distant from ordinary conventional daily patterns, just as the gull's death failed to live up to the expectation of "an immense and monumental process." It is a wisdom of how to be whole and yet mortal in a universe where God has carved us on the palm of his hand, or where death is a natural culmination of life. It is the beauty of the moon, shining through the window.

Chapter Nine

TOWARD A NEW VISION OF DEATH?

IN THE LITERATURE WE HAVE JUST SURVEYED, WE find both the denial of death so well documented for American society, and a variety of attempts to say *something* about it that will ring true. The denial comes at many levels: the protagonists deny, they hide the truth from their families and friends, and they are frequently shunned and excluded, sent to the "moon" when it is known that they are terminally ill. Yet the need to tell the story, to speak what no one normally wants to hear, to replace lies with truth, fuels all of our narrators. They cannot keep silent. Their words, and the publicness of their tales, belies a simple generalization that denial is the way Americans still face death. We find, then, that our study captures American society at loose ends: no longer content with silence, removed from the atmosphere of Andrew Malcolm's 1950s, when everything linked to illness, suffering, and death was pushed off until someday. Today, when persons get sick, die, and grieve, more and more wish to find room for such critical experiences within a landscape of human life. But although all our authors share this wish to move beyond pure denial, they do not know in which direction one should move. They do not speak with one voice.

In fact, the autobiographical mode works because, modestly, each narrator speaks only for him or herself. That is all that the majority of them claim to do. It is not yet time for a society-wide, publicly recognized and accepted alternative to denial and silence—at least not as to the deeper meanings of illness and death, to which our narrators bear witness. Even a commonly heard statement from "the death awareness movement," namely that "death is a natural event," does not reach the level of such a publicly accepted alternative. For a few narrators, such as Terry Tempest Williams, attending carefully and lovingly to "nature," the world of the nonhuman environment can become part of the human encounter with death. But for the majority of our narrators, the meaning of "natural event" is thoroughly obscure, perhaps because with few exceptions, they are on the whole ignorant and distant from the natural world, or at least uninterested and unfamiliar with its complexities. They attend instead to the unique personal relationships of the protagonists and tell how these fractured or endured. They observe the minute details of caretaking, of the protagonists' medical progress or deterioration. They chart an inner landscape filled with intimations of mortality, and learn first-hand death's single privacy. Within the context of our narratives, to say that "death is a natural event" may mean no more than that it is acceptable as subject matter for a writer.

As we mentioned in the previous chapters, some narrators present a strong resistance to going beyond the particular, the individual, the authenticity of this set of events that happened to this particular person. For Barbara Peabody, Gerda Lerner, and others who express this perspective, no generalized universal vision of death, whether as natural event or transition into the afterlife, would be desirable. Holding to the particular means refusing not only spirituality in the terms defined in the previous chapter, but the quest for an understanding of death that American society as a whole may accept and find meaningful.

We note, however, that it is no longer the case that denial and silence characterize what our society as a whole accepts as normative in regard to death. Instead, we find that first-person narratives of dying, death, and grief have a role we believe is likely to be needed for a while to come. Without a society-wide, articulated, shared vision of death that will inform public policy or become a taken-for-granted background to specific discussions, the closest we will come is the view that, like religion, one's view of death is a private sphere matter. Audre Lorde, Diane Rubin, Max Lerner, and each of our authors is entitled to have her own individual say, to tell his own stories, and bear witness to their own and their loved ones' suffering. They are not, in the ideology of the private sphere, as described by Luckmann (see chapter 1), entitled to impose their own idiosyncratic perceptions and intuitions on the rest of us. Even Kübler-Ross' famous five stages seem to some like the imposition of a false uniformity that stifles the autonomous individual's right to die in four, or six, or no stages at all.

We, in turn, are not obligated to hear them and their views by any requirements of our major institutions and their norms. If we, searching for fragments with which to construct our own identities, *wish* to hear and attend to them, that is our choice, an expression of autonomy. Within their own stories, they generate a sense of moral authority that tries to make a claim on the reader. But the claim made by any autobiography is a restricted one: "Listen to my story! Yes, this really happened! Someone was here!" Autobiography is the vehicle for bearing witness, not for commanding that a new worldview be adopted by all. Although we can see how the majority of narrators find death as destruction and loss meaningful, while ignoring death as punishment for sin, the particular ways that they convey what is lost or destroyed are (as we saw in chapter 7) diverse and to some extent incompatible with one another. Even those whose identities rely upon religious traditions do so in a manner finally compatible with the limits of private-sphere identity and its restricted claims.

When we label the situation we have described here a "transition," we thereby assume that it represents a midway place on a journey to a new, shared, publicly articulated vision of death. But perhaps this situation may be our long-term one. American society may not ever replace a lost religiously based vision of death with one equally public and firmly accepted. The situation where autobiography is the favored and appropriate vehicle may be here to stay. This implies that the very hope for a shared society-wide vision about death and illness is misguided. At best, we will have tolerance for differences at the private level, and techniques to adjudicate and adjust for incompatible beliefs at the public level (for example, where health care policy options such as advance directives or active euthanasia are at stake). In that case, not only will the flow of autobiographies not cease, but these may increasingly be felt to be the only legitimate way to approach the topic.

However, we will continue to think in terms of a transition period, a time when saying something is necessary, but no one yet feels authorized to speak for all. Death, illness, and grief are major human experiences, and no society which forgets them in favor of youthful, deathless humanity can live with the latter for very long. The era of denial and silence lasted, really, only from around the turn of the century (at the earliest) up through the 1950s and 1960s (at the latest). To imagine our current situation as continuing forever is too unlikely, even if we cannot make good guesses about the future vision of death that Americans will eventually create and accept.

Moreover, the decades when the majority of these accounts appeared coincide with rising awareness of a crisis in the healthcare system of this country. The crisis on the surface is one of resources and finances, not directly of meanings. The cost of healthcare is out of control. A large percentage of our population has no health insurance coverage. Drugs are too expensive, medical tests are done unnecessarily, and fear of malpractice lawsuits adds to the costliness of care. While high-tech medicine is glamorous and attracts research money, primary care, especially in rural areas, becomes unavailable. All of these problems, now familiar and under discussion for sweeping reform, lurk in the background of many of our accounts. Autobiography is not, however, the preferred genre for airing them; as we have seen, our authors are discrete to the point of prudishness about the financial aspects of their illnesses. But the healthcare crisis, in the sense of the public financial crisis, does, we believe, play a role in our narrators' grasping after elusive and highly personal meanings for death.

For underneath the public health crisis is a philosophical crisis: what are the legitimate goals of medicine? What ought to limit the hopes we may place upon it? When should we abandon the framework of "cure" and turn, instead, to the need for "care" in the face of impending and inevitable death? As we saw in chapter 4, medicine from the bottom up reveals more clearly the negative face of technology from the patients' perspective. Many of our narrators find an alternative in hospice care that is genuinely helpful and which philosophically satisfies them. Yet, even if room can be made for hospice, whose philosophy of "low-tech, high-touch" is a welcome relief from the more publicized face of American medicine, will this answer to the deeper need for a society-wide vision of how to bear witness to life-threatening illness and death? "Even so, we were still in hell," Diane Rubin reminds us, after praising and thanking her hospice team. Are catastrophic illness and death truly and inevitably so hellish that this is why American society can still find nothing publicly to say about them? Not all our narrators would agree. If "hell" signifies despair in the face of suffering, then many would vigorously deny Rubin's claim as anything more than a true statement about her experience.

But suppose the situation of American medical practice undergoes significant changes, of the kind often suggested in our narratives. Adjunctive therapies are completely integrated into mainstream allopathic practices; no one is forced to choose either one or the other. Doctors are trained to be more humane, so that their education rewards caring and healing rather than primarily technical expertise. Doctors are remunerated on a different scale, so that primary care and family practitioners are paid better than surgeons. Not only are advance directives (Living Wills) universally acknowledged as valid, and everyone encouraged to sign them, but death-prolonging measures and procedures for the terminally ill become a thing of the past. Neither doctors nor their patients' families would normally even consider such steps, considering them cruel as well as medically useless. Hospice is the norm for care for the dying. These changes would be applauded by almost every one of our narrators.

Yet all these changes themselves depend upon an altered philosophy of health, illness, and death—not just altered financial incentives. Changes in our societal vision of health, illness, and death are certainly on the way—in their own fashion; our narratives collectively as well as individually testify to that trend—but the changes are not yet here. Attempts to cut costs may bring them about, but without some level of philosophical shift, an option that will work financially will be rejected as morally (or politically) unacceptable. Active euthanasia, the direct killing of a patient by a doctor, is the best known example of such an unacceptable option.

Behind the kind of changes listed, and desired by many of our narrators, there is another one more basic: a shift away from the central belief of allopathic medicine that disease is caused by specific organisms. Against these bacteria and viruses, doctors can shoot "magic bullets" to affect cures, drugs that will kill disease but leave the rest of the patient's body unharmed. The hope for such magic bullets against AIDS, cystic fibrosis, Alzheimer's Disease, and, of course, cancer, is not one our narrators are willing, or likely, to renounce. Nor, seemingly, is medical research, which goes on as if such solutions were a possibility. The large majority of our narrators, like the large majority of the general population, believes in this vision of medicine's task, and trusts that researchers' quests for cures and vaccines are worth funding. Even when the researchers themselves become far more cautious and skeptical (as in the case of AIDS now), the assumption that research can create cures remains pervasive. Several of the AIDS sufferers in our narratives doggedly hope to hang on long enough for the "cure" to arrive. Raising money to fight the disease is the motive behind Glaser's (pediatric AIDS), Deford's (cystic fibrosis), the Massies' (hemophilia), and other work in our collection. This hope for magic bullet cures is exactly the kind of publicly voiced, universal belief that our society does *not* share in regard to death's meaning.

What if, shortly in the future, several such magic bullets were found to make AIDS and cancer both easily treatable and completely curable conditions? What if curing patients with either disease became no more complex or dramatic than the cure for someone in the earliest stage of Lyme Disease, when three weeks worth of antibiotics will usually do the trick? Since cancer and AIDS account for the overwhelming majority of our narratives, and together are the most dreaded diseases Americans can imagine, would such miraculous and marvelous medical news significantly reshape the American landscape of death, making the quest for a way to speak of it unnecessary? In other words, if our narratives are really about cancer and AIDS, and not death in itself, then eliminating the two diseases would let us all sink back into silence and denial. Persons would continue to die of heart, kidney, and blood pressure conditions, just as they die in car crashes: but the flood of autobiographical narratives would perhaps be reduced to a trickle. Or would it?

At present, we find that even to consider such a scenario requires us to accept the impossible, or at least the highly unlikely. The war against cancer begun in 1971 may not have been lost, but early detection and not magic bullets is the reason. As for AIDS, the individual ailments it spawns can be treated. But there, too, the magic bullet theory of disease does not work, or does not work fast enough to prevent the epidemic and the opportunistic diseases it spins off (such as the renewed appearance of tuberculosis) from wreaking havoc and catastrophe. To predict unrealistically hopeful medical developments and speculate on how these would affect Americans' need for autobiographical statements about sickness and death seems doubly unwarranted.

In fact, if our narratives teach us anything, they ought to make us timid about grand predictions, about charting future trends. The human world is impinged upon by the world of viruses, bacteria, weird genetic abnormalities, and so on. Like our protagonists who can no longer assume that, having always been healthy, they will remain so, we are aware of how such an alien, microscopic, and seemingly arbitrary force such as a virus can drastically destroy a human organ, a body, a world. This is one of the reasons why philosopher Alasdair MacIntyre believes that the so-called social sciences are inherently unable to be scientifically predictive (MacIntyre 1984, 100). Human processes, causes, and forces work within a world that includes viruses, and so on, the behavior of which lie outside of what sociologists or psychologists can take into account. At the worst, should the AIDS epidemic continue unchecked and affect America to the same extent that it is affecting Uganda, we will have a flood of new narratives similar to *Eric* and *Ellen*, tales told by mothers of teenaged victims of the disease. Moreover, the comeback of tuberculosis has already produced *Grandma Cherry's Spoon*, a memoir of an earlier generation's struggle to forge lives for themselves amid families ravaged by the pervasive presence of the "white plague."

Whether or not this fearful future, or the rosier one of cures and benevolent healthcare reforms, emerges as the real future, we believe American society will continue to need and read first person mortal narratives. As yet, there is no shared vision of how dying, death, and grief ought to impact and transform the world of the always-young, deathless, autonomous individual. When such a vision becomes visible, when its outlines are seen more clearly, then the experiences of our narrators may play a different role. Some will be recognized as prophets, ahead of their day, able to foresee a framework of authentic meanings and live fully within it. Others will become mere historical curiosities, whose works will evoke a subtle repulsion in the reader, just as the Victorian death-bed scenes now do for many of us. Already, the ideology of an early example, Gunther's *Death Be Not*

Proud, strikes us at times this way; when Johnny Gunther refers to his terminal brain tumor as his "bump," we feel we are peeking back at another era's pretensions and evasions that no longer feel right to us. Will the readers of the future find Terry Tempest Williams' *Refuge* dated in its romanticized vision of nature's destructive cycles? Or will her book be lauded as a strong and powerful statement of what will come to seem obvious connections between nature, bodies, and the renewal of life and spirit? A work such as Lynn Caine's *Widow* still seems honest and forceful after nearly twenty years; in the future its matter-of-fact charting of a widow's craziness may strike readers as tedious and unnecessary.

For the readers of the present and the near future, however, autobiographical narratives are a resource and a promise. If these authors can bear witness to suffering, dying, and death, it is evidence that others can learn the secret of how to endure and even be healed as they travel into death, or watch their loved ones make that journey. The underlying tensions and paradoxes of these narratives will feel real, describing struggles that are not artificially manufactured nor easily avoided. The narrators' passion to bear witness, to memorialize, to retell how "someone was here" will find an echo in our own urge to become storytellers. The proper response is not to revere or idolize Gunther, Williams, or any of the others, to use them as substitutes for our own creative efforts. The best response to others' narratives of first person mortal may be to begin to record one's own.

In Our Own Two Voices: Concluding Postscripts

Lucy Bregman: Here, for the first and last time, I will speak as a Christian, having avoided a theological reading of our narratives in the interest of laying out the themes their authors themselves found important. Now, however, I want to stress the distance of many of them, including many of the professed Christians, from the spiritual resources of Christianity. Death issues Christians faced in past ages included death as the gateway to judgment before God, death as punishment for sin, and death as the great equalizer of rich and poor, great and small. Such famous texts as John Bunyan's *The Pilgrim's Progress from this World to the Next* and Dante's *Divine Comedy* offer a world where death, eternity, God, and divine judgment all must be encountered. The perspective of these turns death into something fearful, not because it is physically painful, but because it is intrinsically linked to sin and judgment. To see God is to die; to die is to meet God, and be answerable to him for one's life. Death is therefore aweful, not because it is the end of everything, but because it is not. It is the consummation of what one truly is. The dying fear death, but the dead souls of Dante's *Inferno* yearn for what they fear; they are drawn down to the level of Hell to which their inner characters correspond. These ideas form part of the eschatology, the traditional Christian cluster of four Last Things: Death, Judgment, Heaven, and Hell helped shape the traditional landscape of faith.

These ideas are absent, totally absent, from our narratives. Christians such as David Watson and Madeleine L'Engle are as disinterested in this traditional spiritual landscape as are secular Jewish narrators such as Gerda Lerner or the Rabin family. Even in their most positive and most hopeful expressions, eschatological themes (such as the arrival at one's goal, the Celestial City, after a lifetime of pilgrimage) are just not part of what contemporary Christians want to say about dying and death. Watson and L'Engle may believe that they and their loved ones will continue on in heaven, but about this hope they say almost nothing; it remains outside the drama for even conservative Watson, whose dilemma is over healing. As for JoAnn Kelley Smith (*Free Fall*), Sandra Albertson (*Endings and Beginnings*), and William Stringfellow (*Second Birthday*), any otherworldly focus to their faith was rejected as anachronistic, escapist, and immature.

But not only Christian eschatological motifs are absent. So are rival eschatologies, such as those associated with New Age spiritualities. There are no tales where hope for reincarnation plays any role whatsoever. References to the near-death experiences popularized by Raymond Moody (*Life After Life*), which one would expect to find scattered throughout our accounts, are extraordinarily scarce. This eclipse of eschatology marks our literature, then, even when some forms of eschatology are alive and well elsewhere in America. Ours is a landscape Dante and John Bunyan would find incomprehensible and depleted, of earth and not of eternity.

Can Dante and John Bunyan nevertheless still teach us something about death, something which even the most spiritually aware of our narrators might need to know? In what sense, if at all, can traditional Christian eschatology become a resource for persons in search of a spiritual perspective on death? Or is the traditional cluster, the four Last Things, so hopelessly irrelevant to the late twentieth century, to postmodern persons, that to pursue such a question is a waste of time? Perhaps Christianity should shed such doctrines and become a religion of life, not death, as Judaism has been.

I do not think this is the appropriate path to take. Not because I accept literally and totally John Bunyan's or Dante's imaginative portrayal of eternal realms, but because a world of earth only, history only, persons only, slips into becoming Hell. This may be one of the warnings from Barbara Peabody and Diane Rubin, from Eric Robinson and Elizabeth Cox, a message that they themselves were unable to decipher, but which we ought to heed. Even their human landscape becomes incredibly depleted. We ought not to spurn out of hand alternative perspectives from which to revision our own spiritual situation.

And yet, it is very easy to judge personal narratives by abstract theological standards, and Christians have a long history of spurning the particular, the embodied, the concrete in favor of the universal, the transcendent, and the eternal. This in spite of being followers of an individual, historical person whose life and death were as unique and unrepeatable as any of those charted by our narrators. In fact, after having read first person mortal narratives—by Christians, Jews, the nontraditionally spiritual and all the rest—I come back to the passion narratives of the Gospels and reread these not as theological statements (although I know they are that) but as the story of Jesus' dying: his preparation and symbolic rehearsal for his death at the Last Supper, his bitter aloneness at Gethsemane, and his death among strangers and enemies. The details of the four accounts vary, but all four have details, and are filled with concrete events. Who was there, what Jesus said, what exactly happened at the tomb on Easter morning—the story has to include these, or it would not be a story at all. To read the story as story, and yet as revelation, becomes easier, not harder, after I have read so many other stories by and about persons facing death, whose narrators feel compelled to bear witness. Even the multiplicity of the accounts—"the Passion in four voices"—now appears an intrinsic part of their meaning. There is no supranarrative, in whose text all incompatibilities are smoothed away. Real stories don't work this way. I can celebrate the achievement of our twentieth-century narrators and thank them for their voices, their contributions

to our society's dilemmas with death. I can also thank them for revealing to me the story most central to Christian faith as story, as narrative
of dying and death, as I had not heard it before.

Sara Thiermann: When I reflect on what constitutes my call to stories,
or the call that stories have for me, I can easily take hold of a number
of strands or paths to track. One strand comes out of my interest in
twentieth-century European philosophers whose works point to the
importance of language: I think of Paul Ricoeur, who wrote

> Our existence cannot be separated from the account we give of our-
> selves. It is in telling our own stories that we give ourselves an identity.
> We recognize ourselves in the stories that we tell about ourselves.
> (Ricoeur 1985, 214),

and Martin Heidegger, often quoted as saying "Language is the
house of being." I came to understand philosophy of language and
contemporary hermeneutics to be saying, in part, that we understand
human experience, individually and collectively, through language,
through narrative, and we understand it in a way that is not disclosed
by any other expository or analytic form. Put differently, we understand ourselves *primarily* through narration. One's sense of self is
generated through the telling of one's life stories, or self-narrative,
and our narratives are also imbued with and embedded in our tradition or larger group identity. In fact, we find it hard to separate
ourselves from the enterprise we call "narrative" since we are always
already knee deep in it.

Another strand has been my own private writing experience with
journaling and story projects. In spite of early violation of my personal journals (I was informed that they had been discovered and
burned), some stronger part of me attempted to prevail, and I found
in following my need to write down my experiences, that the recording and rereading of my own personal narrative has taken me beyond
my original understanding of myself and my situation. I found as well
what Anais Nin described: "Not only a companion . . . but a source of
contact with myself . . . a place where I could tell the truth and where
nobody would look" (Nin 1981, 160). Although the concern "nobody would look" seems less important today, I am of two minds
about how readers of my journals might experience what they find

there. I sense possible discomfort at finding highly personal material perhaps, as yet, unknown or unsuspected, yet I would feel vaguely reassured that having read, they might better understand who I was.

The work of novelist Amy Tan has inspired me to envision other uses for personal narrative. In *The Joy Luck Club*, Tan underscores the importance of passing on family narratives to family members and succeeding generations. In *The Kitchen God's Wife*, the narrator's mother must tell her daughter the story of her life, as yet untold, in order for the daughter to truly understand who her mother is, and ultimately who the daughter, herself, is. In addition, an auntie must also tell the stories of the mother as a young woman. Perhaps because my own mother died before she could tell my daughters stories of their mother when she was a little girl, I find Tan's narratives particularly compelling.

I find personal narrative useful in my work with families, catastrophically ill persons, and particularly with bereaved persons. Giving voice to narrative can provide those who are ill with a sense of distance from the immediate situation as the writer/narrator becomes a reflective observer. The rewards may be psychological self-repair, a sense of new life through the creation of a text, and the transformation of a threatening situation into an art form that can be shared. In the doing, one may find a sense of control amid chaos, the creation of something to be remembered by, the discovery of a safer way to communicate than talking when feelings are pushing to be given form. The healing power of stories is always evident in bereavement. In addition, much of the factual data of a bereavement assessment is arrived at by way of narrative. Developing a coherent story can be "whole-ing," therapeutic—narratives give one the space to objectify, externalize, process, and communicate the reality of one's situation. Much of the work, or tasks, of mourning (recognizing the loss, feeling the pain of the loss, experiencing the feelings and giving them expression, reworking the relationship and reinvesting in life) is accomplished through internal or external storytelling, through playing and replaying the "tapes" of the relationship with the deceased person.

Through my own spiritual path, Buddhism, I have gained a deep appreciation of the interconnectedness of all beings and the spaciousness to hear the stories of illness, dying, death, and loss in that light. The stories in our collection are arresting because, for the most part, they feel intensely real and uncontrived. It has been both exciting and a great privilege to learn from our narrators. Through sharing our discovery of these stories, Lucy and I were led deeper and deeper in our exploration of this genre, and we have spent many, many hours together talking and writing. The experience of collaborating on this project has fed my soul.

Each of us has a strong impetus to tell her own stories, to anchor them in time and place. We do this as individual members of our own lifestyle enclave or social group. We may do this understanding, perhaps implicitly rather than explicitly, that the telling of one's own story often takes us all far beyond the personal yet brings us together in a most intimate fashion.

REFERENCES

Albertson, Sandra. *Endings and Beginnings*. New York: Random House, 1980.

Alsop, Stewart. *Stay of Execution*. Philadelphia: Lippincott, 1973.

Aries, Philippe. *The Hour of Our Death*. Trans. H. Weaver. New York: Alfred Knopf, 1981.

Augustine. *Confessions*. Trans. R. Warner. New York: New American Library, 1963.

Barrett, Marvin. *Spare Days*. New York: Arbor House, William Morrow, 1988.

Bellah, Robert, et al. *Habits of the Heart: Individualism and Commitment*. Berkeley: University of California Press, 1985.

Blakely, Mary Kay. *Wake Me When It's Over*. New York: Times Books, 1989.

Blumberg, Rena. *Headstrong*. New York: Crown Publishing Co., 1982.

Bregman, Lucy. *Death in the Midst of Life*. Grand Rapids, MI: Baker Book House, 1992.

Brody, Harold. *Stories of Sickness*. New Haven: Yale University Press, 1987.

Brooks, Ann M. *The Grieving Time*. Garden City: Doubleday, 1985.

Broyard, Anatole. *Intoxicated by My Illness*. New York: Clarkson Potter, 1992.

Bruchac, Carol, Linda Hogan, and Judith McDaniel (eds.). *The Stories We Hold Secret*. Greenfield, NY: The Greenfield Review Press, 1986.

Butler, Sandra, and Barbara Rosenblum. *Cancer in Two Voices*. San Francisco: Spinsters, 1991.

Cabot, Richard, and Russell Dicks. *The Art of Ministering to the Sick*. New York: Macmillan, 1951 (1936).

Caine, Lynne. *Widow*. New York: Bantam Books, 1975.

Chodorow, Nancy. *The Reproduction of Mothering*. Berkeley: University of California Press, 1978.

Cousins, Norman. *Anatomy of an Illness*. New York: Bantam, 1979.

Cox, Elizabeth. *Thanksgiving: An AIDS Journal*. New York: Harper and Row, 1990.

DeBeauvior, Simone. *A Very Easy Death*. New York: Pantheon, 1965.

Deford, Frank. *Alex: The Life of a Child*. New York: New American Library, 1986.

DeMille, Agnes. *Reprieve*. Garden City: Doubleday, 1981.

Dreuilhe, Emmanuel. *Mortal Embrace: Living with AIDS*. Trans. L. Coverdale. New York: Hill and Wang, 1988.

Des Pres, Terrence. *The Survivor: An Anatomy of Life in the Death Camps*. New York: Pocket Books, 1977.

Evans, Jocelyn. *Living With a Man Who Is Dying*. London: Anthony Blond, Ltd., 1971.

Fay, Martha. *A Mortal Condition*. New York: Coward-McCann Inc., 1983.

Frank, Arthur. *At the Will of the Body*. New York: Houghton Mifflin, 1991.

Gee, Elizabeth. *The Light Around the Dark*. New York: National League for Nursing Press, 1992.

Gilligan, Carol. *In a Different Voice*. Cambridge: Harvard University Press, 1983.

Glaser, Elizabeth, and Laura Palmer. *In the Absence of Angels*. New York: G.P. Putnam's Sons, 1991.

Gould, Joan. *Spirals*. New York: Penguin, 1988.

Graham, Laurie. *Rebuilding the House*. New York: Penguin, 1990.

Greene, A.C. *Taking Heart*. New York: Simon and Schuster, 1990.

Gunther, John. *Death Be Not Proud*. New York: Harper, 1947.

Halberstam, Michael M.D., and Stephan Lesher. *A Coronary Event*. Philadelphia: Lippincott, 1976.

Hammond, Phillip (ed.). *The Scared in a Secular Age*. Berkeley: University of California Press, 1985.

Hawkins, Anne H. "A Change of Heart: the Paradigm of Regeneration in Medical and Religious Narrative." *Perspectives in Biology and Medicine* 33, (Summer 1990).

Heller, Joseph, and Speed Vogel. *No Laughing Matter*. New York: Avon, 1986.

Henking, Susan. "The personal is the Theological." *Journal of the American Academy of Religion.* 59, number 3:511–526 (Fall 1991).

Hodgins, Eric. *Episode: Report on the Accident Inside My Skull.* New York: Atheneum, 1964.

Holleran, Andrew. *Ground Zero.* New York: William Morrow, 1988.

Hostetler, Helen. *A Time for Love.* Scottsdale, PA: Herald, 1989.

Ireland, Jill. *Life Wish.* New York: Jove Books, 1987.

Jagger, Alison, and Susan Bordo (eds). *Gender/Body/Knowledge.* New Brunswick: Rutgers University Press, 1989.

Jury, Mark. *Gramp.* New York: Grossman Publisher, 1976.

Kleinman, Arthur. *The Illness Narratives.* New York: Basic Books, 1988.

Konek, Carole Wolfe. *Daddyboy: A Memoir.* St. Paul, Minn: Graywolf Press, 1991.

Kübler-Ross, Elizabeth. *On Death and Dying.* New York: Macmillan, 1969.

Lear, Martha. *Heartsounds.* New York: Simon and Schuster, 1980.

LeGoff, Jean. *The Birth of Purgatory.* Chicago: University of Chicago Press, 1984.

L'Engle, Madeleine. *The Summer of the Great-Grandmother.* San Francisco: Harper and Row, 1974.

L'Engle, Madeleine. *A Two-Part Invention.* San Francisco: Harper and Row, 1988.

Lerner, Gerda. *A Death of One's Own.* New York: Bantam Books, 1974.

Lerner, Max. *Wrestling with the Angel.* New York: W.W. Norton, 1990.

LeShan, Lawrence. *Cancer as a Turning Point.* New York: E.P. Dutton, 1989.

Levit, Rose. *Ellen: A Short Life Long Remembered.* New York: Bantam Books, 1974.

Lewis, C.S. *A Grief Observed.* New York: Bantam, 1976 (1963).

Lifton, Robert J. *The Broken Connection.* New York: Simon and Schuster, 1979.

Lorde, Audre. *The Cancer Journals.* San Francisco: Aunt Lute/Spinsters Ink, 1980.

Luckmann, Thomas. *The Invisible Religion.* New York: Macmillan, 1967.

Lund, Doris. *Eric.* New York: Perennial Library, 1989 (1974).

Lynch, Dorothea, and Eugene Richards. *Exploding into Life.* New York: Aperture/Many Voices Press, 1986.

MacDonald, Betty. *The Plague and I.* Philadelphia: Lippincott, 1948.

Maier, Frank. *Sweet Reprieve.* New York: Crown Publishers, 1991.

Malcolm, Andrew. *Someday.* New York: Harper and Row, 1991.

Mason, Bobbie Ann. *Spence + Lila.* New York: Harper and Row, 1988.

Massie, Robert and Suzanne. *Journey.* New York: Alfred Knopf, 1975.

May, Gerald. *Care of the Mind, Care of the Spirit.* San Francisco: Harper-SanFrancisco, 1982.

May, William. *The Patient's Ordeal.* Bloomington: Indiana University Press, 1991.

McIntyre, Alasdair. *After Virtue.* Notre Dame: University of Notre Dame Press, 1984.

Meryman, Richard. *Hope: A Loss Survived.* Boston: Little, Brown, 1980.

Monette, Paul. *Borrowed Time: An AIDS Memoir.* New York: Avon, 1988.

Money, J.R. *To All the Girls I've Loved Before.* Boston: Alyson Publications, 1987.

Munday, John, and Frances Wohlenhaus-Munday. *I Wasn't Ready.* Ocean City, Md.: Skipjack Press, 1991.

Murphy, Robert. *The Body Silent.* New York: Henry Holt, 1987.

Nin, Anais. "The Personal Life Deeply Lived." In *The American Autobiography,* edited by Albert E. Stone. Englewood Cliffs, N.J.: Prentice-Hall, 1981.

Noll, Peter. *In the Face of Death.* New York: Viking, 1989.

Nouwen, Henri. *A Letter of Consolation.* San Francisco: Harper and Row, 1982.

Olney, James. *Metaphors of Self.* Princeton: Princeton University Press, 1972.

Pascal, Roy. *Design and Truth in Autobiography.* Cambridge: Harvard University Press, 1960.

Paton, Alan. *For You Departed.* New York: Charles Scribners, 1969.

Patterson, James. *The Dread Disease.* Cambridge: Harvard University Press, 1987.

Peabody, Barbara. *The Screaming Room.* San Diego: Oaktree Publications, 1986.

Pearson, Carol Lynn. *Good-Bye, I Love You.* New York: Jove Books, 1988.

Permut, Joanna. *Embracing the Wolf.* Atlanta: Cherokee, 1989.

Perry, Shireen. *In Sickness and in Health.* Downers Grove, Ill.: Intervarsity, 1989.

Petrow, Steven. *Dancing Against the Darkness.* Lexington, MA: D.C. Heath & Co., 1990.

Phipps, Joyce. *Death's Single Privacy.* New York: Seabury Press, 1974.

Rabin, Roni. *Six Parts Love.* New York: Scribners, 1985.

Radner, Gilda. *It's Always Something.* New York: Simon and Schuster, 1989.

Rice, Rebecca. *A Time to Mourn.* New York: Plume, 1991.

Ricoeur, Paul. "History as Narrative and Practice." *Philosophy Today* *29(3–4), Fall 1985.*

Ritchie, Douglas. *Stroke: A Diary of Recovery.* London: Faber and Faber, 1960.

Robinson, Eric. *One Dark Mile.* Amherst: University of Massachusetts Press, 1989.

Rollin, Betty. *Last Wish.* New York: Warner Books, 1985.

Rose, Xenia. *Widow's Journey: A Return to the Loving Self.* New York: Henry Holt, 1990.

Rosenfeld, Stephen. *The Time of Their Dying.* New York: W.W. Norton, 1977.

Ross, Ellen. "Spiritual Experiences of Women's Autobiography." *Journal of the American Academy of Religion* 59(3), Fall 1991.

Roth, Philip. *Patrimony.* New York: Simon and Schuster, 1991.

Rubin, Diane. *Caring: A Daughter's Story.* New York: Holt, Rinehart and Winston, 1982.

Sacks, Oliver. *A Leg to Stand On.* London: Duckworth, 1984.

Sarton, May. *After the Stroke.* New York: Norton, 1988.

Sattilaro, Anthony. *Recalled by Life.* Boston: Houghton Mifflin, 1982.

Schreiber, LeAnne. *Midstream.* New York: Viking, 1990.

Schwerin, Doris. *Diary of a Pigeon Watcher.* New York: William Morrow, 1976.

Seigel, Bernie. *Love, Medicine and Miracles.* New York: Harper and Row, 1986.

Shin, Nan. *Diary of a Zen Nun.* New York: Dutton, 1986.

Shilts, Randy. *And the Band Played On.* New York: St. Martins Press, 1987.

Simonton, O. Carl, Stephanie Matthews-Simonton, and James Creighton. *Getting Well Again.* New York: Bantam Books, 1978.

Smith, JoAnn Kelley. *Free Fall.* Valley Forge: Judson Press, 1975.

Snow, Lois. *A Death With Dignity.* New York: Random House, 1975.

Sontag, Susan. *Illness as Metaphor.* New York: Farrar, Strauss and Giroux, 1978.

Southard, Samuel. *Dying and Death.* Westport: Greenwood Press, 1991.

Spohr, Betty. To Hold a Falling Star. Stamford: Longmeadow Press, 1990.

Steinfels, Peter, and Robert Veatch (eds). *Death Inside Out.* New York: Harper and Row, 1975.

Stringfellow, William. *A Second Birthday.* Garden City: Doubleday, 1970.

Sutliffe, Marjorie. *Grandma Cherry's Spoon.* Santa Barbara: Geronima Press, 1991.

Tan, Amy. *The Joy Luck Club*. New York: Putnam, 1989.

Tan, Amy. *The Kitchen God's Wife*. New York: Putnam, 1991.

Trautmann, Mary Winfrey. *The Absence of the Dead Is Their Way of Appearing*. Pittsburgh: Cleis Press, 1984.

Trull, Patti. *On With My Life*. New York: G. P. Putnam's Sons, 1983.

Truman, Jill. *Letter to My Husband*. New York: Penguin, 1987.

Tsongas, Paul. *Heading Home*. New York: Vintage, 1992 (1984).

Walker, Daniel. *The Decline of Hell*. Chicago: The University of Chicago Press, 1964.

Watson, David. *Fear No Evil*. Wheaton: Harold Shaw, 1984.

Weingarten, Violet. *Intimations of Mortality*. New York: Alfred Knopf, 1978.

Weintraub, Karl. "Autobiography and Historical Consciousness." *Critical Inquiry* 1, June 1975.

Wertenbaker, Lael Tucker. *Death of a Man*. Boston: Beacon Press, 1974.

West, Jessamyn. *The Woman Said Yes*. Greenwich: Fawcett, 1976.

Whitmore, George. *Someone Was Here: Profiles in the AIDS Epidemic*. New York: New American Library, 1988.

Wilber, Ken. *Grace and Grit*. Boston: Shambala, 1991.

Williams, Terry Tempest. *Refuge*. New York: Pantheon, 1991.

Williams, Wendy. *The Power Within*. New York: Simon and Schuster, 1990.

Young, James. *Writing and Rewriting the Holocaust*. Bloomington: Indiana University Press, 1988.

Zaleski, Carol. *Otherworld Journeys*. New York: Oxford University Press.

Zorza, Victor, and Rosemary Zorza. *A Way to Die*. New York: Alfred Knopf, 1980.

INDEX